Tim LaHaye's books always entertain, educate, and thrill, but *Thunder of Heaven* takes it to a new level. I never thought the End of Days would cost me so much sleep!

Glenn Beck
number one *New York Times* bestselling author

Tim LaHaye writes about the prophetic future with such accuracy and passion that once you get started reading what he has written, you do not put the book away until it is finished! In our generation, he has led the way back to a proper appreciation of the prophetic writings of Scripture. Everywhere I go, I meet someone who has read one of Tim's books and been blessed by it. This book will continue that tradition!

Dr. David Jeremiah
senior pastor of Shadow Mountain Community Church
founder and CEO of Turning Point

Dr. Tim LaHaye writes about the future with the kind of gripping detail that others would use to describe the past. I've been reading Tim LaHaye's books for over thirty years, but *Thunder of Heaven* may be his best yet!"

Mike Huckabee
former Arkansas governor

THUNDER OF HEAVEN

Other Books by Tim LaHaye

The End Series

Edge of Apocalypse (with Craig Parshall)

Thunder of Heaven (with Craig Parshall)

Revelation Unveiled

Finding the Will of God in a Crazy, Mixed-Up World

How to Win Over Depression

Anger Is a Choice (with Bob Phillips)

*The Act of Marriage: The Beauty of Sexual Love
(Tim and Beverly LaHaye)*

*The Act of Marriage after 40: Making Love for Life
(Tim and Beverly LaHaye with Mike Yorkey)*

TIM LaHAYE
& CRAIG PARSHALL

THUNDER OF HEAVEN

THE END SERIES

ZONDERVAN®

ZONDERVAN.com/
AUTHORTRACKER
follow your favorite authors

ZONDERVAN

Thunder of Heaven
Copyright © 2011 by Tim LaHaye

This title is also available as a Zondervan ebook. Visit www.zondervan.com/ebooks.

This title is also available in a Zondervan audio edition. Visit www.zondervan.fm.

Requests for information should be addressed to:

Zondervan, *Grand Rapids, Michigan 49530*

This edition: ISBN 978-0-310-31811-8 (softcover)

Library of Congress Cataloging-in-Publication Data

LaHaye, Tim F.
    Thunder of heaven / Tim LaHaye and Craig Parshall.
      p. cm. — (The end series)
    ISBN 978-0-310-32637-3
    1. End of the world — Fiction. I. Parshall, Craig, 1950 - II. Title.
PS3562.A315T48 2011
813'.54 — dc22
                                          2011010567

Published in association with the literary agency of WordServe Literary Group, Ltd., 10152 S. Knoll Circle, Highlands Ranch, CO 80130.

Cover design: James Hall
Cover photography: 123RF®
Interior design: Michelle Espinoza

Printed in the United States of America

12 13 14 15 16 17 18 /DCI/ 23 22 21 20 19 18 17 16 15 14 13 12 11 10 9 8 7 6 5 4 3 2 1

THUNDER OF HEAVEN

PART 1

An Ill Wind Blowing

We can absorb a terrorist attack.

President Barack Obama, quoted in
Obama's Wars by Bob Woodward

Under the last administration, as well as under this one, it has been the United States' policy not to build a missile defense that would render useless Russia's nuclear capabilities.

Testimony of the Secretary of Defense before
the Senate Foreign Relations Committee, July 2010

Al Qaeda's continued efforts to access chemical, biological, radiological, or nuclear material pose a serious threat to the United States.

Testimony of FBI Director Robert Mueller
before Congress, March 2010

ONE

In the Near Future

In a small warehouse in Howard Beach, a few miles outside the fence of JFK International Airport, Hassan was going over the details with his two partners. He stared into the eyes of Farhat, the young Turkish man who was fidgeting with a set of car keys. Hassan had his doubts about him but kept them to himself. The mission was too important to risk just because Farhat hadn't given himself completely to the cause. Farhat's level of commitment had to be probed. Hassan was afraid that his young recruit was more concerned about his pretty girlfriend back in Istanbul than he was about the mission.

"Farhat," Hassan began, "the time has come. Are you with us?"

"Yes. Why do you doubt me?"

"I don't waste time doubting. I believe. I decide. Then I act."

Farhat nodded and looked over at the third man, Ramzy, a Palestinian on loan from Hamas. With his arms crossed, Ramzy looked uninterested until he spoke up. "Fine. Then we start." Ramzy motioned to several large fuel tanks in the corner of the warehouse. "But what about those?"

Hassan smiled and said, "Don't smoke." He held a sat-fone, the newest generation of digitally encrypted satellite cell phones. He clicked it on and waited until a woman inside the terminal answered.

"Talk to me," said Hassan.

"National Airlines Flight 433 to Denver is boarded, waiting on the tarmac. Clearance has not yet been given. I will tell you when it starts taxiing down the runway."

"I will be waiting," said Hassan. "Remember. We'll need two minutes lead time."

The woman said, "I will make you proud."

After clicking off the sat-fone, Hassan barked to Farhat, "Recite your role in the plan again."

Farhat swallowed hard and spoke, "I wait inside the van. I do not start the engine until I see your text on my Allfone. I have ten seconds to read it before it self-deletes. Then I turn on the ignition. Wait for you and Ramzy. If I see police or security, I turn off the van, get out, and walk over to tell you, but I don't run. If the mission is completed, then we all get in, and I drive exactly three miles per hour over the speed limit — no more, no less — to our destination. Don't run red lights. Obey all stop signs."

"The route?"

"Shore Parkway to I-278."

Hassan put his face close to Farhat's. "One correction," said Hassan. "Not *if* the mission is completed. Get that straight. We will complete the mission. We must not fail." Then, to put a point on it, Hassan poked a finger into Farhat's chest and said, "*Sha-Ja-'a* ..." Farhat wrinkled his brow. Hassan smiled. His one-word mandate to Farhat to "have courage" was meant as a warning.

"*Allah Ackbar!*" Hassan yelled out.

Now they would wait. But not for long.

□□□

Deborah Jordan settled into seat 14A, next to the over-wing emergency exit on the 797 parked on the tarmac of JFK. First class was filled, so she had settled for coach on her flight to Denver. At least she had extra foot room in that spot and no overhead storage compartment above her seat. Too bad, though, that her father's private Citation X jet was getting security upgrades and was unavailable, otherwise she'd have asked for a ride. Not that commercial flights bothered her; she didn't have a rich-kid attitude. She just wanted to get home to her family's sprawling log mansion in Colorado. It was their family retreat. Sure, she loved their New York City penthouse, which was close to her father's Manhattan office. But the place in the Rockies held a special attraction for her.

She studied the slow pack-animal parade of passengers as they shuffled down the aisle and stuffed bags into the overhead compartments.

As she put her purse on the floor by her feet, she stuffed her hand into the embossed leather bag and pulled out a small magazine, *National Security Review*. After buckling her seat belt, she sat back and tried to focus on her reading.

Just then, a man in his early thirties shoved his carry-on into an overhead, took the seat next to her, and flashed her a smile. He wore a golf shirt — too tight, she thought — maybe to show off his biceps, which, she had to admit, were impressive. A chiseled face and something interesting about the nose. It was off-kilter, like it had been broken. Short hair. Blue eyes. *Uh-oh. He caught me looking.*

The man smiled again. Then Deborah, after tossing a tight-lipped nod in his direction, turned her attention back to the magazine. When the jet was full, an attendant bent over in her direction. There was a courteous smile and the standard question: was Deborah willing and able to activate the emergency exit door next to her if the need arose?

"Absolutely. No problem."

The attendant disappeared, and the man next to her leaned toward her. "You sure about that? I'd be glad to help out."

The grin on his face told her two things. First, he was taking a clumsy stab at flirting. Second, it was a lame attempt at an icebreaker.

"Thanks, but I can handle it."

Still managing a smile, he added, "I'm sure you can. Just trying to be friendly."

□□□

On the other side of the country, LAX airport seemed normal enough. Flights mostly on schedule. A few backups. Although no one seemed to know why, the security status had been raised for the TSA workers screening passengers at the X-ray machines. But then, that had happened before. The security staffers in the dark blue shirts simply increased their number of random carry-on inspections.

Outside on the tarmac, a couple of uniformed airport cops slouched against an LAX Ops police squad car. They talked casually, squinting behind their Ray-Ban sunglasses in the glare of the California sun.

One block outside the LAX perimeter, two men stood on the roof of an apartment building. One was a Muslim ex-military veteran from Chechnya. Next to him was an American-born Arab recruit from the U.S. Army. The location was ideal. It was on the line between Highway 405 and the tall, rectangular airport control tower with the spiked exterior that looked like some kind of giant Lego construction. When everything went down, it would be a short drive to 405, where they could then drop the hammer and merge into the crazy fast traffic from Los Angeles and escape the disaster scene. They would leave behind their signature: an exploding inferno and a mass of fatalities.

TWO

The good-looking guy next to Deborah kept glancing at her magazine. Then he moved from looking at the magazine to taking in her pretty face, softly square with double dimples and dark eyes.

She braced herself. *Great. Okay, here it comes.*

And it did. He nodded toward the publication and said, "So, national security stuff. You work for a defense contractor?"

Deborah had to make a quick decision. *Engage? Or activate avoidance measures?*

She decided that limited engagement was the safest course. Then she could get back to the article she was reading about "nuclear deterrence in an age of asymmetrical warfare."

"No, not with a defense contractor."

"Military detail then?"

Deborah weighed her answer. "Not exactly." Without looking up, she added, "Technically not."

"Intriguing. Okay. Then you're in one of the academies." He eyed her closer. "Air Force? Naw. I'm Air Force. You don't fit the profile ..."

Deborah tried to keep up the stone face. *Profile? What profile is this guy talking about?*

"Not Navy. Not reading that kind of stuff. So that leaves West Point, right?"

Deborah didn't realize she was blushing. Her seat partner kept talking. "Wow, direct hit. Oh, sorry. Didn't introduce myself. Ethan March. Formerly lieutenant major, United States Air Force. Now civilian. Glad to meet you, Miss ..." He reached out to shake her hand.

Deborah threw him a side look and offered up a quick handshake and a short explanation. "You're right. I'm West Point."

"Graduated?"

"One more year."

"Congratulations. In advance."

"Thanks. And you, Mr. March?"

"I go by Ethan. Defense contracting. Until recently ..."

That got her attention. "Which company?"

"Raytheon. Just got laid off. Part of defense downsizing from Washington. Go figure."

Deborah gave a nod, but she still looked underwhelmed by the chatty guy next to her.

Ethan March made a rapid recovery. "I've been lucky though. Been around the block with some of the best."

She couldn't resist. "Oh? Like who?"

"Well, for one, I had the privilege of serving under the great colonel Joshua Jordan."

Deborah dropped her magazine and broke into a grin, which slowly lapsed into laughter.

Ethan flashed a look of disbelief. Then he said with some disgust, "Army. Can't believe it. You folks don't know how to honor a true-blue Air Force hero like Colonel Jordan!"

When she stopped laughing, she explained, "You don't understand. You said you served with the 'great Joshua Jordan ...'"

"Exactly. At McGill Air Force Base."

"Well, Joshua Jordan is my father. Which I guess makes me ... well, his almost-great daughter ..."

Now Ethan was the one blushing.

"Oh man. Plane going down. Mayday, Mayday ..."

Now they were both laughing.

She reached her hand over. "Let's start this again. I'm Deborah Jordan. Good to meet you."

They shook hands again, but this time he held on a little longer.

"I'm honored to be sitting with you. Figure that. Joshua Jordan's daughter."

THREE

Inside the cockpit of Northern Airlines Flight 199 at Chicago's O'Hare airport, the copilot was reading off the preflight checklist. When he got to one item he paused. Then the copilot read it out. "Primary countermeasures."

Pilot Bob Blotzinger, a veteran of twenty years of commercial flying, flicked the little toggle switch, and the green light on the instrument panel lit up. He said, "Check."

"Secondary system."

"Check."

The copilot stopped again for a second. Then, after turning around to make sure the cockpit door was closed and they were alone, he asked, "What's the deal with that?"

"With what?"

"The secondary. You know, the RTS?"

"Hey, I'm just the pilot. Ask Northern Airlines. I only work here."

"Come on, Bob. Humor me. Did the FAA really approve the Return-to-Sender defense system or not?"

The pilot gave it some thought and tossed his first officer a tired look. "Okay. This is only what I heard, so don't quote me. Apparently the FAA clears the RTS for installation in commercial jets, right? But then Homeland Security gets involved and says, 'Whoa, wait a minute. This is national security stuff.' So it starts getting complicated. Like it always does. Now you've got a battle between two agencies. So they decide, okay, leave it installed. But each airline and each airport can jointly decide whether the system gets activated. Anyway, the FAA wants to see if having it physically installed jinxes anything in your avionics — which it shouldn't, from everything I know — but that's their compromise."

"But you're not answering me. Are we able to use the RTS or not?"

"No. Not really. Not automatically. Have to call it into air traffic control. Give them the alert. Get their permission first. Ridiculous."

The pilot waved his hand toward the preflight log in the copilot's hand.

"All right. So, sign off on the preflight, will you? I want to get to Dallas."

The copilot tilted his head as he listened in his headset to a message from the tower. He followed that with a nod. "Good news. They've moved us up. We're on deck."

□□□

By the time Flight 199 started taxiing down the runway at O'Hare, across the country, at JFK, Deborah's Flight 433 to Denver was next in line for takeoff. At LAX the Los Angeles to Las Vegas flight was in the same position.

As the Chicago flight rolled toward takeoff, two men hunched together inside the Ulema Salvage Yard in Schiller Park, just outside of the O'Hare perimeter. An Indonesian man shouldered a FIM-92A Stinger missile launcher. His brother stood next to him, reading the quick-text messages from the other cell groups in Los Angeles and New York.

Just outside the Ulema Salvage Yard, the driver of the getaway van, with its engine idling, sat behind the steering wheel. He was watching the two-man Stinger team get ready.

The brother's sat-fone rang. He took the message and seemed electrified. "Takeoff is confirmed for Flight 199 to Dallas," he yelled. "It's coming…" A few seconds later they could hear the big jet approaching in the distance.

□□□

While Flight 199 was taking off from Chicago, Flight 433 out of JFK was slowly rolling down the runway. The 797 straightened its alignment for takeoff. The pilot eased the throttle forward. The jet started to accelerate. Then the pilot powered it up for takeoff.

As the 797 raced down the runway, Deborah felt the familiar centrifugal force pulling her back into her seat. At that moment her purse tipped over on the floor, spilling the contents. Lipstick, compact, coin purse, Allfone cell, pens. Everything.

For a split second she tried to fight the impulse. But she did it anyway. She quickly unbuckled her seat belt so she could reach down and stuff the contents back into her purse.

□□□

For Blotzinger, this was only his third time flying the new 797. He had eighty-eight souls on board, including the crew and flight attendants, as he taxied the big jet into position for takeoff from O'Hare airport.

Moments later Blotzinger gently lifted the big jet off the runway. Their flight path took them over Schiller Park, but when the jet was directly over Ulema Salvage Yard, the copilot noticed something. A blip on the radar screen — a blip streaking right toward them. Suddenly the attack-warning buzzers went off in the cabin, and a yellow light started to flash.

The copilot blurted out, "Bob, incoming — "

Blotzinger hit the countermeasures button. The flares designed to deflect heat-seeking missiles blew out from the underbelly, but they were not close enough to the Stinger missile to distract it. The missile kept streaking toward its target.

Blotzinger could see what was happening. "Fire the RTS!" he screamed.

The copilot hit the control for the RTS antimissile system while Blotzinger swung the big jet into an avoidance pattern.

Their eyes were riveted to the screen.

But for some terrifying reason the linear blip kept coming, closing in at a blinding speed, heading right for the belly of the jet.

The RTS should have worked. Should have instantaneously transmitted a data-capturing/data-reconfiguring laser beam aimed straight for the guidance system in the missile. Should have reversed the flight path of the FIM-92A Stinger that was streaking toward the jet and turned it around, sending it back to its source.

But something had gone horribly wrong.

The last sound on the cockpit voice recorder was a millisecond-long scream of the copilot when he got a glimpse of the long steel cylinder full of explosives momentarily flashing into sight just before it struck.

There was an unearthly blast. And in one blinding explosion they were all gone.

On the ground a man was walking his dog. He screamed and jumped at the sound of the sky exploding into fire overhead. His dog howled and cowered on the ground. When the man looked up, he saw the fireball expanding in the air. Then he screamed again. He saw the charred pieces of the fuselage, cockpit, and wing assembly falling from the sky all around him and crashing onto the streets and houses of his Chicago suburb.

□□□

Soon National Airlines Flight 433 out of JFK would be winging its way high in the sky over the warehouse where Ramzy nestled the missile launcher against his shoulder. Standing directly below the now-open retractable skylight, Ramzy peered through the clear pane of plastic on the launcher's viewfinder, ready to line up the big 797 jet in its rectangular lines.

□□□

As Deborah bent down to stuff the spilled items back into her purse, Ethan March joked, "No seat belt? Leave it to the Army to ignore flight regulations ..."

At that moment, the cockpit crew heard a shrill warning bell. The copilot pointed to a flashing light on the flight deck. An oblong object on the LCD screen was streaking toward them.

The copilot shouted, "Oh my G — "

The pilot thrust his finger down on the primary countermeasure button. A flare shot out from the underbody of the jet toward the incoming heat-seeking missile in an attempt to detract it. But the missile kept coming.

More alarm bells rang.

The security screen flashed: "6 SECONDS TO IMPACT."

The pilot punched the button marked "RTS." A laser beam shot out of a small orb on the belly of the National Airlines jet. The beam struck the missile's guidance system right behind the heat-seeking tip.

The pilot knew he had to put distance between the heat of his jet engines and the approaching missile, so he tried to bank into a twenty-degree yaw to the left. Passengers screamed as magazines, jackets, and purses flew into the air.

In an instant, Deborah, still out of her seat belt, felt herself being lifted violently into the air. She would have smashed straight into the ceiling — headfirst, with the force of an automobile crash — if Ethan March hadn't instantly reached over her and blocked her with his arms and held on to her. Up front, a stewardess lay unconscious on the floor, having hit her head against the bulkhead before she had buckled into her jump seat.

□□□

Five hundred feet away, the RTS laser beam had triggered the guidance system of the missile into a mirror image of its trajectory. The infrared head of the missile was deactivated, and the Stinger began a turning loop away from the jet. The missile was now on a path back to earth at fifteen hundred miles per hour, returning to the warehouse where it had been launched.

On the ground, Ramzy couldn't afford to wait even a few seconds to verify his hit. The Stinger missile left a visible plume behind it and they had to clear out of the launch area before they were sighted. He hurriedly repacked the launcher into the case. Hassan was already sprinting toward Farhat and the van.

That is when Hassan, standing outside, thought he saw the glint of something in the air — a thin metallic object streaking through the sky toward them.

It was the last thing he would see.

When the missile struck the warehouse it ignited the fuel tanks. There was a flash and a deafening roar as the warehouse disintegrated in the enveloping ball of fire. Hassan, Ramzy, and Farhat were consumed instantly. Four workers on the loading dock of the neighboring building were taking a break. They never knew what hit them. The shock wave from the blast blew them a hundred feet from the building, which imploded behind them. Its windows sprayed broken glass in a shimmering mist as the walls buckled. The sonic blast could be heard all the way to the New Jersey shore.

□□□

In the cockpit of Flight 433, the LCD screen on the flight deck was flashing "FIELD CLEAR," and the buzzer ceased. The pilot corrected his flight path.

Deborah found herself in a heap on Ethan's lap with his arms still locked around her. She climbed back into her seat as their hearts banged in their chests.

Deborah threw a glance up to the ceiling of the plane, realizing what might have happened. She managed a smile and turned to Ethan. "Thanks. Really."

In the cockpit, the pilot radioed the tower. "Permission requested to use RTS secondary countermeasures per FAA rules. Over."

"Hey, what happened? What the — "

"Permission requested for RTS."

"Don't understand — "

"Look, I'll just take that as permission granted. Thanks, tower. Over."

□□□

Two minutes later, the men on the roof near LAX airport were monitoring the Los Angeles flight to Las Vegas. They had already received an ecstatic voice message on their sat-fone from the Chicago cell group: "Plane down! Plane down! Allah be praised!"

Now the Chechen was helping the Arab missile expert shoulder the Stinger launcher.

"Hear it? Listen. That's our jet!" he cried out. Then he added, "We have to bring it down like our brothers in Chicago."

The missile man aimed his launcher. The 797 was appearing off to the left. His aim would be exact. He pulled the trigger, and the missile blew straight up into the sky, leading the approaching jet perfectly in its approach.

In the cockpit, bells went off. The copilot automatically slammed down on the countermeasures button. Two flares shot out, heading for the incoming missile.

The pilot next to him was yelling. "What is it? What is it?"

But before he could get a response, he could see it on the screen. The flares had diverted the heat-seeking missile from its trajectory slightly, but just slightly. The pilot and copilot could see the missile for a split second. The pilot prayed aloud that the missile would not hone in on the heat from his engines.

"Get away ... get away ...!"

The missile shot past the jet with a trail of smoke. It kept traveling due west and eventually fell harmlessly into the Pacific surf, a half mile offshore.

Three hours later, a group of Navy SEALS and the L.A. bomb squad located the missile and defused it. For some reason, the explosive never detonated.

The RTS system hadn't been utilized.

FOUR

In the Colorado Rockies, Joshua Jordan and his wife, Abigail, had been riding their horses. Earlier that day they had taken the pass that wound through the tall pines and eventually ended at the barn near their log mansion. Now the ride was over, the horses had been stalled, and they were walking in the door of their massive retreat house. Both were wondering when they would hear from their daughter, Deborah, who was soon expected at the Denver airport.

Joshua migrated to the big family room, with its high-timbered crossbeams, and turned on the Internet television set. Then he took a few steps back and dropped into a cowhide chair. On the end table were pictures from his years in the Air Force, before he'd started his own defense-contracting company. One framed photo showed Joshua and a former president, shaking hands after his successful surveillance flight over Iran. Another showed him with several members of the Joint Chiefs of Staff. The third, his favorite, showed Abigail back when she practiced law with a D.C. firm; she was heading down the steps of the federal courthouse in Washington after arguing a case to the Court of Appeals — one of many she would win.

Suddenly, Joshua's attention was drawn to the ticker scrolling across the bottom of the screen.

NORTHERN AIR FLIGHT FROM CHICAGO CRASHES ON TAKEOFF. FEAR NO SURVIVORS. FLIGHTS FROM LAX AND NEW YORK TURNED BACK.

Joshua yelled to Abigail, who dashed into the room. Joshua pointed at the message that was still scrolling.

A look of panic came over Abigail's face. "Flight numbers ... what flight numbers?"

"They haven't given any. What's Deborah's flight out of JFK? Where'd you write that down?"

Abigail dashed to her study.

Joshua was trying to make sense out of it.

Three flights in three parts of the country. One crashed. Two turned around. This is sounding terribly familiar ...

F1VE

Washington, D.C.

Mike Leaky sat at his desk eating a Cuban sandwich and slurping Mountain Dew from a plastic bottle. He was hitting the Dew because he needed an energy boost. He'd been out late partying the night before.

His job at the U.S. Geological Survey, National Climate Change and Wildlife Science Center, was to analyze weather data, specifically on global warming. Sometimes the endless stats all seemed to blur together. Like today. He chugged more Dew while he reviewed the latest printout in the empty computer room.

As he studied it, he groaned, "Oh, no, man. No ..."

It seemed clear that he had entered the hundred-year average rather than the one-year average. So he loaded the parameters into his computer once again, this time making sure he was asking for the one-year average. He punched Enter and waited.

Bored, he decided to wander down to the office of his supervisor, Dr. Henry Smithson. When he got there, Smithson and Ernie, his assistant, were glued to the little Internet television set.

When Mike started to ask what they were watching, Smithson put his finger to his lips and pointed to the screen. There was footage of the smoking, charred wreckage that had landed in the Chicago neighborhood.

Smithson said, "This is awful. No facts yet. The NTSB is investigating but isn't talking. Someone on the ground thought they saw an explosion in the air. Just to make sure, other flights are being cancelled. Know anyone flying today?"

Mike shook his head.

"Me neither."

Smithson hit the search function on his remote, and on the right-hand column of the screen a series of weblogs and Insta-News articles appeared. All were reporting the same thing. Smithson scrolled down. After fifteen more entries, all nearly identical, one finally looked different. It was from a new web-and-wire service called AmeriNews. The headline read: MISSILE SITED IN CHICAGO, HEADING FOR DOOMED PLANE . . .

Ernie chirped out, "Hey, lookit that!" and pointed to the headline.

Smithson just grunted back, "AmeriNews? You got to be kidding, Ernie. Bunch of crazies. Members of the flat-earth society."

He clicked off the Google search and enlarged the TV footage. Mike hung around for a minute, watching the gruesome coverage, then looked at his watch and figured he should get back to work.

In his office Mike checked the screen, hit the Print button, and after a few seconds collected his papers. He sat down with the earth-temperature average index and reached for his Cuban sandwich. He took a big bite and savored the crunchy thinly sliced dill pickle and the spicy meat. It was just the way he liked it. He chewed once. The side of his cheek bulged.

Then he saw it — at the bottom of the last page of the index.

He nearly choked. He coughed and gagged. He was so dumbfounded that he'd forgotten to keep chewing.

This can't be right. No way.

He scanned every page, following the trail of data, point by point, until he got to the end. It made sense mathematically. It all fit — except for the one-year average. That had to be wrong again. But it wasn't. It was correct. He checked it. For a moment Mike felt as if he was about to have an out-of-body experience. "I must be going nuts."

Or was it something else?

If the data was correct, it meant that the newest average worldwide temperatures were climbing to dangerous levels. Catastrophic global warming had finally kicked into overdrive. Due to carbon dioxide emissions from cars and factories? Of course. There could be no other scientific explanation. At least not one that was respectable.

When Mike realized what that meant he snatched the papers and sprinted down the hall like a maniac, his frenzied footsteps echoing off the linoleum floor. He reached Smithson's office.

Dr. Smithson and Ernie were still watching television when Mike burst in. His frantic entrance made the Ph.D. of climatology and his research assistant whip around in their chairs. Mike raised the papers in the air. His face had the stunned look of a pedestrian who almost got hit by a bus.

"God help us. It's happening ..."

SIX

In the conference room of Eternity Church in Manhattan, the small group of men had their own special custom for meetings of this kind: no cell phones, no wireless handheld devices. That meant they were temporarily cut off from the news of the day and that they could focus on the subject at hand with a hydraulic kind of intensity.

Today they felt a palpable atmosphere of anticipation, though no one said it aloud. It was like being on the beach when the tide suddenly sucks back and you know a tsunami is about to hit.

The chairman of this small biannual conclave was Peter Campbell, head pastor of Eternity Church, which was housed in a historic brown-brick cathedral in downtown New York. Forty-three, athletic, and with a calm kind of kinetic energy, he had a passion for the study of Bible prophecies.

The other six members of the group had the same passion. Two of them were professors at seminaries. Two others were pastors. One of them was the head of the Israel Study Institute in Jerusalem. And then there was the oldest, "Doc," a retired president of a Bible college, who had authored expositions on the books of Daniel, Ezekiel, and Revelation and during his long ministry had picked up a master's degree in archeology as well as a Ph.D. in Semitic languages.

They had spent the last hour in prayer. Each felt a crushing burden for what they saw off on the thin line of the horizon.

A seminary professor led off. "We've met here together for the last three years, contemplating and debating, wondering what we would do if this day ever came in our lifetime. And now it's here."

"And yet," one of the pastors said, "we all know the admonition from our Lord, standing on the Mount of Olives — "

Another pastor chimed in, quoting " 'Of that day and hour no one knows, not even the angels of heaven, but My Father only.' "

One of the seminary theologians had a point to make, the same idea that he had voiced before. "But remember what event the Lord is referring to in that passage. Not the events leading up to His coming, but rather, the actual occurrence of His physical appearance. Which means that we might be able to identify the preappearing events, the stage setting, so to speak, with great accuracy. While still not knowing the actual day or hour of the second coming of Christ."

"Doc" cleared his throat loudly. The room grew quiet as he took a swig of water. He removed his tinted glasses from his wrinkled face and put them on the table. He was not prone to speak quickly. He would choose his words carefully, like a sculptor cutting a face out of marble, with each blow calibrated just so. He knew that every word, like a chisel on stone, had consequences.

His voice was weak and had the tremolo of age. "Great events cast long shadows. Can we deny that we see the shadows of these epochal events approaching? Some are even at our doorstep. Jesus upbraided the Pharisees, didn't He, for failing to read the signs of the times? Will we be like them, failing to tell the world the very thing that we see? While the world is saying it is a good day because it's morning … friends, we realize that the sky is red. How can we stay silent?"

No one spoke for a full minute. Finally Peter Campbell said, "I believe, just like the apostles of old, that we have 'to declare what we have seen and what we have heard,' tell the truth — unvarnished — and let the chips fall where they may."

No one dissented.

So it would begin.

SEVEN

After three desperate hours in their Colorado retreat, Joshua and Abigail Jordan finally heard the voice of their daughter. They were both on the line. Abigail blurted out, "Deb, are you all right?"

"Our flight got shaken up a bit. I have a few bruises, but I'm okay."

Abigail sighed, "Thank You, God. What in the world happened?"

"Mom, I'm not sure. The plane took a dive. Things flew everywhere. Then we returned to JFK. They've been interviewing us nonstop but not giving us information."

As a former Capitol Hill lawyer, Abigail wanted the backstory. "Which agency questioned you? The NTSB?"

"Yeah ... National Transportation Safety Board. Right."

"Anyone else?"

"Guys in suits. Probably FBI. Gee, why don't I remember for sure?"

That caught Joshua's attention, and he immediately asked, "Why'd they turn your flight around?"

"I don't know, Dad. One minute we were taking off; the next minute the plane goes into ... well, it almost seemed like evasive maneuvers, and then everything went crazy ..."

"Any talk about this being connected to the Chicago plane?"

"What?"

Joshua realized his daughter knew nothing about the Chicago crash. He decided to drop it. "Never mind, honey. Just let us know how soon we can see you."

"While jets are being grounded they're giving us priority on the new westbound *Flashtrain*. I'll board today and be in Denver tomorrow and with you guys by tomorrow afternoon."

Joshua, a decorated colonel in the Air Force and former spy-plane pilot, had cut his teeth on military flying, not commercial, but he knew something about flight-incident investigations. His most recent stint as the premier antimissile defense contractor with the Pentagon had also brought him into contact with many federal agencies: the NTSB, the FAA, Homeland Security, and the National Security Agency among them. By now he'd already guessed that his daughter's flight was somehow connected to the Chicago disaster.

"Oh, there's something I have to tell you," Deborah said. She didn't give either parent a chance to process before she continued, "I'd like to bring someone to Hawk's Nest ... so you can meet him."

Abigail threw a look across the log-beamed living room to Joshua, who was sitting by their five-foot-tall fieldstone fireplace.

"Explain, dear," Abigail said in a tone freighted with a parent's expectation, "exactly who you're talking about?"

"Mom, this guy is former Air Force. And Dad, guess what? He worked in defense contracting with Raytheon."

Abigail pushed a little. "How long have you known him?"

"Well, just a few hours ..."

Across the room Abigail was shaking her head. It wasn't adding up.

Joshua said, "Sweetheart, this isn't making sense. You're probably shaken up."

"Dad," she began, and her parents could hear the depth of emotion in her voice, "he saved me during the flight, kept me from getting a broken neck or cracking my skull."

"Deborah, what on earth?" Abigail had had enough. Now she was going to launch into one of her skillful, impassioned cross-examinations. Seeing that, Joshua waved his hand toward Abigail, as if to say, *Not now. This is too sensitive for a phone conversation.*

Abigail decided to pull back. "Darling," she said, "just come home quickly. We love you so much, and we're glad you're safe. Your brother's coming in a few days. Hopefully flights will be back to normal by then. Cal's in Boston. We'll all be together. I can't wait to hug you."

After they clicked off, Abigail strode over to the sofa where Joshua was sitting and dropped down next to him. She grabbed his powerful hand and ran her other hand through her hair. Joshua, as usual, was doing the stoic thing, but she could see he was carrying a two-hundred-pound weight on his chest. They sat silently, absorbing what their daughter had told them, scant as it was. It sounded like something terrifying had happened. Abigail said she wanted her daughter home "ten minutes ago." How frustrating it was that that their private jet was down with repairs. Could they charter another private jet to pick Deborah up?

Joshua shook his head. "Abby, I know what you're thinking. I'm there too. But by the time we lined up a charter, she could be heading home. Let's stick with the plan. Besides, I don't want to flag Deborah to the federal folks."

"You think something's going on, don't you? This was not just a random plane crash ..."

"With all we've learned and seen, we have to expect anything."

They disappeared into their own thoughts.

Abigail broke the silence. "Josh, what she said ..." The words caught in her throat. "She said someone *saved* her on that flight ..."

Joshua was rocked by the fact that his daughter's life had been at risk, but he was also thinking about the Chicago flight and the fact that the FBI had interrogated Deborah and the other passengers from her flight — four states away. He couldn't shake the feeling of catastrophe. And responsibility. Both jets were 797s, and he knew something about them. He had designed the RTS antimissile system installed on those planes, and he had a vested interest in commercial air safety. His own daughter had been on a National Airlines flight with his RTS device on board. He had to find out why the Chicago flight ended in disaster. And right away. Was this just a tragic air accident? And if so, then maybe it was pilot error. Or equipment failure. Major wind shear at takeoff?

One thing he did know: there was a possible explanation for the crash that he was dreading. He wasn't a person who prayed, a religious type, like his wife. But what he said silently in his head sounded awfully similar.

Please, don't let it be that ...

EIGHT

Washington, D.C.

At 5:45 a.m., William Patch, retired Navy admiral and now national-security advisor to the president, was hunched in the back of a government limo as it motored along the Washington Parkway. He had no idea which route his driver was taking because it changed every day for security reasons. Patch wouldn't have gawked at the scenery anyway. Most days, like today, he was absorbed in the contents of the leather-bound folder on his lap. It contained the latest national-security data that he was to present in his briefing to President Virgil Corland, scheduled for 6:30 a.m. There were the standard State Department memos, diplomatic cables, a Homeland Security report ... the usual.

Recently the Department of Agriculture had begun filing its own reports. They wrote about the growing dust bowl in the Midwest; and their concern was that the unending drought, coupled with the bizarre pest infestations, had decimated American agriculture, putting a lot of farmers and food industry workers out of work. The DOA's latest speculation was that those conditions might create "increased domestic unrest and possibly create homegrown, right-wing terrorists." Patch thought it was bunk, that it would take the national-security focus off the real threat. And he said so. The intelligence guys, the Defense Intelligence Agency — the DIA — and the CIA had agreed with his assessment. But the mood in the situation room had been different lately. Politics was trumping everything — not that political realities weren't

34

factored into every decision made in Washington when it came to war and peace: Bay of Pigs, Vietnam, Kosovo, Persian Gulf 1 and 2.

But now there had been a seismic sea change. It wasn't just about politics either. Geopolitics was running everything. Now there was talk from the president, and even more from Vice President Jessica Tulrude, about a "global security coalition" and less talk about American interests.

Patch's file also contained a short summary of his briefing from the CIA. As usual, when it came to the agency's written outline for Patch — and for everyone else, for that matter — the CIA kept it concise and cryptic. The spy guys wanted to keep things up their sleeve until the last minute, until it was their turn to brief President Corland.

This morning Patch's file had memos from the FAA and the NTSB concerning the Chicago air catastrophe of the day before as well as the near misses at JFK and LAX.

He looked over the photos of the crash scene and spat out several of his favorite sailor's cuss words as he looked at the carnage. He came to a one-page statement from the office of Vice President Tulrude. He read it carefully. Then a second time.

He swore again, this time even louder, trying to vent all of the steam out of his system before the meeting.

On the other hand, he thought, *maybe I should just tell the vice president where to go and be done with it.*

In Patch's mind, there was a cancer in the White House, and it wasn't coming from the Oval Office. It was coming from a little farther down, from the VP's office in the West Wing.

Forty-five minutes later, in the situation room in the basement of the White House, the president's national-security advisors were seated in the black-leather executive chairs around the long walnut conference table. On the walls, digital screens flickered with intelligence data, charts of international hot spots, and, today, a cascade of images from the crash of Chicago Flight 199.

President Corland was flipping through a report. His face was pale and haggard; his skin, an unhealthy pallor. In the harsh glare of the ceiling lights, he looked even worse. The president brushed his hand over his partially balding head as he read. He looked up and started the meeting.

"Let's begin with you, Admiral. This air crash and the other two flights ... no question about who was behind this?"

"No question. *Al Aqsa Jihad*, a splinter group of Al-Qaeda."

"What's their beef with the United States? ... as if I have to ask."

"Our support of Israel."

"Right. Okay. What are we doing to round up these murderers?"

The deputy director of the FBI chimed in, "We have a dragnet around the greater Chicago area. Same with Los Angeles. We have solid leads. We'll find them. We have positive IDs on several of them already. As for the Long Island group, we believe they were all killed in the attempt."

"How'd they get their hands on heat-seeking missiles?"

There was an awkward pause. Admiral Patch filled in the blanks. "There's evidence that Arab sympathizers within the military transferred Stinger missiles to enemy hands."

Helen Brokested, the director of Homeland Security, a tall, bland-looking woman with close-cropped hair, was shaking her head vehemently. "Mr. President, the facts are very much in dispute on that. We have to be careful not to make hasty accusations based on racial profiling."

Vice President Tulrude, sitting at the president's right, nodded, her pageboy hairdo waving. She held her finger out, like a place marker for her turn to talk.

"Yes, I agree with Helen," she said. "Mr. President, let's get this train back on track. The real question is where we go from here."

Admiral Patch pulled out the note in his file from Tulrude. He said, "Madam Vice President, it appears that your suggestion is that we tell the American people very little about the incident."

"Just what they need to know, Admiral."

"So," Patch continued, "you really think that we should tell them only one missile was fired — the one that downed the Chicago flight — and nothing about the JFK and LAX near misses?"

"Admiral, that's what my note said," Tulrude snapped, pointing to her memo, which was now on the conference table. "Mr. President, we could deep-six the entire airlines industry if this gets out of control. I've already given all of you my advice, that we lift the lockdown on commercial flights we imposed when this happened. This nation is tottering on financial catastrophe. Before the missile strikes all but one of the airlines had already gone into bankruptcy, failed to reorganize, and are now under federal control. Our foreign credit is precarious. What we say publicly about these incidents is going to be crucial. And even more importantly, there's our international partnerships, our new global coalition. There are worldwide values at stake here. The new global society we are trying to build. Peace, gentlemen. Peace."

"You know, they used to call this the National Security Council," Patch growled. "Now it's sounding like the United Nations glee club."

"That's all, Admiral," the president responded. "I understand your devotion to national security. Everyone does. But we have to work as a team here."

The CIA liaison from the Office of Collection Strategies and Analysis raised his hand. "Mr. President, we have some data."

"Let's hear it."

"About the FBI report, the wording, I mean. You heard it in the briefing just now. The statement was that there was an 'attempt' to launch a missile at Flight 433. That report implies that the suspects were blown up when the missile, which they tried to launch, somehow detonated in the warehouse before being fired. But we have a visual from the NSA. It picked up what looks like a missile heading toward the 797 jet, but then it does a U-turn in the last third of the flight pattern and heads back to the warehouse where it exploded. Also, in the first interview with the folks in the cockpit, the pilots said that the alarms and the deck screen indicated they were under attack—"

"Wait just minute." Tulrude was waving her hands.

But the CIA guy plowed ahead. "So it looks as if the RTS, the Return-to-Sender system on Flight 433, successfully turned around the incoming—"

"Now you just wait right there," Tulrude sputtered. "The final report, the very last one, says just the opposite. That the cockpit crew renounced their previous statement about the missile alert warnings going off and about some incoming missile. They admit they were mistaken."

"Looks like that missile wasn't the only thing that did a U-turn," Admiral Patch muttered, loud enough to evoke a few chuckles. Then, with a heavy dose of cynicism, he added, "Of course, there's no chance that those pilots were pressured to say that ..."

President Corland threw him a wearied look but said nothing.

"I want this on the record," Jessica Tulrude shot back, slightly red in the face as she threw a pointed look toward the CIA liaison. "I want to know how and why the CIA is getting domestic surveillance data from satellites tasked by the National Security Agency. That is a major breach of privacy of American citizens — and is probably illegal. You people have no business using satellites to spy on American citizens or on American soil. Was permission obtained from the FISA court for this?"

The CIA guy was nonplused. "This data regarded foreign actors inside the United States trying to shoot down our planes — "

Tulrude dug in. "I repeat, domestic spying that is probably illegal — "

Brokested jumped into the fray. "There's enough dispute here, Mr. President, that I think we should be careful about what we say publicly. I suggest that we go along with the recommendations of Madam Vice President, and limit our statement to the following — that a missile was fired at the Chicago flight, and the onboard RTS system failed to stop it, resulting in the tragic destruction of the Chicago flight. Period. Nothing about the LAX or the JFK flights being at risk. At least for now."

To the left of the president, Hank Strand, his chief of staff, had a suggestion. "Mr. President, a thought. We could simply say that the LAX and JFK flights were rerouted back to their airports based on preliminary security information. Out of an abundance of caution. The pilots on both flights would back us up on that."

President Corland sighed and asked his chief of staff a simple question: "Would that be the truth?"

Hank Strand grimaced, tried to smile, and then said, "Well, in a manner of speaking."

"All right," Corland said. "I'll think on it, Hank, and get back to you in a few hours. Now, good day, ladies and gentlemen. Thank you all."

When everyone had cleared out of the room, Vice President Tulrude and the president's chief of staff stayed behind. The situation room was impenetrable in terms of security, acoustics, and privacy. And they knew it.

Tulrude started. "Well, I bet this changes Corland's decision about who's going to be on his list for the Medal of Freedom."

Hank Strand looked worried. "Don't be so sure."

"You're kidding."

"No, I wouldn't joke about something like that."

"He's got to be nuts if he doesn't change his mind ..."

"Madam Vice President, I'm telling you, things are different with him lately. I'm not saying we are losing control ..."

"Let's hope not ..." Then she thought about something. "Are the White House physicians still talking about the same diagnosis for Corland?"

"Yeah. TIA. Transient Ischemic Attack."

"Next time he has one of his blackouts I could demand an immediate transfer of power to myself. Constitutionally I could do it and Corland knows it. So what are you noticing?"

"He's less compliant. More unpredictable. And he's changing course on some policy issues. I'm worried about whether he'll keep his promise to you ..."

Tulrude tapped a painted fingernail against Strand's chest. "Just make sure he does. He's got to know he can't run for a second term. I've kept my part of the bargain. I haven't told the press about his medical condition. Now he has to keep his by putting his seal of approval on me publicly and then declaring he won't run again."

She couldn't resist another jab at the president. "Did you hear him today? His question ... 'Would it be the truth?' he asks. Since when did he become such a Boy Scout?"

Hank Strand was about to say something, but Tulrude cut him off. "You're sure Corland's not keyed into the fact that I've been meeting with you behind his back?"

"No chance."

"So when's he announcing the recipients of the Medal of Freedom?"

"Tomorrow."

"And the ceremony?"

"I think he wants it quick. In a few days. In the Rose Garden."

Jessica Tulrude gave a disgusted shake of her head and turned to leave. She tossed out one last comment as she left. "I'm glad I won't be there. Especially if he still insists on hanging a medal around Joshua Jordan's neck. That would be political suicide for him if he's still holding onto to the crazy notion of a run for a second term."

With that, she stopped in her tracks. A thought broke through like sunlight. Her face relaxed. It was no longer the hard, bitter look the vice president would occasionally flash when things didn't go her way; instead, it was the look that she had been working on for her public appearances and the photo ops. Now she was smiling and nodding with her own personal revelation.

Virgil Corland aligns himself with the controversial weapons dealer Joshua Jordan. Corland's ratings crash, making it even more difficult for him to change his mind and seek reelection and forcing him to stick with our plan. I distance myself and push forward to the primaries. People start thinking, why was she ever vice president anyway? She should have been president. Yes, this could be a good thing.

NINE

Boston, Massachusetts

Cal Jordan looked absently from the front window of the crowded main room of the Reardon Art Gallery and out at the traffic on Harrison Avenue. For a moment he was oblivious to the seventy-four patrons, art aficionados, and buyers politely milling around with glasses of punch in their hands, taking in the array of paintings with their heads cocked forward to study every detail, pointing and talking to each other in hushed voices, as if they were in a cathedral. He had even forgotten, for one brief moment, that three of the paintings on display that day were his.

There was a time, not long ago, when Cal would have thought it incredible that his art would be on display in a place like this, that even as a college student he would find his work in the company of some of the East Coast's best artists.

But he wasn't thinking about that or the cordial, well-heeled manners of the art enthusiasts around him. His mind was elsewhere … back in a dark, ugly place … hands tied, duct tape over his mouth, staring into the face of a sadist.

In that harrowing place, only two things stood between Cal and certain death: God and his father, Joshua Jordan. Sometimes he wondered whether he confused one with the other, taking his father too seriously, with too much fear and awe, and not having taken God seriously enough.

But in the cold, sickening fear that had paralyzed him during that incident, Cal cried out to God from the bowels of his soul. The NYCPD bomb squad eventually showed up and rescued him, but he suspected at that moment, and later knew for sure, that his father had been the one behind his rescue. *Of course.*

Which made Cal wonder what he was doing now at an art gallery in Boston. He was having second thoughts. He was sensing a change of heart about what he wanted to do with his life. But was it really because of his own prayerful sifting and weighing, or was he just trying to please his father?

After his rescue, he naively thought that things would be different with his dad. But he came to realize that, yes, in matters of life and death some things can change in a heartbeat. But other things don't, at least not that quickly.

Then a familiar voice interrupted his thoughts. "Wow, I am so impressed, Calvin Jordan. At the Reardon Art Gallery ..."

He turned around to see the pretty face of an ex-girlfriend. "Karen, what are you doing here?"

"In town for a family thing. My folks read the blurb in the paper about the show and saw your name."

Cal smiled even though he and Karen shared some painful memories. "So, I don't see you on campus, but suddenly you show up here for my art show in Boston ..."

"Yeah, I've been super busy. Music. Drama club."

"And still dating Jeff?"

Karen reached out and squeezed his forearm. "I'm sorry how that all happened ..."

"I'm over it. Really."

"I tried to call after the news about what happened. I couldn't believe it. So scary. Oh my gosh ..."

"Thanks. I know. I got your messages. My fault. After all that, I wasn't in the mood to return calls."

She nodded and shifted uncomfortably. Then she said, "You look ... I don't know ... different. Bigger. Wow, you really do. You look good. Been working out or something?"

"Yeah. Keeping in shape. Doing some weight lifting. Physical conditioning."

"After what you went through, yeah. No doubt."

"Well, not just that. Just wanted to do it. For myself, I guess …"

Then Cal heard another voice. "Mister Jordan, you've been avoiding me." Cal turned and saw the bearded face of Alvin Reardon, the proprietor. He had a strained smile. "I told you I wanted to chat while you were here …"

Karen gave Cal's hand a quick squeeze. "You've got business. I'll let you go. Congratulations on the show."

When Karen had stepped away, Reardon got right down to details. "Your work is getting a very positive response."

"Good. Thanks."

"Now it's time to expand, I think, get you loosened up as an artist, get more edgy, find your real artistic center. Your still-life work is impressive in technique, but there's more to art than technique."

"What are you getting at?"

"You like to paint traditional stuff: bowls full of grapes with curtains blowing in the background, a worn Bible on the table. That's fine. A certain kind of passive energy there. But you need to break out. That's why I brought you here."

"I thought I was here because you liked my paintings."

"You're here because of your potential. I would like to bring you along. I want you to bust out of the box you're in."

"I didn't know I was in one."

"You are whether you realize it or not. Your mind-set is too … well, static. Conventional."

"What's wrong with that?"

"It's boring. Look, I know you got this Christian thing going. Okay. What you do with your time on Sunday mornings is your business. But if you are going to be a successful artist, you need to explore the reality beyond your personal beliefs."

"Like …?"

"Take Salvador Dalí. His crucifixion piece, for example. Jesus floating on a cubic cross, hovering over a chess board. You could use religious iconic symbols if you want, that's up to you, but break out of your stuffy, churchy traditionalism."

"You know, Mr. Reardon, I just changed my major."

"What are you talking about?"

"I'm leaving the art department at Liberty University."

"You mean you're going to an art academy? That's great news ..."

"No. I mean I've decided not to major in art."

"That's ridiculous."

"No, I don't think so. There's nothing wrong with art. I'll always enjoy it. But I feel like I'm supposed to be doing something else with my time."

Reardon had the look of a racing fan who had just bet on the wrong horse. He stretched out his arm and swept his hand out to take in the whole of his gallery. "What could be more important than this to an artist?"

Cal shrugged. "That's what I am about to find out."

TEN

Joshua and Abigail were sitting across from their daughter, Deborah, and her new friend, Ethan, in the big living room of their Colorado lodge. The log mansion was nestled in the foothills of the Rocky Mountains with land stretching all the way down to a winding river. The family loved the retreat. For Joshua particularly it had been a haven from the world, a safe house from the forces of destruction, from men whose aim was to spread chaos and death. At Hawk's Nest he could keep some of that at bay.

Deborah, with some help from Ethan, had just described their experience on Flight 433 the day before. The boarding. The takeoff. The wild deviation of the big jet. The gut-wrenching experience of the big 797 being jolted into a drastic turn, and Deborah being grabbed by Ethan, keeping her from being tossed up into the ceiling. Then the flight's return to JFK, and the interrogation of passengers.

Her parents listened, unmoving. They took turns peppering her with questions. Finally Joshua said, "Two things are clear. First, your jet was responding to an actual security threat, not just a perceived one. Those pilots must have known they were at risk."

Ethan was nodding fiercely. "Colonel Jordan, copy on that. I think you're absolutely right, sir."

Joshua turned to him. "And the second thing, Ethan, is that your quick thinking probably saved my daughter from a fractured skull, or worse. How can a father find the words to thank a man who does that?"

"No need, sir. I'm proud to be of service to your family. Your service and bravery on behalf of the nation, Colonel — "

"Retired, Ethan. Now a civilian. You can call me Joshua."

"That'll be hard."

"Well, I can't pull rank and order you around anymore."

"So you do remember me, sir, when I served under you at McGill Air Force Base?"

Joshua nodded. He was silently recalling the details of a few nasty incidents involving Ethan. The drunken bar fights, the violation of flight rules. But Joshua was not going to dress down the man who had protected his daughter. Not a chance in a million.

"I remember you, Ethan. And here you are. So my daughter says you worked with Raytheon."

Just then the phone beeped. Abigail picked it up. "Hello, Ted," she replied. "Great to hear from you." She fell silent and turned toward Joshua, her expression growing somber. She winced and said, "Josh, you'd better take this in the study."

Joshua quickly stepped around the corner, dodged into the library, to his big desk with the multiple computers, and closed the door behind him.

"Ted, what's up?"

Ted was the chief weapons-design engineer for Jordan Technologies. "Josh, bad news . . ."

"Tell me . . ."

"The jet crash . . . the one on the news . . ."

"Out of Chicago?"

"Right. Flight 199. It went down because of a missile strike. Our sources in the Pentagon say that the White House is about to release an official statement."

"What — "

But before Joshua could formulate his next question, Ted jumped in. "There's something else. That flight was outfitted with an onboard RTS unit when it was struck."

"Did the pilot launch our Return-to-Sender laser?"

Silence.

"Ted. Talk to me. Did the pilot — "

"He tried to."

Joshua hesitated, as if he'd been punched in the solar plexus.

Ted kept talking. "Reports are that the pilot went through the launch sequence for the RTS. They've retrieved the cockpit voice recorder and the flight data recorder from the wreckage. No word yet on that. But the tower said the pilot announced hitting the RTS button after the primary countermeasures, the flares, failed. But the RTS didn't stop the missile."

"How many … my God, Ted … how many — "

"There were eighty-eight on board."

"Did anyone — "

"They're all gone, Josh. All dead."

When Joshua had collected himself, he said, "I want all your data transferred to me so I can review it here at Hawk's Nest — on the secure line. Everything you've got on that flight: our install on that 797, all our protocols, the verification of the test runs, the sign-off by the FAA on that particular jet. Whatever you have on the crash. Everything, Ted. I want everything. And I want it stat."

After he hung up, Joshua turned in his wooden swivel chair to look through the window, out to the tall trees and the impenetrable line of mountain peaks in the distance.

His insides were numb, as if he'd received an anesthetic, but his mind raced wildly.

More than that, there was the awful, crippling inner torque, the crush of responsibility bearing down on him like a ten-ton weight. The solitude of Hawk's Nest had been broken. The world was pressing in.

ELEVEN

Harrat-Ithnayn, Western Desert of Saudi Arabia

Like the surface of another planet, the wasteland stretched around him as far as the eye could see, a place with hellish temperatures and brutal terrain.

Robert Hamilton, Ph.D., had dismounted his camel and was surveying the landscape of hardened black basaltic lava that had cooled into hostile, jagged rocks. His young assistant, Finley, was snapping digital photos. Back with the camels, Maher, their Saudi guide, was swishing his hand to keep the flies away.

The two volcanologists had driven their Land Rover off the highway and into the desert for a few miles, where they met Maher, who was waiting with the camels. The Rover was no use from that point on. The terrain was impassable by motor vehicle. It was studded with half-ton basaltic rock bombs that had been tossed out of the volcano that had erupted just a few weeks earlier. Deep crevasses had recently ripped through the ground during the earthquake that accompanied the geological disruption. In the distance, a great volcanic cone rose from the table-flat desert during the recent eruption.

Hamilton took off his wide-brimmed field hat and mopped the sweat that was beading on his bald scalp. He marveled at the scene in front of him.

Finley stopped snapping pictures, studied his mentor, and said, "Dr. Hamilton, do you need some water?"

Hamilton shook his head.

Finley sheltered his eyes with a hand as he looked up in the general direction of the baking sun and said, "I promised Mrs. Hamilton I'd make you take it easy."

"Not possible in this place. There's nothing easy here. Just look at all of this, will you, Finley?" He motioned toward the giant volcanic cone.

But Finley was still concerned. "Perhaps you can sit down for a few minutes ..."

Hamilton shook his head and laughed. "Finley, stop worrying. I'm not dying yet. I'll let you know when the time comes. Relax. Enjoy."

After swabbing his face with a rag, Hamilton took a few more steps toward the volcano. Then he started talking, almost to himself, as though he was delivering one of his lectures at the University of Hawaii where he taught. "Back in 1256, not far from where we are now, during the Muslim holy days and the beginning of Jumada al-Akhira, the people were gathering in Madinah for prayers at the Mosque of the Prophet. That's when the earthquakes started. The ground cracked open. Underground, the basaltic magma was building. Then the eruption. Fire in the sky, followed by two solid months of volcanic activity. Lava flows for fifteen miles. The Muslims fled for their lives. They must have thought it was the end of the world."

Hamilton paused, reflecting. He swung around to face Finley. "But then, after that eruption, silence. For nearly eight hundred years — until now. Of course, there have been others like this one here in the Middle East. That eruption on the island of As-Tair off the coast of Yemen in 2007. That was impressive. Volcanic ash a thousand feet in the air. And other ones in different parts of the world. The Iceland eruption in 2010. But you see, Finley, folks don't realize how this region in particular, the whole of the Middle East, from the Saudi Peninsula to Syria, is riddled with fault lines and volcanic fields."

Finley smiled and nodded. "Maher says that he's got us a motel room in Al-Amair. If we leave now we can make it before sundown."

"We've got camping gear with us, for heaven's sake."

"I'd hate to deal with your wife, Dr. Hamilton. If anything happened — "

"I finished the first round of chemo more than two weeks ago. I'm as strong as an ox."

"Could you humor me, Dr. Hamilton? Please?"

Hamilton shook his head. This was a major opportunity, once in a lifetime perhaps. In view of everything else in his life, he needed to nail this down with scientific precision. He wanted to start on his journal submission and hopefully get it published, as a follow-up on some of his earlier published work. Time was not on his side, and he knew it.

He spoke with resignation. "Fine. All right. Let's head back. But we need to start tomorrow before sunrise and make the most of the day."

Hamilton was almost back to the camels when he stopped and looked back at Finley. He poked a finger in his direction. "Do you realize how big this is?"

Finley smiled, but Hamilton looked him in the eyes, knowing that his assistant didn't really understand. "Finley, this is global — historic. What's going on here is scary stuff. I've got to get my data together and tell the climate people and global-warming organizations. They've got to be told — right away. Mind you, people are not going to want to hear this. The human race doesn't like bad news. Especially the kind that upsets their applecart."

TWELVE

Eighty-eight dead. No survivors. That thought threatened to swallow Joshua whole.

Somehow he managed to keep his MIT-educated engineer's brain trained on the task before him. Failure analysis. Why had the RTS system failed on Flight 199?

Then there was the fighter-pilot side of his brain too, never compromising, needing complete command and control, not satisfied with anything less than a fully successful mission.

But the mission had failed. Terribly. So terribly that as Joshua studied the information on the computer screen he had to tell himself not to think about the extended families of those eighty-eight people, the grieving husbands, wives, children, grandchildren. How many? What if each passenger left only two surviving family members behind? That would be nearly one hundred and eighty shattered lives. Heartbroken and weeping. What if each had left three behind ... and then again, what difference did a game of numbers make in the face of something so awful? As a military man, Joshua was used to the concept of casualties. He had seen them killed on missions and when things went bad while testing experimental aircraft in the desert.

This was different. These were civilians. When they bought their tickets they hadn't signed up for the hazards of war. He caught himself. He had to steel himself to the task at hand.

It was now a little before four in the morning, and Joshua had been in his study since receiving Ted's phone call. His team had sent him a dump of electronic data, and Joshua was scanning it for anomalies. Nothing jumped off the screen. He ran integrated consistency tests, his own software invention to cross-check each RTS unit, but he came up with nothing. He started to dig down into the granular details of each system of the Commercial Flight Return-to-Sender Laser Defense Unit that he and his group had adapted from the original RTS design plan in order to arm civilian aircraft.

At this point Ted and Carolyn who was the chief of weapon physics hooked up with Joshua on a conference call. They double-checked everything on the final production protocol, item by item. The digital circuits, in case there had been an electrical failure. The digital logic design. Even the schematics for the diode array inside the laser. Then the onboard computer settings. The data-capturing directorate inside the laser, which commanded the laser beam to copy the signal inside the guidance system of the incoming missile. And the mirror-reverse command, which would instantaneously load the opposite trajectory into that enemy guidance system. All of the functions that were designed to operate while the approaching missile was traveling more than a thousand miles an hour. Those systems were all checked, and they should have worked — all of them.

After several hours on the telephone, Carolyn spoke up. Besides Joshua, she was the one most responsible for the overall operating principals behind the RTS. She was known for her bluntness. "We're chasing our tails."

Joshua dismissed that. "No, we're missing something here. We have to stay on this until we find it."

Carolyn wouldn't budge. "Josh, just hear me out. We're working with half the picture until we find out what the black box says and what the voice recorder picked up in the moments before the plane exploded. Till then we're just working blind."

Ted the diplomat, intervened. "I think she's saying it's not logical to start on the premise that the RTS failed, that it was a production defect or design flaw. Maybe it's something else — "

Joshua cut in. "Like what? Like maybe a flock of birds hit the engines?"

Carolyn said, "Come on, Josh."

"No, you come on. Both of you. We can't look for the easy way out. Eighty-eight people dead — that's the body count. We need to find out why. You're saying we should assume pilot error in firing the RTS? Is that what you're saying? I don't think so …"

"We're not saying that," Ted countered. "Just that I was with you, re-member? At the White Sands missile-test range when we ran through the commercial jet RTS tests. Ten out of ten. Perfect scores all the way around. Then the tests by the Defense Advanced Research Agency and the Missile and Space Intelligence Center. No glitches. The RTS took everything the Pentagon could throw at it."

Carolyn broke in again. "You know what's going to happen, right? The other defense companies with their lasers, the traditional ones that act simply as blunt-force weapons, blasting things out of the air, that sort of thing, are going to tell the Pentagon to dump us and start working with their lasers. They'll say the RTS comes with too much risk. And the politics behind this … you have to admit, Josh, we've been working in a political cyclone ever since the North Korean thing. Sure, RTS worked during that crisis last year, saved New York from the incoming North Korean nukes. But Congress and the press — they treated us like Nazis, for crying out loud."

"We're off track," Joshua said.

But Ted needed to counter something else. "Listen, Carolyn, your point about the blunt-force kind of lasers … we all know why they don't work well: too heavy, too bulky. They have to intercept at too close a range. And if they miss the target, they blow up some innocent plane. The solid-state ones are still lacking, and the chemically ener-gized lasers are like elephants. But the RTS is like a cheetah, except it's got the IQ of Einstein. Let's keep reminding ourselves what your RTS laser defense, Joshua, has achieved. It doesn't blast missiles out of the sky, which is still too hard to do accurately. Instead it captures data from a guidance system and recalibrates it with the speed of light. That's revolutionary. Anyway, let's keep an open mind … maybe, like Carolyn says, our assumptions are all wrong. Maybe it wasn't installed properly."

"Our staff supervised the installations on the commercial jets."

"Then maybe another factor?"

"Look, people," Joshua said with fatigue in his voice, "we have to face the possibility that we screwed up. And now there's a death toll."

"I'm not ready to take the rap for that," Carolyn bulleted back, "not until we know every fact — and we're far from that right now. And one more thing …"

Joshua asked, "What?"

"Like Ted says, our RTS is the best thing we've got to protect Americans from offensive missiles. The best. Period. Start doubting that, and more Americans are going to die."

There was a knock on the door of Joshua's study. Joshua put Ted and Carolyn on hold. Abigail was there in the doorway in her pajamas.

"Just wanted to see how you're doing."

"Not good. You should be asleep."

"Are you kidding? Ted told me a few things when he called, so I have a pretty good idea about what's going on and what's in your head right now."

Joshua snapped back, sharper than he should have, "So it's Abby the mind reader?"

"On this I am. You're shouldering the responsibility for the deaths of all those people on the Chicago flight. It was a horrible thing, but you can't put this on yourself."

"And why not?"

"Because it's too early in the investigation to start taking blame."

"Why is everyone trying to get me to shirk this thing?"

"No one's doing that."

"Sure you are. And Ted and Carolyn too. I'm the only one willing to admit failure."

"Or maybe …," Abigail started to say.

"What?"

Abigail's eyes flashed. "Maybe it's your maddening perfectionism, Josh, your obsession. Whether it's missile defense or your children or —"

"This isn't about me."

"I think it is. You're too quick to beat yourself up. You're a glutton for punishment over this RTS thing ..."

Joshua shook his head.

Abigail bowed hers. "Sorry. That was a rotten thing to say."

After a few moments of silence, Joshua said, "I've got to get back to my conference call. I'm flying out early tomorrow, back to the office. The jet's ready."

"Cal's going to be disappointed. He's arriving tomorrow afternoon."

"He'll understand."

"He said he had something to tell you."

"Whatever it is, it'll have to wait." Then Joshua softened. "Look, tell him we'll definitely talk, okay?"

Then Joshua thought of something. "Did Ethan March stay overnight?"

"Yes. I put him in the guest wing. That all right?"

"Fine."

"Speaking of New York, I didn't tell you ..."

"What?"

"Got a letter from Pastor Campbell. It was a thank-you for the gift I sent from both of us, the one for the Eternity Church inner-city project. He said he was looking forward to another round of golf with you, you know, when you're back in the city."

Joshua didn't answer. Golf seemed absurdly irrelevant at the moment.

"Okay, I'll leave you alone." As she was about to leave, she added, "I'm just thankful we have our daughter, considering what could have happened."

Joshua nodded. He was embarrassed that his RTS analysis had distracted him from the fact that Deborah was safe and sound ... thanks to Ethan.

But when Joshua looked back to where Abigail had been standing, she was gone, and the door was closed.

THIRTEEN

In the City of Taraz, at the border of Northern Kyrgyzstan and Southern Kazakhstan

It was a fine day for planning death and mass destruction.

Particularly for the silver-haired Ivan Radinovad, Russia's debonair chief of special operations. For several years he had headed up a secret project, something called Невидимый Медведь — "Invisible Bear." Now it was on the verge of final, devastating implementation.

Radinovad leaned back in his chair and looked around the room. He was pleased with his new strategic headquarters. He had taken over the old stone-walled museum situated on the ancient Silk Road. The museum was part of the mausoleum of Manas, who was a folk hero and an ancient mythical figure in Central Asia. Considering the discussion he was about to have, there was a certain poetic symbolism in his selection of this place. According to legend, Manas sported a variety of magical weapons, and when he died, his widow put a false inscription on his grave to trick his enemies so they wouldn't desecrate his resting place.

So there it was. Advanced weaponry and deception. Nothing could epitomize Russia's plan better than that.

And Kyrgyzstan was a good choice to house Russia's secret meetings for dominance, which involved its partnership with Iran and North Korea. It was remote and would avoid the global scrutiny of Moscow or its other major cities. Over the years Russia had gathered back its union of former Soviet republics.

Russia's concerns about a watching world were justified. It had provided missile technology to North Korea. And back in 2010, Russia had successfully defied the world and provided enriched uranium to Iran for its nuclear program and had even helped build its reactors.

But Iran wasn't the focus of the meeting that day with Radinovad. Today it was North Korea's turn.

The Russian looked across the table at the emotionless face of Po Kungang, North Korea's head of offensive nuclear ambitions. Po turned to his left and right. Both of his North Korean assistants gave him a quick head bow of agreement.

Po was a man of considerable power in his country. He had worked personally under Jang Song-taek, the man selected to insure the transition of succession from Kim Jong-il to Kim's son, Kim Jong-un, shortly before the elder Kim's death. But Jang had been more than just a pencil-pushing bureaucrat. He ran the National Defense Commission. He was cold, unstoppable, and brutal. And for Po Kungang, he had been Jang's most promising disciple.

"So, then, it is done," Po announced. "And you will implement this through ... intermediaries."

The Russian nodded. "Yes. We have good connections. Well-trained cell groups. And the scientific muscle to put this together."

"Good. North Korea will have its revenge. But like your Russia, we need the cloak of anonymity. The international community will have suspicions about who's behind this attack. But they must never have proof. Now these cell groups ... they must not be sidetracked by their own personal zeal ..."

"That won't be a problem. They share a common purpose with us. They've always dreamed of a nuclear strike, and now it is going to happen. A great opportunity. They won't disappoint."

"And the ships?" Po asked.

"We have the final route picked out. It is still easy to transfer ownership and thus switch shipping names and flags at each port without raising suspicions. We will move your ship with the nuclear material and the detonator to the first port. Meanwhile, the weapon hardware, which has been quality-controlled by our scientists, will be on another ship. They will eventually meet up in Durban, and the components will continue on to the shores of the target. Then inland, the two bombs will be assembled and driven to their destinations."

Po nodded vigorously. "And that ...," Po said, his granite face breaking into a rare expression of joy, "is when the great flower will bloom."

The North Korean cupped his hands and slowly, delicately, expanded his fingers, like a street mime, in the graceful arching shape of a blooming flower. But that wasn't it. Po was simulating the image of a nuclear mushroom cloud rising in the sky.

Now they were all smiling.

FOURTEEN

HAWK'S NEST

"I'm not some giggling school girl. I'm a grown woman. Somehow you seem to forget that."

Abigail was studying her daughter's posture. Resistant. Arms folded over her chest. Abigail tried the reasonable approach. Sort of. "Of course you're a grown woman, but I'm your mother. My job doesn't end just because you're in the top three of your class at West Point. In terms of your life, maybe Dad and I aren't president and vice president anymore, but we still serve on your cabinet."

"Cute analogy," Deborah sighed, "but I need the freedom to exercise my own judgment when it comes to relationships. Okay?"

Deborah didn't wait for an answer. She rose from her porch chair. She pretended to study the mountains and the morning sun now rising over the peaks, yet her posture gave her away. She thrust her hands in her jeans, agitated, and rocked back and forth on her toes.

Abigail had a momentary thought as she looked at the empty rustic chair that her daughter had just vacated. It had been fashioned out of intertwined tree limbs. Abigail had lovingly picked it out at a crafter's shop in the mountains when they first moved in. *How little my children understand the love that went into picking out that furniture — something masculine and rugged that Josh would like; something comfortable for the family in sit in, to dream in, to make memories in.*

Abigail glanced over at her daughter and her resistant posture. *Yes, you're a woman, my darling daughter, and I do love you so. But you still have so much to learn.*

Abigail had been surprised by her daughter over the last twenty-four hours. Deborah had been glued to Ethan's side until this morning, when he announced he was taking a jog. Deborah wanted to join him, but Abigail talked her into joining her on the porch. Deborah seemed ready to fall for this man, who was still a near stranger, even if he had been her gallant rescuer. Abigail realized she still had things to learn about her own daughter.

"Deb, sit down."

"That sounds like an order."

"Come on. Stop the game playing. Just sit with me for a few minutes."

Deborah cocked her head with a look of futility and dropped into the chair.

"Darling," Abigail began again, "all I did was to remind you to guard your heart. That's all."

"No, it's much more than that. I can decipher your mom-talk. Translation: you're telling me, 'Don't get involved with Ethan March.' Don't deny it. I know you too well, and that's exactly what you're implying. You've sized him up and already have a verdict."

"Not at all. Just take things slowly. You know very little about him."

"Like what? Mom, this isn't a marriage proposal we're talking about. I'm just trying to get to know him."

"As a Christian, you can't be unequally partnered with a nonbeliever. The Bible's clear on that. I didn't come to the Lord until years after I married your father. He's a great man and a good husband. But you know how I've struggled with the fact that he hasn't made the same commitment to Christ I have. My advice is to handle first things first, like finding out where Ethan is spiritually."

"Well, if you cut me some slack and leave us alone, maybe I could do my own personal intel, get some private time with him, and find out."

"And there's an age difference. He's seven years older."

Deborah gave an exasperated grunt and threw her head back.

Then Abigail spotted Ethan in the distance, running toward them, returning from his jog. She had to talk quickly. "Just take your time. That's all. I respect you, trust you, love you. Which means I'll always give you straight talk, especially about things that are really important."

As Ethan jogged up to them, he slowed to a walk, hands on his hips as he panted.

Deborah tried not to stare, but she couldn't help it. Ethan was in a pair of sweatpants and a tank top with the words "Big Dog" in large letters on the front. His arms and torso were well-muscled, almost sculpted. He hadn't shaved yet. He was handsome, and she had already memorized his slightly skewed nose, but now realized that he had a scar on his left cheekbone.

While Deborah stared at Ethan, her mother was staring at her.

Ethan flashed a big smile. "Good morning, ladies."

"Good morning, Ethan," Abigail started. "Have a good sleep?"

"Perfect. Thanks." He turned and took in the mountains in the distance. "Man, this place is magnificent."

Before her mother could respond, Deborah jumped in. "Ethan, how about you and I go horseback riding? We could pack a lunch. It'll be a blast. I bet you haven't been given the official Hawk's Nest tour. Come on, I'll show you around."

Deborah reached out and took his arm. As they walked away, she threw her mother a look as they rounded the side of the house.

Abigail was left on the porch alone. She knew that her children were, well, not children anymore. Was she having problems letting go? Or did she have fears about her own role in life right now? She had been an accomplished and successful lawyer on Capitol Hill, but being a mother was different. It defined her — down to her soul.

She sat down and put her feet up on the rough-hewn log coffee table, leaning back, closing her eyes, and she did what she did whenever she felt confused — she prayed. There was never anything high church about it, just plain talk to her Heavenly Father. She hadn't known her own father very well; she was ten when he died. But God was always there, even if she sometimes ached for the Lord to be there in the flesh.

As she prayed, she lost track of time. It must have been a half an hour later when she heard car tires crunching over gravel. She opened her eyes. Her son, Cal, was climbing out of his Jeep with his suitcase in his hand.

She strolled down the porch steps, gave him a long hug, and peppered him with kisses.

"How'd your art show go? I am so sorry Dad and I couldn't make it, but you know how proud we are. Your father was fit to be tied when he learned our jet had developed a minor gauge problem. Not a big deal apparently but you know your father. Anyway, by then we couldn't catch a commercial flight. "

"Don't worry about it mom. The show was ... oh, interesting, I guess. Where's Dad?"

"Had to fly to New York at the break of dawn. Finally got the gauge problem fixed. And some security upgrades. Anyway, I know he wanted to see you, but he's got a real crisis on his hands."

Cal's voice was tinged with cynicism. "Dad handling some crisis? Yeah. That'd be something new."

Abigail replied with a sly smile, "Hey, mister, he's bailed you out of a crisis or two."

Cal gave her a funny look. His eyes narrowed. "Yeah. I know. You have no idea how much I still think about that."

She nodded and waited for more. When it didn't come, she asked, "Can I fix you breakfast?"

"I'd love it. I've been driving straight for two days. I couldn't wait to get here."

As they walked inside, Cal seemed buried in his thoughts.

"What's on your mind?" Abigail asked.

"A question."

"What?"

"Oh, it can wait. At least 'til I get some food in me."

"Come on, don't keep your mother waiting. If I feed your belly, you have to satisfy my curiosity."

Cal stopped and set his suitcase down. "The subject's kind of a *downer.*"

"Try me."

"I keep thinking about it. About almost getting killed."

Abigail didn't speak. She just waited, with a look that said she loved him no matter what.

"And it's about ... *him*," said Cal. "I've been thinking about him lately. Don't know why. We haven't mentioned his name for a while. I guess we've been trying to forget it."

"Which name?" she asked even though she already knew.

His face twisted a little and his mouth was pulled tight. "Atta Zimler."

The name belonged to the psychopath who, for one short terrifying moment, had Cal in his grip. It was a name that the family had tried to forget as things returned to normal.

As she looked at her son, she saw the man in him, even though, considering what he had endured in that harrowing episode, her impulse was always to coddle him a bit, try to protect him. Abigail had been a tough, no-nonsense trial lawyer, but when it came to Cal, the risk was always that she would be too soft. She never worried about being too hard on him. She didn't have to. Josh, with all his good intentions, always played that part well.

Cal kept talking. "I was just wondering. You know ... whether Zimler is dead or not. I know the FBI told us he might have been killed, but I need to know ..."

His jaw flexed and his face tightened, but Abigail could see that this was not fear. It was a new kind of resolve that used to belong only to his father.

He finished the thought, "... whether he's still out there somewhere. I need to know that."

FIFTEEN

Desert Palm Bank, in the Dubai World Trade Center, United Arab Emirates

"Mr. Jorgenson, welcome."

The banker reached out to shake hands with the customer who was carrying a briefcase. The customer looked the part of a Swede. The man's hair had been dyed blond. He had blue contacts in his eyes and had endured the sacrifice of staying shaded from the sun to keep his skin from tanning. While the customer had been spending the last few days on a rented yacht in the Dubai marina he had to wear long sleeves and a ball cap. What a drag.

The banker continued. "I'm sure you remember the procedures for our safety deposit boxes."

The customer smiled. "Yes, I certainly do."

The banker would have no way of knowing how well the man with the briefcase understood the security procedures. In fact, this "customer" had visited the commercial section of the tower before — during its construction. He had cased out the bank, and particularly the safety precautions being installed, even as it was being built. He was a man who kept tabs on potential high-dollar hits like this one, targets that could help fund the lavish globe-trotting lifestyle to which he'd become accustomed. His mobility was necessary for other reasons too — like the fact that Interpol, Scotland Yard, France's Direction Centrale de la Police Judiciaire, and the FBI were all looking for him.

"Come this way," the banker said. He led the customer into a frosted-glass cubicle with a soft chair and a small table. The cubicle led to a locked steel door, which, when opened, led down a dead-end hallway filled with safety deposit boxes and a video touch screen.

"I'll leave you to your business. If you need anything, Mr. Jorgenson, just let me know."

With that, the banker left the cubicle and closed the door behind him.

The customer set down his briefcase and opened it. He took out the credit card of Rolf Jorgenson. He walked over to the big metal door and swiped the card in the locking device. A green light on the door lit up. He heard the heavy click as it unlocked, pushed it open, with the briefcase in his hand, and looked to his right at the touch screen. He tapped in the security code that Mr. Jorgenson had given him — under duress. That was before things got even uglier for the Swedish broker who dealt in precious gems.

Now came the only part that presented a mild obstacle. The customer looked at a box on the screen that read in a dozen different languages: "Place Palm Here for Biometric Identification."

He reached into his briefcase and pulled out a spray can and a small plastic case. He snapped the case open and pulled out a tissue-thin polymer cutout of a right-hand palm print. It had been taken from Mr. Jorgenson in a manner that insured a painstakingly perfect duplication. The customer carefully laid the tissue-thin imprint across his own hand. Then with his left hand he used the latex spray to mist a fixative over the polymer imprint of Jorgenson's palm, securing it temporarily to his own.

He placed his palm onto the screen and tapped the button.

For a few seconds nothing. Then the screen lit up. "Identification confirmed. Hello Mr. Jorgenson. You may now proceed to access your lockbox with your key."

He wanted to say something to the surveillance cameras in the corners of the ceiling but didn't. Something viciously cynical like, "So sorry Mr. Jorgenson wasn't able to be here. He would have sent his regrets, but that was impossible. They have probably found him by now with his neck broken and his right hand cut off. Who could have done such a thing?"

Instead, he smiled at the cameras and walked past the security boxes until he came to Jorgenson's. He slipped the key in and opened the small door. A bundle of papers and a black velvet bag were inside.

He pulled out the bag and strolled back to the cubicle. The light was better there. He tucked a jeweler's glass over his eye and spread the contents of the bag on the table. Two dozen large, brilliant diamonds glinted with an inner fire.

Yes, this would do. He would get a quarter of a million, maybe a third of a million, for them if he was lucky. Usually that was chump change, but now money was tight. He had to be more discrete than usual. His last client, Caesar Demas — the international business celebrity, a friend to the vice president of the United States, and a chum of the secretary general of the U.N. — had not paid him for his last job. At least not the second half of the contracted job. That came as no surprise, of course, because the American job didn't work out the way that he and Demas had planned.

But for Atta Zimler, the customer in the bank's security cubicle who was impersonating a Swedish diamond broker, there was no such thing as failure. It was just a matter of delay. He had every intention of finishing what he'd started the year before in a New York City train station. And when he was through, and he offered Demas what he still hoped to obtain, then he would get his money from Caesar Demas. Or else.

After he had placed the bag of diamonds in his briefcase, secured the lockbox, and unlocked the frosted-glass cubicle, he strolled back, his Italian-made shoes clicking on the marble floor of the bank lobby.

Always looking for an opportunity, he spotted some mints on the counter outside the window of a pretty bank teller. He walked over. He put his hand into the dish and pulled out a small candy.

"I was looking for something sweet," Zimler said to her with a smile as he lingered at the window.

SIXTEEN

In the Manhattan office of Jordan Technologies, Joshua and his research and development team had worked around the clock for two days on their design data for the commercial version of the RTS laser antimissile system. They had found nothing to explain the failure of RTS to stop the terrorist missile that downed the ill-fated 797. His engineers had theories, but no real answers.

Joshua was in his office with Ted. As Joshua looked out the window to the New York skyline, he thought back to something his weapons physicist, Caroline, had said. So Joshua put the question to Ted. "How soon can we get the data from the black box and the voice recorder?"

Ted said, "The FAA isn't the problem. The real issue is getting the okay from Homeland Security to share the data with us. That'll be a high hurdle."

"I don't understand," Joshua complained. "We designed the system. We're part of the team."

"Yes and no. Don't forget that the Feds placed all kinds of restrictions on a pilot's ability to hit the RTS button — like getting permission from the tower first. It's all part of their concern about the consequences if a missile is turned around in a highly populated area. The RTS could result in huge casualties on the ground —"

"But we explained we were working on refinements to minimize collateral damage. Until then, our current RTS is the best thing going. They can't blackball us."

Ted pulled out his handheld wireless Allfone, clicked on the headline news, and said, "Maybe this will explain."

Joshua looked at the screen. His stomach turned.

The headline read: "Return-to-Sender Failure Cited for Chicago Air Disaster."

"You'll notice," Ted said, "that the media guys don't report that terrorist crazies shot a missile at the plane and that's why it fell from the sky."

Ted took his Allfone back and started searching for something else. "Like we've said all along," Ted noted, "the biggest obstacle is always the politics." He swooped his finger over the screen. After a moment, he said, "Found it. Yeah, I wanted to see what AmeriNews had to say. They're the only ones giving you a break."

Joshua kept his mouth shut. If anyone on his tech team could be trusted to be discrete, it was Ted. Even so, Joshua had never shared with Ted his connection to AmeriNews. Joshua had been intimately involved with this controversial new entrant into the electronic media, the first to finally bust open the media monopoly that the White House had willingly allowed to develop and exploited for political purposes. The Roundtable was a secret group of like-minded business, political, and financial leaders with Joshua at its head. Together they had launched AmeriNews to counter the encroaching information censorship that had taken place throughout the country. Joshua had been so absorbed in receiving the RTS documents that he missed the headlines on his own news service.

"Okay," Ted said, "AmeriNews reports — and this is just two hours ago — that they are questioning whether the Feds are being forthright in the investigation of the Chicago air disaster."

"Any details?"

"No. Not yet. Just speculation. Wish they'd give us some specific information."

Joshua knew why they couldn't. Phil Rankowitz, the Roundtable's media leader for AmeriNews, must not have been able to dig up anything either, even with the help of his high-octane team of investigative reporters.

"Okay, Ted," Joshua had to admit, "I dreaded finding some design flaw in our commercial RTS. Frankly, I can't see it yet. But I don't like not knowing either. Thanks for assembling the team and putting together all the schematics so quickly. Good effort. I'm flying back to Hawk's Nest — as soon as Billy fuels up the jet."

After Ted left, Joshua called Phil Rankowitz and talked to him about the upcoming meeting of the Roundtable at his Colorado estate. "Phil, I just read your headline blurb."

"About the Chicago jet shoot-down?"

"Right. What do you know that I don't? And what aren't you able to say yet on AmeriNews?"

"Only one thing. There's a blogger who keeps popping up with stuff that drives the media moguls and the White House crazy. He runs something called Leak-o-paedia. Remember the old days of WikiLeaks, the blog that used to post high-level leaks and cause all kinds of chaos? Well, this is the next generation, but with a twist. This guy is different. He doesn't just get classified documents and dump them into the public sphere. He does the old-fashioned, high-definition kind of investigative reporting where there's honest-to-gosh high-level corruption, then posts his stories before he gets shut down."

"Who is he?"

"A former investigative reporter named Belltether ... used to work at a newspaper before print journalism went the way of the dodo bird."

"What's his angle?"

"Not sure, but one of our AmeriNews stringers says he heard from a friend of a friend who knows Belltether that he's working on a scoop on the Flight 199 attack."

"I think you've got something up your sleeve, Phil."

"I do. If his story checks out, we may want to buy it as an Ameri News exclusive. Belltether doesn't sound like he's rolling in dollars. If he's a former print reporter, he's probably living off a diet of grub worms by now. I'm sure we could work a deal with him, offer him money to hire him for an exclusive, give him our platform."

"Sounds like a plan. I've got some things of my own I need to bring up at the Roundtable. See you in a couple of days at Hawk's Nest."

After the call, Joshua hit speed dial on his Allfone for an encrypted number.

It rang three times and a man picked up. "Patriot" was all he said.

Joshua could tell it was Pack McHenry, the head of the private unit of former spies and ex-intelligence "spooks" that the Roundtable occasionally worked with.

"Pack, we need to talk. I've got a crisis."

"By my book, you've got more than one. Which crisis are you calling about?"

Joshua pondered that and said, "The missile attack on Flight 199."

"We're still working on that. Nothing new. But I expect something to break any day."

"What other crisis are you talking about?"

"National security. The nuke threat. The things I'd mentioned to you and the Roundtable some time ago but could never nail down. It looks like we'll have something for you in forty-eight hours."

"Perfect. We're meeting in two days."

"I'll connect with you and your group via encrypted flashmail video. But be forewarned ..."

"Oh?"

"It won't be pretty."

SEVENTEEN

At Hawk's Nest, before the Roundtable met, Joshua took his son, Cal, aside. "I know you wanted to talk ..."

"Nothing urgent. But yeah, I'd like to talk, Dad."

"How about after the Roundtable conference?"

Cal was nonchalant. "No problem."

Joshua nodded. He was tempted to pursue it. He loved Cal. The terror episode of the year before had made him appreciate his son even more. Even though, strangely, it hadn't seemed to have brought them any closer together.

He clapped Cal on the shoulder before striding into the conference room in the working wing of his lodge. Every chair around the huge table was filled. The wall of windows offered a breathtaking view of the mountains, but no one was taking in the view. They were staring at something else.

All eyes were on the wall-sized InstantSat video screen at the end of the room. The supersecure flashmail satellite feed was about to start. The Roundtable included some of America's most successful entrepreneurs, media executives, former politicians, judges, and retired military leaders. Most were multimillionaires; some were worth more. All were powerful influences in their fields.

Abigail was at the table. Retired judge Fortis "Fort" Rice had insisted that she head up the group's legal unit, although with Joshua acting as the chair, she kept a low profile.

One new member was in attendance, a recently retired special agent from the FBI, a paunchy fellow named John Gallagher, who looked slightly out of place. He wore a crumpled suit and a golf shirt that didn't match his jacket. While at the Bureau he had a reputation for two things: an eccentric approach that put him at odds with FBI protocol and an effective knack for cracking terrorist cells.

Joshua stood up and addressed the group. "In a minute, you will hear the voice of one of our most trusted allies. I am one of the few people here who knows his identity."

Joshua gave John Gallagher a quick glance. The former special agent was the only person in the room, besides Abigail, who knew who Pack McHenry was. Gallagher had dealt with McHenry's Patriot group, a private cadre of security and intelligence gurus, during the nerve-rattling incident at New York's Grand Central Station. That was where Gallagher had first come into contact with Joshua, Cal, and the rest of the Jordan family. At that time, Gallagher, as the chief of the Bureau's New York terrorism unit, had long been tracking Atta Zimler, still number two on the FBI's most wanted list. The episode at the train station was as close as he'd ever come to Zimler.

But not close enough.

Joshua continued. "Our contact's voice will be altered and his image scrambled, but his information will be unimpeachable. You will know him only as the Patriot. He leads a group of volunteers, all of whom formerly worked in the national security system or law enforcement. His group decided, as we have, that the fate of our nation hangs perilously in the balance. Our leaders are either incapable or, worse, unwilling to take the steps necessary to save us. So the Patriots decided to take responsible action, as we have. You are about to hear about the grave threat that our country is facing."

The video screen lit up. In the live feed, a man was sitting at a desk, his face digitally blurred.

"Good day," said the image. "As I proceed, if anyone has questions, don't hesitate to interrupt me. We have credible information that a nuclear strike inside the United States is imminent. I'm talking *within* American shores. I know Joshua has mentioned this to you before, but only in general terms. Today I can be more specific. Our agents have traced this threat to the Russian Federation. Reliable sources indicate that meetings orchestrated by Moscow have been held at a special location in Kyrgyzstan. We believe the two other nation states involved are North Korea and Iran. It appears that Kyrgyzstan is the strategic planning site for these attacks."

Former senator Alvin Leander, a short, feisty man with a bald head, shot out the first question. "Why Kyrgyzstan, for crying out loud?"

The man on the screen was precise as he explained. "We have to start with Russia's overthrow of Kyrgyzstan in April of 2010. In subsequent years, America retreated from its military air base there. The U.S. gave up our military base near Bishkek, which we had been using for our war in Afghanistan before we withdrew militarily from that country. As a result, it left Russia in unchallenged control of Kyrgyzstan. Russia managed to take control over the entire Collective Security Treaty Organization, the regional security coalition of all the former Soviet republics. With Kyrgyzstan firmly in Moscow's lap, and a slow, steady process of putting all of its neighboring republics back under the Russian thumb, we see something amazing and very dangerous: the former Soviet empire has been entirely reconstructed — without any international condemnation or sanctions from the U.N. And this time without the need for a bloody revolution. Of course the current administration in Washington is aware of this but has opted to treat the rise of Russian power diplomatically. They don't see the risks.

"There is one more thing ...," the man on the screen added.

There was a pause. Leander said, "We're waiting."

"That Kyrgyzstan site is being monitored. A North Korean nuclear expert attended a meeting there. But we have intelligence that Iran is also involved."

"So you think Iran is in on this nuclear plot?"

"Exactly."

"Against the U.S.?"

"Iran may have a role, but their main interest is Israel. As we know, Iranian leaders have long harbored the desire to obliterate Israel. The other player, North Korea, has long despised our nation and wants to retaliate against the United States for destroying one of their navy vessels with the successful use of Mr. Jordan's RTS system. So, that's the playbook and the players."

Retired general "Rocky" Bridger, a stocky man with short salt-and-pepper hair, jumped in. He took off his reading glasses and tapped them on the table. "What's the operational plan for the attack?"

"We don't have anything definitive yet, but some data indicate that portable nuclear devices are involved."

Bridger followed up. "Have you shared this with our government?"

"Of course. Central Intelligence Agency, Defense Intelligence Agency, and the FBI. I've sent this to all of my contacts."

"And?" Bridger wondered out loud.

"At first, some interest. But as time goes on, we have no assurances that our leads will be followed up on — and some evidence that they never will."

"How would you know if they had or hadn't? You don't have the same resources as the government."

"I can't reveal sources, General, but we have friends in critical positions along the chain of command. They report that the data we shared with key federal agencies was ... well ... treated like a patient declared DOA in an emergency room."

Now Gallagher piped up. "Are you saying there's a cancer in the government?"

"Mr. Gallagher, I'm not at liberty to speculate. That's one thing we don't do. I'm tempted ... but just can't go any further. The new consolidation of national security agencies, while that has had some advantages, has one big disadvantage: there are now fewer people at the top who have the power to decide when to pursue and when not to pursue a threat."

Gallagher wouldn't let up. "Well, let's assume that there's something rotten. How high? Attorney General? Higher than that?"

Now Joshua turned to the former FBI special agent and had to draw the line. "John, our contact said he won't speculate. We have to leave it at that."

Gallagher shrugged with obvious displeasure.

"I have a question," Joshua said. "You said portable nuclear devices. How do you know?"

"The device that triggers a nuclear bomb is called a neutron initiator. Now Russia's always known how to make them. They were in the nuke race with us for years. Supposedly, since the New START Treaty with the U.S. under President Obama, they were going to stop further testing and development of offensive nuclear weapons, but we know differently. And at the same time, we were hampered in developing antimissile defenses. Even your own RTS is arguably forbidden under the START treaty, at least according to the Russians. But Russia started partnering with North Korea and Iran to get them to do Russia's bidding in the nuclear race. That way they could look clean but act dirty. Years ago, all the way back in 2009, everybody — U.S. intelligence, the Brits, the International Atomic Energy Agency — all had evidence that Iran was experimenting with uranium deuteride, used as a neutron source for the trigger system for nukes. But now, one of our contacts in Kyrgyzstan tells us he's seen documents passed between the Russian nuclear scientists and the North Koreans, and between the Russians and the Iranians. These papers show plans for the manufacture of very small neutron initiator systems, so small that the entire nuclear weapon could fit into the size of, say, a funeral coffin or the bed of a small pickup truck. We've also been told something else — and this is critical — that there was some kind of transportation timetable."

Joshua zeroed in on that. "You're talking transportation of a weapon?"

"No. Weapons. Plural. Two of them."

The next question was the most important one, and everyone in the room knew it. Gallagher leaned forward, his hands flat on the conference table as if he was going to vault off a gymnastic side horse at the Olympics.

Joshua asked, "What's the timetable?"

The man on the screen leaned back in his chair and delivered the bad news.

"The clock's already ticking."

EIGHTEEN

There was no tidy ending to the Roundtable meeting. It was the only time that Joshua had failed to forge some kind of consensus before adjourning. Pack McHenry, behind his scrambled image on the screen, ended the session by indicating that his volunteer agents would be at the disposal of the Roundtable, but if no coordination could be forged with Joshua's group, he said his people would be forced to go it alone.

"The only problem," the Patriot explained, "is that we lack the resources and political clout of your group. I'm not sure my group of former intel operatives, acting alone, could stop this thing."

"What do you want from us?" Senator Leander blurted out. "You're telling us our nation's going to be blown up with nuclear weapons and that the government isn't heeding your warnings. So tell us straight … what do you want us to do?"

McHenry didn't hesitate. "We need you to take the lead. You've got a retired four-star general and a former FBI terrorism expert right there in the room with you. Your group is led by an Air Force flying ace who has given the Pentagon the cleverest antimissile device in military history. You've got a former U.S. senator and a retired federal judge. We need you to coordinate this, make the judgment calls, forge the plan, and we'll give you all the assistance we can." Having turned the responsibility over to the Roundtable, the Patriot signed off.

Senator Leander, as usual, was cynical. After the video was turned off, he complained, "I think the Patriot wants us to take the rap for this little adventure if his intel turns out to be bad. If we go cowboy on this thing, chasing down and harassing some guys who turn out to be vacuum-cleaner salesmen rather than terrorists with a suitcase bomb, who do you think the Department of Justice is going to go after? We'll all end up serving jail time."

Phil Rankowitz was astonished. "Alvin, for crying out loud, you know this Patriot group worked with Joshua and Rocky during that Grand Central Station incident. They saved the day. Joshua and his son Cal are both alive because of them — and, of course, because of John Gallagher here sticking his neck out."

Gallagher looked away. He didn't handle commendations well.

Beverley Rose Cortez, a self-made billionaire, pledged five million dollars payable immediately as a down payment to "stop these blood-thirsty terrorists." But just as soon as she said that, she hedged. "But *only* if you can tell me exactly who the people are, the ones in this nuclear plot ... can anyone tell me that?"

As usual, Judge "Fort" Rice had hung back, weighing things. When Joshua asked for his opinion, Rice just shook his head. "I keep going back to what the Patriot said — I jotted it down — he has 'no assurances' that the government had followed up on these leads ... For me, that's too vague. I need more. How can he be sure? This is where we have to decide who we trust and who we believe. I can't accept the notion that the CIA and the FBI would just disregard a threat like this — if in fact it's a credible one. And that's a big *if*."

Rankowitz wanted Abigail's take on the judge's comment. She tried to be diplomatic. "I respect your analytical approach, Judge, your desire for some kind of legal certainty, but I'm not sure that's the right approach. If this really is an imminent threat, we have to make judgments on the facts as they are presented, not as we wish they were."

The judge wouldn't shift. "Burden of proof. That's the legal standard we ought to use, Abby. For me, legal analysis is all we have to rely on. Bottom line is that he didn't meet my burden of proof. It was his job to convince me of the facts ... and he didn't."

Gallagher tried to choose his words carefully. "Judge, remember one thing. This is not the same CIA and FBI that I joined years ago.

A lot of it has to do with all the political ropes and chains that have been looped around everything they do now. They're men and women, brave ones too, working in unbelievably dangerous situations, but now they have to do it in a crazy political and legal straightjacket. The people at the top are the ones responsible for that. Plus, you heard what the Patriot said about the dangerous downside of this new consolidation of the security agencies at the top — fewer people make the decisions. I agree one-hundred percent."

Joshua suggested that they carry the meeting over to a second day, but people had other commitments. Instead they would link up by encrypted conference call in seventy-two hours. Joshua and Gallagher resisted the delay, but the rest wouldn't budge. Joshua got the feeling that, as much as the group wanted to believe the threat was both real and imminent, they had too many lingering doubts and that clouded everything.

That night, as Joshua and Abigail sat alone on the back porch outside their bedroom suite, looking at the stars, he expressed his own doubts. "Maybe I should have pushed harder."

"That isn't your job."

"No?"

"Of course not. You chair the Roundtable, you lead the discussion, but these are accomplished men and women. They're not junior staffers you can order around. They have to make up their own minds."

"Listen to us ... talking as if this was some bad policy in Washington that we want changed. This is a nuclear strike against our nation!"

"I was there, dear, remember?"

"Well, it surprises me you aren't as agitated as I am ... hours are ticking by ... men coming after our cities with weapons of mass destruction, and what are we doing? Wasting three days till we meet again by phone."

"What would you suggest?"

"Something. Anything. Seventy-two hours is an eternity when national security is on the line."

"What then?"

"I'm calling Pack McHenry, putting together a tighter plan. Then when we have our conference call I'll lay it all out. An up-or-down vote."

"A plan in three days to stop a nuclear attack? You don't even know the target or how the nukes will come into the country ... Josh, how are you going to do that?"

He had no idea, but he wasn't going to admit it.

They fell silent. He looked up and recognized one of the constellations. Up in the black void of the sky were the cold, twinkling lights of Orion. Suddenly he felt tired, but his mind kept clicking and churning.

He changed the subject. "I want to talk to Cal tomorrow."

"He wanted to see you today, but the minute you got back from New York you buried yourself in your study ... then into the Round-table ..."

"Why does that sound a little like an indictment?"

"No. Just a wifely observation. Talk to him, Josh."

"I will. In fact, I told him as soon as I was done with the Roundtable we'd get together. He seemed okay with that."

The phone rang. Joshua got up and trotted into the bedroom to catch it.

Abigail could hear his voice growing more animated as he talked.

After he hung up, he came back out to the porch. But he had a startled look on his face. "Abby, guess who that was? Patsy. From the office."

"The Jordan Technologies Patsy? The new receptionist?"

"Yes."

"A little late, isn't it?"

Joshua flopped back down on the chair next to Abigail. A smile was spreading on his face. "You know how you asked me a minute ago how I could pull all this together ... a plan to stop this horrendous thing from happening?"

He answered his own question.

"I just got an idea."

NINETEEN

There were catcalls and shouts from the curb in downtown Manhattan and they threatened to drown out the proceedings. A handful of reporters and a dozen onlookers had gathered in a semicircle around the front steps of the Eternity Church for a press conference, but the noise across the street forced everyone to strain to hear what the pastor was saying as he stood outside the old, brown-brick cathedral.

Several NYPD cops kept the small mob of protesters from getting out of hand. Most of them had wandered down from an unrelated demonstration on Wall Street a few blocks away. With the unemployment rate at seventeen percent, and eleven states on the verge of bankruptcy, the public was in full-blown panic. The protesters had hit the streets to blame the "robber-baron capitalists" for the nation's financial woes. But when they heard that a Bible-toting pastor was preaching about the "end of America" a few blocks away, some of them decided to head over to the church and redirect their fury.

A bearded man in a dirty sweatshirt shouted over to the press conference from the opposite curb. "Hey, quit bringing God into this, you idiot! It's the capitalist system that's rotten. My kids don't have any food. You can take your Bible and — "

A cop grabbed both ends of his nightstick and blocked the man at the chest from walking in the direction of Rev. Peter Campbell, who was standing on the top step in front of the church. Two members of the pastor's Bible-prophecy group were standing behind him.

A female reporter with a wireless microphone took a step toward

Campbell. Her cameraman, who had a quikcam linked to a satellite feed, was right behind her. "What do you say, Reverend Campbell, to that man who can't feed his family? You talk about God's coming judgment, but with our economic problems, do you think people are listening to your message?"

Campbell had to raise his voice to be heard. "Our message today isn't just about God's judgment; it's also about God's grace and His plan for redemption. We want people to see the signs of the times and realize that the coming of Jesus Christ is imminent. We can't tell you the day or the hour, but it is very clear as we speak that Jesus is once again approaching the door of human history—"

"What kinds of signs?" another reporter shouted.

"As mentioned by Jesus in the gospel of Matthew: earthquakes. We've seen fourteen major earthquakes around the world in the last twelve months, and now the volcanic eruption in Saudi Arabia. Jesus predicted these things would be the 'birth pangs' of the cataclysm to come. The book of Job says that God 'shakes the earth out of its place, and its pillars tremble.' These signs are reminders that the Lord has something He wants to tell us."

"And what about our national financial mess?" a man from an Internet news service asked. "Are you saying that's from the hand of God?"

"I am saying—the Bible is saying—watch for the signs. Jesus also predicted famine. Here in the United States, we haven't pulled out of the dust-bowl effects of this drought we are seeing in the Midwest, or from the virus that has been killing off our livestock, or the collapse of many of our financial institutions. The dollar is plunging. We have to get the big picture. Think back to some history. The BP oil disaster along the Gulf Coast. Remember that? Resulting in the halting of offshore drilling. Then promises of renewed drilling. Administrative delays. Another spill. Another shutdown of drilling. Then our government dives into our strategic oil reserves, which become depleted. And when that happened, and when OPEC refused to supply us, where did we turn? To Russia. Why is that important? Because in Ezekiel ..."

But Campbell was interrupted by a volley of eggs. He was hit in the head and face.

The reporters and cameras immediately whirled around to take in the scene across the street, where cops were zip-tying the hands of a few of the egg throwers. More screaming and scuffling.

Pastor Campbell's press conference had disintegrated.

A young Asian man in a T-shirt and baggy cargo pants stood on the sidewalk. He had been walking by but stopped when he heard the pastor's comments. As he walked up the stairs, Campbell was still wiping his face as two of his friends helped him into the church.

"Hey," the Asian man shouted.

The other two men held their hands out to block his way, but Campbell turned toward the Asian man. "So what do we do?" the young man asked. "What now?"

Campbell smiled. "Come inside. Let's talk."

□□□

In the lobby of the Climate Change Office of the U.S. Geological Survey in Washington, D.C., Dr. Robert Hamilton had been waiting for nearly two hours. He was usually a patient man, but his foot was tapping incessantly. His patience had just run out. The papers on his lap were important — more important than his own battle with cancer and the ill effects of the chemo he'd endured. After a long and undistinguished career, Hamilton had stumbled on a discovery so stunning that it's magnitude almost defied quantification. He had his hands on a devastating assessment of an impending geological crisis. He ran through his vocabulary: *apocalyptic, disastrous, catastrophic.* All those words fit. It went far beyond his original thesis — simply that global warming trends had been spiked because of increased volcanic activity. Now the government scientists needed to know it too.

In his agitation, Hamilton glanced nervously through the office window to check the weather outside. The sky was darkening. *Drat. I didn't bring an umbrella.*

Finally, a secretary breezed in and motioned to Hamilton. "Dr. Smithson will see you now."

Hamilton grabbed his expandable folder, bulging with papers, and nearly sprinted into the inner office.

Smithson was startled by Hamilton's hasty entrance. He stood up and reached over the desk for a handshake. "Bob, good to see you again. It's been awhile. What brings you here from the glorious state of Hawaii? Still teaching?"

"Yes, and doing a lot of fieldwork — which is why we need to talk — "

"Sure. For a volcanologist like you, there must be plenty to study on the islands."

"Well, Henry, lately my fieldwork has been in the Middle East — "

Smithson cut him off. "Interesting. So what can I do for you?"

Hamilton started to pull papers from his folder. Smithson gave a tight-lipped smile and glanced at his watch.

"Henry, this data is startling. Some shocking trends are developing — with potential effects on the global-warming debate."

"Well, you've come to the right place."

"Right. Henry, I needed to show you my computations. I'm aware of the extrapolations your people have made, based on spiking global temperatures. I know you are preparing to present them at the International Climate Conference."

"Yes. Thank goodness the United Nations pulled together this emergency conclave. You know, Bob, it might be best ... rather than take your time to explain this now, just send me an e-datafile."

"This can't wait. I need your assessment of my conclusions immediately."

"I don't think that's going to happen."

Hamilton gritted his teeth and tapped his finger on his file. "You don't understand. An environmental cataclysm is coming, and it's going to blow your global-warming ideas sky-high."

"Come on, Bob. Leave it alone. Your expertise is in volcanic activity. Leave the climate-change stuff to the experts, okay?"

"Henry, for heaven's sake, you've got to review this data."

"Bob, you want the truth? You've been a thorn in our side. Every one of us who has spent our careers on the problem of global warming has had to put up with you. I remember the meeting in Reykjavik ... and then in Amsterdam. Frankly, you were an embarrassment. We hold these conferences on climate change, trying to salvage this planet — and you keep turning up like a bad penny, with your cockamamie theories. Why don't you give it a rest?"

"No, I can't do that. Will you please look at my findings — "

"Fine. Send me the e-datafile, and when I get the time I'll look it over — *when I get the time.*"

Hamilton could almost feel yet another door hitting him on the backside. He shoved his papers back into the folder. "Henry, you know what's really sad about all this?"

"What?" Smithson was now on his feet and scooting around his desk to escort Hamilton out of his office.

"What's tragic is that you're missing the really big catastrophe, the forest for the trees. I can see it coming, but you can't ..."

"What I can see," Smithson said with a grimace, "is that I'm late for my next meeting. Take care, Bob."

Hamilton played one last card. "I happen to know you have some spaces still open for presenters at the climate conference. I want a speaking slot. Bill me as a dissenting opinion. You owe me that. Let's at least have a debate."

Smithson just stared at Hamilton with a raised eyebrow. He leaned down and punched a button on his phone. He tried to call his secretary but she had stepped away. So he called Mike Leaky, his research assistant, to bring a parking voucher for his visitor. A moment later, Leaky showed up and handed the coupon to Hamilton and walked him out through the lobby.

At the elevator, Hamilton turned to Leaky. "Young man, have you heard about any of my older research papers on the connection between global warming and volcanic activity? I'll send your boss my updated data, something far more devastating is on the horizon ..."

There was an awkward silence.

"Good luck to you, professor," Leaky said, but nothing else. His eyes avoided Hamilton's gaze. His mouth parted like he was about to say something, but no words came out. Instead, Leaky turned and hurried back into his office in the government building.

By the time Hamilton made it to the bottom floor, the wind was picking up. A bit of paper swirled into the air. The clouds were black. Hamilton heard a rumbling of thunder as he thought back to his meeting. And then, a memory swept in from somewhere, a line from Shakespeare, *Macbeth*:

> *When shall we three meet again,*
> *in thunder, lightning, or in rain?*
> *When the hurly-burly's done,*
> *when the battle's lost and won.*

For Dr. Robert Hamilton, the outcome was painfully clear. As he prepared to dash to his car, while the thunder rumbled overhead, a thought buzzed in his head like a gnat. Despite his own scientific certainty, Hamilton still couldn't shake that nagging sensation.

I'm tired of feeling like the crazy one.

TWENTY

Deborah Jordan beamed. "Wow, this is awesome. My dad's going to receive the Presidential Medal of Freedom!"

Joshua had the electronic draft of the letter from the White House in his hand. He turned to his son, Cal, who was standing to one side. "Well, first of all, I'm only one of eight recipients. And second, Cal, you actually deserve the credit for this."

Cal shook his head and stumbled for a response. "No way, Dad ..."

"Read the letter." Joshua handed it to Cal. "It mentions my helping in the 'terrorist' incident in Grand Central Station. That was you, right in the middle of it. Or don't you remember ..."

Cal laughed. "Oh yeah, I remember all right."

"Well, your mom and I have to leave today for Washington. I just got the call from my office last night. This thing really came in the bottom of the ninth. The Rose Garden ceremony is day after tomorrow. For some reason my office folks didn't see the letter until yesterday."

Abigail sauntered over and planted a big kiss on his lips. "Ninth inning or not, you deserve it, darling. They should have given it to you after the Korean incident. But ... better late than never."

As Abigail, Deborah, and Ethan moved into the big knotty pine-paneled kitchen for lunch, Cal hung back to talk with his father.

"I wanted to talk to you."

"Right. Absolutely. What's up?"

"I've been thinking ..."

When Cal paused, Joshua chimed in. "I'm all ears."

"Well, here's the deal. I've dropped my art major. I'm going into poli-sci."

"That's quite a change. You sure about this?"

"Been thinking about it for a while. It sort of crystallized for me up in Boston."

"I'm sorry, Cal, that Mom and I couldn't be there. You know the story about our travel problems ..."

"Yeah. No big deal. Mom explained."

"Anyway, having your art show in a prestigious gallery ... that's a real honor. You clearly have talent."

"Thanks."

"Why political science?"

"I guess I realized after the Grand Central Station incident ... that, well, there are important things I want to be part of. There's bad stuff happening out there. I'd like to make a difference, be part of the 'salt and light.'"

Joshua recognized the reference. He'd heard Abby quote that New Testament phrase more times than he could count. That had always been Abby's thing. It was even Cal's thing, and Deb's as well. But not his. He was the religious holdout, even in the face of the near-miraculous rescue of his son. The stumbling, frantic prayer for help that he had uttered — that was answered. God had been there, he was sure of it. Still, the encounter with Christ that the rest of his family had experienced and talked about, he didn't have that. He'd stopped — right at the one-yard line.

"You know what I mean, Dad ..."

Joshua broke out of his thoughts. "Yeah, I do. Making a difference. Your mom and I believe in that. You know that."

"One more thing."

"Sure."

"About the Roundtable group."

"What about it?"

"Well, you and Mom are in it."

"Right."

"I'd like to be involved somehow."

"What do you know about our group?"

"Not a lot. Just tidbits. Helping the country. Protecting it. Defending it. Filling in the gaps where things have fallen apart ..."

"That's a good description."

"I think I could help. If I could just get a chance — "

"Cal, your enthusiasm is great. Really. And I'm impressed that you're so interested in what your mom and I do. It's just that, the Roundtable ... that's not something that you can be part of."

"Why not? I'm not talking about wanting to be a big shot, a decision maker. I'd be willing just to be a low-level assistant of some kind."

"Look, Cal. I'm serious when I say this: I'm keeping you out of the Roundtable for your own good. We're into some pretty heavy stuff, and if things go wrong, it could be very bad for your mom and me. You know about the controversial things we've been doing. People out there are gunning for us. That's fine. We're willing to accept that. But I don't want that for you."

Cal gave him a perplexed look. He wasn't going to let it go that easily. "If this country's really in the kind of bad shape we think it is, then why keep me out?"

"For your protection."

"Yeah, and if this was the Revolutionary War and the British were coming up the driveway, then what? You'd toss me a mussel-loaded rifle and tell me to shoot straight, that's what."

"So, just like that, you're talking like a soldier rather than an artist?"

"Oh, so soldiering is okay for Deb but not for me. Right?"

"She chose the Army life, Cal. You didn't."

"Mom's a lawyer, not a soldier, but she's involved. I want to study politics, make a change, just like you and Mom. I think I've earned this. I was the guy at Grand Central Station who almost got blown up by a terrorist ..." Cal's face changed a little. He had painfully overplayed his hand and knew it. His father had been right there with him that day, in the thick of it, and his dad had willingly risked death, just to save Cal.

Joshua clenched his jaw. "I'm trying to protect you, Cal. Just like that day in New York. It's too bad you can't see that. You have no idea how dangerous this might get for Mom and me, for all of us in the group. But not for you. You're staying out of it. Understood?"

The last question hung in the air. It was rhetorical but had the tone of a military order.

His father tried to wrap his arm around him, but Cal stood frozen where he was. His father said, "Let's get some grub. Carletta has fixed some awesome stuff for lunch."

After the meal, everyone scattered. Abigail went to the master bedroom to pack. Deborah huddled in a corner of the kitchen, laughing with Ethan March. Joshua asked Deborah if he could talk with Ethan, alone. Joshua led Ethan into the big living room.

Before he could speak, however, Ethan blurted out, "I want to congratulate you, sir, on the Medal of Freedom. You're an amazing man, if I can say that."

Joshua gave him a matter-of-fact nod. "Thanks. But frankly, Ethan, I'm a realist. It's an election year. Most likely, the White House is giving me the medal as a way to pick up votes. Don't get me wrong. I'm humbled and honored, but I'm cautious too."

"Cautious?"

Jordan avoided going down that road. "Ethan, are you thinking about staying in defense contracting?"

"Yes, sir. I did well at Raytheon before I got laid off. You've actually been an inspiration for me. Air Force flier. Then into defense engineering."

"Okay, then send me your résumé. I'll take a look. Who knows, maybe we have an opening at Jordan Technology."

"Outstanding, sir. I'll shoot that out to you right away."

Ethan reached out and patted Joshua on the side of the shoulder. "So, you do remember me from our stint together at McGill Air Base?"

Joshua's expression changed. "I remember that you set some flying records."

Ethan's grin got bigger.

"And I recall your getting reprimanded on two occasions for taking joyrides with experimental aircraft without authorization ..."

Ethan's smile faded. "I can explain that sir ..."

"And reprimands in your file about getting into a couple of fights."

"You know about that?"

"I make it a habit of knowing about the men under me. The main thing I recall from your file, Ethan, is that you had difficulty taking orders when you disagreed with them."

Ethan's bravado disappeared. He looked down for an instant but then looked up, straight into Joshua's eyes and said, "With all due respect, sir, I admit my faults ... all of them. But I also recall a story about a decorated flying ace, doing surveillance over Iran's nuclear facilities. When the Iranian radar painted him, and enemy ground-to-air missiles were about to be launched right up his tail, command signaled him to abort. The flier refused and kept his heading. He got the spy shots from the camera in that U-2X ultrasonic jet and returned to base without a scratch. Mission complete. That was one gutsy move that you did, sir, if I may say so. And that flight of yours over Iran is a legend among my flying buddies."

Joshua was suddenly taken aback by Ethan's account. But he also remembered what he learned at his briefing later at the Pentagon about that flight. Something he hadn't told anyone since. There was a reason he hadn't been blown right out of the sky. Somebody else had his back. In fact, a guy on the ground had sacrificed his life to insure that didn't happen.

He looked at Ethan. Young. Talented. Overly eager. Way too cocky. But Joshua saw the potential — and the need for Ethan March to have somebody watch his back.

"Send me that résumé," Joshua said. "But no promises." Then he shook Ethan's hand.

Cal was cutting through the big living room, with its mammoth fieldstone fireplace and bear rug on the wall. He glanced over just as Ethan was thanking Joshua for something and the two were shaking hands.

Cal stopped, struck by what he saw. His face tightened. When his father caught him out of the corner of his eye, Cal continued walking, through the room, out the front door, and down the front-porch steps without stopping.

TWENTY-ONE

Joshua had a plan. He'd come up with it earlier on the porch but kept it secret from everyone except Abby. His idea was to use the White House ceremony as an opportunity to slip the intelligence he'd received about an impending attack against the U.S. directly to the president. Joshua trusted Pack McHenry's intel sources, but just being at an event with the commander in chief wasn't enough. The real obstacles were the political realities he knew all too well. He had met with presidents before. Merely being honored with a Presidential Medal of Freedom wouldn't guarantee him private, confidential access to the most powerful man in the world. That much he knew.

And there was another matter to consider, his founding of the Roundtable itself. He had recently asked Abby to give him legal advice about any legal liability the group might have for its activities and how close they were to the edge of danger. When he did, she just gave him one of those knowing looks. She'd already done her homework even before he'd asked — typical of Abby. But when she told her husband what she'd come up with, she adopted her serious lawyer posture.

She cited the federal laws against "seditious conspiracy": 18 United States Code Section 2384. Abby said that in the hands of a skillful, mean-spirited prosecutor, the meaning of the word "force" in that criminal law could actually be stretched to cover some of their plans to help protect the United States from foreign threats. Every member of the Roundtable, especially Joshua, could be made to look like a wealthy criminal vigilante interfering with U.S. policy — in effect, running their own shadow government. It was a real risk. It didn't matter that they loved their country or believed the nation's leaders were failing its citizens and imperiling its safety from enemies foreign and domestic. The point remained, in the end, that their clandestine activities could land them all in jail.

Maybe he was just being paranoid, but the facts were undeniable. Not long ago, Joshua had boldly defied a congressional subpoena in his effort to protect the proprietary design of his RTS antimissile system to keep it from falling into the wrong hands. Then there was the contempt-of-court charge brought against him by a federal judge over the same issue, forcing him to go into hiding to avoid service of federal papers. Sure, things finally worked out and the charges were dropped — thanks to Abby's brilliant maneuvering — but he knew that some people in the White House were still trying to bring him down.

What if his inclusion in the Medal of Freedom event was just an elaborate trap, to get him close enough so the Feds could grab him on some charges he wasn't even aware of yet? And why did they instruct him that only one family member could accompany him to the ceremony? But his anxiety over all that seemed absurd. Why would the administration bestow a medal on someone just so they could arrest him?

☐☐☐

As the president of the United States addressed the small audience in the Rose Garden ceremony, Joshua was still wondering what had truly brought him to that place.

He found himself in a row of eight recipients, all standing behind President Virgil Corland. The president spoke from a podium embossed with the familiar presidential seal, as press cameras whirred and fluttered. They had a great shot. The sprawling trees of the White House lawn framed the event, and far off in the background stood the white obelisk of the Washington Monument. Joshua looked out and located Abigail's warm, loving face.

Joshua had not been prepared for how haggard the president looked: tired eyes, pale, sunken skin. He realized why the administration had denied the cameras any close-ups.

When it came time for Joshua to receive his medal, Corland said it was for recognition of his "acts of bravery and civic duty in foiling a criminal plot at Grand Central Station, which not only threatened the life of his own son, Cal Jordan, but also posed a threat involving America's national security." Joshua thought it was strange to get a medal for that; he'd have walked through hell to save his own son. That's just what a father does.

Most likely the president was ramping up for his reelection campaign and wanted to pander to voters who supported a strong national defense. But beyond that, Joshua got the feeling that he was there, in this glittering Rose Garden ceremony, because he was a chess piece in some kind of high-stakes political game.

When it was over, the president went down the row of medal recipients and shook hands with each of them. Joshua noticed that he took the time to converse at length with every other medalist, but when he got to Joshua, he simply gave a quick shake, silently smiled, and then moved on without saying a word.

When those on the dais dispersed, the president was quickly ushered by his staff and Secret Service detail back inside the White House. Joshua strode over to Abigail. Around his neck was the blue ribbon, and dangling from it was the white five-pointed star edged in gold and laying against the background of a red pentagonal shield.

Abigail reached out to touch the medal. Her smile was uncontainable, a gentle explosion of love, passion, and pride.

She was about to say something when her eyes darted off to something behind Joshua. Before he could turn around, Joshua felt a hand on his arm. Two square-shouldered men in suits stared at him from behind sunglasses, with tiny electronic ear buds in their ears.

"Mr. Jordan, please come with us."

"What's this about?" Joshua asked.

"You need to come now, Mr. Jordan ..."

Abigail tried to keep things light. "I hope our Medal of Freedom winner here isn't in some hot water," she said with a halting attempt at a joke.

The men didn't smile.

"I'm not just his wife," Abigail said. "I'm also his lawyer."

One of the men, ignoring her comment, said, blandly, "Mrs. Jordan, you need to go back to the check-in tent beyond the West Wing. Wait there for more information."

Joshua turned to Abigail. He looked her in the eye but was staring right into her heart. "Don't worry, Abby. I'll be right back."

"You'd better be," Abigail snapped, loud enough for the two men in suits to hear.

She kept her eyes on Joshua as he walked away, sandwiched between the two federal agents, until they disappeared in the milling crowd of smiling families and glad-handing politicians.

PART 2

The "Gods" of Climate

The National Oceanic and Atmospheric Administration released data showing that, from January to July, the average global temperature was 58.1 degrees. That was 1.22 degrees over the average from the 20th century, and the highest since 1880, when reliable records began. Although, NOAA experts say global climate change isn't the only reason 2010 has been so hot — an El Nino event earlier in the year pushed temperatures up.

David A. Fahrenthold, The Washington Post, August 14, 2010

At a gathering held during the climate summit of spiritual leaders from Christian, Buddhist, Hindu, and other traditions, I asked those in the audience to listen to the voice of the Source as it spoke through the leaders assembled.... They reinforced my view that these spiritual values, more than science and data, might be the basis for true human partnership among our leaders to achieve their ultimate objectives and avoid the cataclysms of melting polar ice, vanishing permafrost and glaciers.

Wangari Maathai, 2004 recipient of the Nobel Peace Prize
and the United Nations' "Messenger of Peace"

More science and more technology are not going to get us out of the present ecological crisis until we find a new religion, or rethink our old one.

Lynn White, U.C. Berkeley professor,
from a 1967 article in Science

The filling of a spiritual vacuum by environmentalism creates an ever greater spiritual vacuum. The environmental religion based on climate change catastrophism is itself a catastrophe that we inflict upon ourselves at huge intellectual, moral, spiritual, and economic cost.

> Dr. Ian Plimer, award-winning professor in the School of Earth and Environmental Sciences, University of Adelaide, Australia

TWENTY-TWO

The United Nations General Assembly, New York City

The U.N. had urged the Conference on Climate and Global Warming to hold its emergency session in the General Assembly chambers. The consensus was that a mind-bending climate disaster was fast approaching. What better place to discuss the future of planet earth?

No one was surprised that Dr. Robert Hamilton had not been invited to speak, not even at one of the smaller breakout sessions. Henry Smithson had used his influence to ensure that. But a few of his professional colleagues suggested that Hamilton's controversial theory should be heard, maybe at some future conference.

Vice President Jessica Tulrude gave the opening address. She talked tough about the need for "the community of nations to forge a courageous agreement to save our way of life, no matter what the political backlash." Several climatologists reported on their findings, and they all agreed, with only minor variations, that the recent planetary spike in temperatures presented a worst-case scenario. Earth was now in the early stages of catastrophic global warming as a result of human-created carbon dioxide emissions. Admittedly, it had happened faster than anyone had calculated, but the question now went far beyond abstract theory. It was a question of human survival.

Some of the morning editions of the international news outlets had previewed what would be discussed at the conclave. The global conference sponsors had given them talking points, couching the issues in less-than-apocalyptic terms so that the general population wouldn't react with riots, but the message was dramatic enough to still ring like a fire bell. The press release read:

> The nations of the Earth must construct a new way of solving climate problems as a global community, and it must be accomplished immediately. International climate law must be preeminent and binding on every human being, on every enterprise and business, on every nation. Global cooperation of all citizens of Earth will be our urgent mission. Our survival as a species depends on it.

It was Romanian ambassador Alexander Coliquin's address that was to draw all the presentations together. The plan was for him to introduce Caesar Demas, the international financier and consultant to numerous heads of state, second richest man in the world. Demas was privately reputed to be the most powerful nongovernmental person in the world. As it turned out, Coliquin's remarks went beyond mere introduction.

Coliquin's warmly intelligent, winsome style was much different from that of the arrogantly brilliant and aggressive Caesar Demas. While Demas had changed the face of international politics by the sheer force of his personality and wealth, Coliquin was more personal, more focused, and he had been, at least up to now, much more private. He had personally supported orphanages in Romania and other former Soviet bloc countries and helped to start leper hospitals in Africa, but he ferociously avoided media interviews about his good-Samaritan gestures. Coliquin was younger and enjoyed glamorous good looks, but like Caesar Demas, he was gifted with genius. With a Ph.D. in international finance from the London School of Economics, and another degree from the Sorbonne in Paris, Coliquin was a masterful communicator. Yet according to some pundits, he lacked the ability to "go for the jugular." His friendly demeanor hinted that he lacked the killer instincts of a truly successful geopolitician.

But things would change that day.

Earlier a limo had stopped near the north plaza of the U.N. building.

The door opened. When Alexander Coliquin's ridiculously expensive custom-made Berluti wing tip shoes stepped out of the black sedan, more than a thousand adoring fans were waiting to cheer him. No one knew how the climate activists had learned of his arrival. For them, he was the combination of a rock star and a latter-day Albert Schweitzer. The conference delegates had apparently never considered the possibility that Coliquin had already gained a following among the ecology and global-warming groups. Some conference leaders speculated that Coliquin himself must have orchestrated the impressive lovefest outside of the U.N., but they couldn't prove it.

Their underestimation of Coliquin was even more surprising given his track record in promoting the CReDO. With his acumen in finance, he was a natural promoter of this new global currency. Even Jessica Tulrude, who sold the Corland administration and Congress on joining the new currency, had to admit that he had a certain administrative genius.

In his address to the more than eighteen hundred delegates at the conference — scientists, politicians, writers, leaders of ecological NGOs, and others — Coliquin explained that he would be introducing "that brilliant, international treasure known as Caesar Demas" but added, "rest assured, though, that I have not come to bury Caesar, but to praise him!"

After the warm laughter died down, it didn't take him long to bring the audience into the core of his sobering message. Borrowing from the poet T. S. Eliot, he warned, "If we do not today begin a revolutionary new approach to controlling the factors that are destroying our climate, then we will see the poet's horrifying vision of a world that ends 'not with a bang, but a whimper.'"

The camera shutters from the media box fluttered like a million locusts as he spoke. He struck a good pose with his athletic physique, well-fitted Italian suit, and Hollywood face framed by boyishly tousled hair. Coliquin previewed the plan that Demas would explain in his remarks: a global treaty giving extraordinary powers to an international climate-control coalition, which would study all industrial sources of

CO_2 emissions and would police with an iron hand the activities of all companies, enterprises, and nations that in any way contributed to global warming.

But there was one lingering question, a practical one. What could bring the community of nations to agree to this startling new approach when so many attempts at global-warming conventions had failed in the past? Doubters pointed to the failed Kyoto Protocols from decades before. What would motivate the citizens of the world to embrace this new way of thinking?

Coliquin had an answer. "The solution to this crisis is not just political," he said, "nor is it just scientific. I believe in the final analysis the real remedy will elude us until we grasp the fact that this is ultimately a crisis of faith. We have in our midst today leaders from all the world's religions. In addition, there are representatives from the World Church Coalition, the Global Coalition of Religions, and many other ecumenical organizations. Most of the denominations of Christendom are represented here in this room. I have met privately with all of these leaders, and it is no accident that they all share a common element of faith — preservation of the earth. Christians believe in the redemptive act of Jesus who died 'for the whole world.' We must finish the work of Jesus and redeem the climate. And doesn't Buddha himself say that nature shows us the way to Dharma? The Hindus know that Krishna was a lover of nature and nurtured it in his lifetime. And the Muslims understand the directive of the Qur'an, that Allah makes us guardians of the earth and 'loves not those who are wasteful of it.'"

With a smile, Coliquin began wrapping it up. "It would seem that God Himself is here today, and I think He's mad at our squandering and destruction of His majestic creation. He's sad that we have failed to solve this problem until now. But more than anything, I believe that God is urging us to unite. One family of people. One opportunity. One great mission. To save our one, common earth. The *only* earth we shall ever have."

The speech was electrifying. The delegates rose to their feet. Men and women from the four corners of the earth were, for one brief moment, united. Their applause thundered through the great chambers of the United Nations.

Coliquin waited until the very last hand had ceased clapping. Then he made the required introduction: "Now for a more important voice than mine. Caesar Demas has been called by the *International Journal of News* one of the most influential men of the century. That is an understatement. Caesar has unparalleled access to the most powerful leaders on the planet. His brilliant global negotiations have brought us to this point, this conference, this moment in history. If we succeed in saving the human race from the disastrous rise in global temperatures, we have one man to thank — our next speaker. Ladies and gentlemen, I give you Mr. Caesar Demas!"

As Demas strode confidently to the rostrum, he gave Coliquin an uneasy smile and a quick handshake. As his introducer stepped away, Demas threw an almost imperceptible glance at Coliquin's back, a look of camouflaged contempt for his scene-stealing speech. But Demas was ready to launch into his own explosive address. Regardless of his feelings about this Romanian upstart, Demas knew that the crowd had been ignited. That was good. Now all he had to do was to fan the flames.

TWENTY-THREE

Joshua Jordan hadn't expected his day would end this way. He sat forward in the chair, his hands cupped in his lap, waiting, anticipating, and tense.

Finally President Corland strolled into the Oval Office. His chief of staff, Hank Strand, was standing off to the side. Strand had greeted Joshua when the Secret Service first led him past the president's smiling appointment secretary, Judith, and then into the historic office. Joshua felt a flush of pride at being an American when he entered that alcove of power and, once again, recognized the Great Seal embossed in the carpet and the famous Resolute Desk in front of the bay windows.

A pale, tired-looking President Corland walked over to Joshua. He sidestepped the ornate oak coffee table that had been a gift from the president of Belarus. Corland reached out and shook Joshua's hand. Corland plunked down on the gold-brocaded couch, an arm's length from Joshua.

The president began with startling informality. He asked about Joshua's wife and wanted to know if she had ever considered rejoining her previous Washington-based law firm, one of D.C.'s most prestigious.

Joshua smiled. "No, she has other pursuits and other clients now."

But Joshua didn't say what he was actually thinking: *No, Mr. President, keeping me out of trouble seems to be her full-time job lately.*

President Corland asked about his daughter, the soon-to-be

West Point graduate, and then asked about Cal by name. "How is he doing? Did he recover from his injuries in the Grand Central Station incident?"

Joshua appreciated that. "Yes, thank goodness his injuries were minor — at least physically — which is amazing, considering what could have happened."

"You were severely injured yourself, saving your son," said Corland. "I read the rundown of what you went through. You're a tough customer."

"I had a lot of help that day."

The president nodded. "By 'help' you mean ..."

"FBI Agent Gallagher, the NYPD, others ..."

More nodding from the president; then he added, "And help from other places? Divine providence, Mr. Jordan? ... It has shaped the history of this room we're sitting in. Do you believe in divine intervention? Your wife was known to be a woman of faith while she was still working in D.C."

Hank Strand fidgeted in the corner.

Corland noticed him. "Hank, come over here and join us."

Strand dutifully walked over and sat at the end of the couch.

The president continued, "So, divine guidance ... where do you stand on that?"

It was a surreal moment, nothing like what he had planned for. An almost out-of-body experience, especially for someone like Joshua. Even as a flier and an engineering genius he had been able to go through life with his feet firmly on the ground.

"I think the way things turned out at Grand Central Station that day ... you might say was a miracle, Mr. President."

"And the North Korean missile episode? That too?"

Joshua thought it eerie that the president of the United States would have put it that way. In his own private thoughts, not even shared with his wife, Joshua had replayed that day in Manhattan: the incoming nuclear missiles from the North Korean ship. The disabled East Coast antimissile defenses. The scrambled jets that wouldn't have made it in time to intercept. Joshua, his team, and their partners at the Pentagon had only one shot at two approaching missiles with the Return-to-Sender laser system. It hadn't even been fully tested at that point. He knew that day — in the hollow of his gut as he stood with his team, every muscle tensed and sweat beading on his back as they synchronized with the weapons guys on the USS *Tiger Shark* to launch the RTS-armed defense missile in hopes of turning the North Korean nukes around — he knew the odds were against him, against catching both missiles perfectly and redirecting their guidance data. But that's what happened. And Joshua knew, deep down, that it wasn't his weapons design genius that had actually saved New York City. Not really.

But something — or Someone — else had.

"Yes, Mr. President," Joshua finally said, "that was a miracle too."

Corland's voice lowered a bit. "You know, some of us, as we get older, occasionally get wiser. Even presidents sometimes wise-up as time goes on. For instance, I fully realize now that God directs the destinies of nations. That much is certain. I also believe he can rescue us individually, save us, preserve us for Himself. If we let Him, of course. *Redemption*. It's an old-fashioned word. My grandmother was a Sunday school teacher. She talked about it all the time, the redemptive power of the cross. I think I've finally come to understand what she was talking about."

Then, without warning, Corland changed the subject. He said he wished he could have given Joshua more recognition, in a more visible way, for Joshua's RTS contribution in the North Korean nuke crisis, back when it had happened the year before.

Joshua remarked that no apology was needed, but he did sense an opening at that moment, a chance to share his pressing intel from Pack McHenry concerning the two coordinated nuclear attacks within the United States.

Not a man to hesitate, Joshua said, "Mr. President, on that issue ... regarding threats against the United States, sir, I have some urgent and disturbing information I need to share with you."

Hank Strand's back straightened as he sat on the couch, one hand on each knee.

Joshua kept talking. "I can't reveal my sources, but you must trust me when I say that they are highly credible."

Corland didn't flinch. "Go on."

"Mr. President, we have information that America is soon going to be under a coordinated nuclear attack, and it will come from *within* our own shores."

TWENTY-FOUR

The commercial freighter, which was flying a Danish flag, was just two days away from the Port of Philadelphia, the largest freshwater harbor in America.

The captain, a Danish transplant from Russia, was in the wheelhouse, checking his logs, making sure the paperwork was in order: bills of lading, commercial invoices. He couldn't afford any unusual inspections, not with the nightmare cargo he was freighting.

He turned to his chief mate and remarked, *"En klar dag for sejlads."*

The sailor smiled back. "Yes, a fine, clear day for shipping."

It would be an easy cruise up the Delaware River to the busy harbor. The channels were deep and easily navigable, ending in a substantially deep harbor, unlike Bridgeport, Connecticut, whose harbor was too shallow. A grounded ship would be a disaster for the mission. And the big, open sea harbors of New York, Boston, and Norfolk had too much heightened security, too much military presence. Of course taking a freighter as far inland as Philadelphia had its own risks. It was an audacious plan, but there was also a great payoff. It was close, so close, to the two targeted cities.

The captain remained ignorant of the cargo's history to deliberately maintain plausible deniability. If he was captured by the Americans, he couldn't confess to what he didn't know, even under pressure. So the plotters kept each of the captains along the route in the dark about the details.

The cargo had previously been split between two ships. The two terrible half brothers had been spawned from two monstrous mothers. Now their containers lay side by side in the hold of the ship. Though they housed deadly potential, they still required final assembly and detonation.

One container had come from a ship belonging to IRISL, the commercial line of the Republic of Iran. It had shipped out of the Port of Bandar Abbas, bound for Karachi, Pakistan. There the name of the ship was changed, as well as its flag, to avoid tracking. But the cargo stayed aboard. From there it shipped out for Durban, South Africa. It was now called *The Tigris*, referring to the Middle Eastern river. But the ancient root of the word meant something else as well — it meant "arrow."

Meanwhile, the North Korean container started its journey in the bottom of a small commercial vessel named *Dai Hong*. When it arrived in Hong Kong, the ship's flag was changed to Indonesian colors. The ship's name was changed too. Now *Asian Flower* was painted on the side of its prow.

After a few weeks, *The Tigris* docked in Durban. A few days later, the *Asian Flower* joined it. The container from *The Tigris* was then unloaded and transferred to the cargo hold of the *Asian Flower* to join its evil twin.

The Danish captain had boarded the ship in South Africa. Once again, the name and flag had been changed, this time to reflect a commercial shipping line from Denmark. His job was simple. Head straight to the Port of Philadelphia. An encrypted satellite tracking device had been installed so that the group of plotters who remained behind in Kyrgyzstan could follow its passage across the sea.

The plan was flawless. No one — none of the vessel watchdogs at the Lloyds international shipping registry office in England, nor U.S. Homeland Security — had picked up the flag and name changes, or the notorious cargo, or the convergence of effort among North Korea, Iran, and Russia. The cargo continued to move to its destination without trouble.

In any one of these harbors — Hong Kong, Bandar Abbas, Karachi, and Durban — bells might have rung, at least for a few of the veteran naval monitors. It was the same route, after all, used a decade before by Iranian ships to carry illegal contraband, including weaponry, in violation of international sanctions.

The Danish captain and the first mate stood behind the seaman at the control panel of the ship. They had rounded Cape May and were well into the Delaware Bay. Soon they would be required to check in with the harbor master and receive a harbor pilot, who would go along for the ride. Pro forma.

Then the docking and the unloading. With that, the pilot's job would be finished, and for America, the nightmare would begin.

TWENTY-FIVE

Deborah Jordan was struggling with the urge to call. It had only been twenty-four hours since she and Ethan had separated at Hawk's Nest. Ethan was at a job interview at a tech company in Denver, while Deborah remained at her family's Rocky Mountain mansion. As she sat next to the phone, she thought about her feelings for him, how surprised she was at the overpowering impulse she felt to contact him. But the logical part of her mind also thought back to her mother's advice, even though she would have been slow to admit she had been listening.

What do I really know about Ethan?

Deborah had been with him as he packed to leave. She asked him directly about the scar on his cheek and his broken nose. Ethan was just as direct: "A barroom brawl with a Marine. Not proud of it, but there it is. I spent some time in the brig."

She couldn't resist a smart-aleck crack: "Just tell me that the Marine didn't win ..."

Ethan guffawed and shot back, "Roger that!" But then, in a moment of honesty he added, "The other guy was a lot smaller."

Almost instantly Deborah had regretted her joke, proof of how mixed up she felt about Ethan.

Deborah had been quick to offer to drive him to Denver. She was glad he accepted. When she got back to her family's house, she was already sorry he was gone.

She thought back to their last few moments when she dropped him off. He had pulled his bag out of the backseat of the car as Deborah stood next to him. He smiled and gently put his hand behind her neck. He bent forward. She wanted a kiss on the lips. She got a kiss on the forehead instead.

"Take care of yourself, Deb. I want to see you again soon . . . if that's okay."

She blurted out, "Anytime. Please call me. I need . . . would like a call. All right? Call me."

He headed into the hotel but didn't turn around again. In just seconds he was out of sight.

It was now a day later and he hadn't called.

On the other hand he was probably absorbed in his job interview. Or whatever.

Deborah sat next to the phone in the great room of the lodge. She had gone riding that morning, through the pasture and down to the river and back. Her big gelding, white with brown spots, used to be her delight. But today riding him just wasn't the same.

She pulled her little Allfone out of her pocket to make sure it was turned on. Then she gazed back at the phone on the table.

A voice came from behind her. "You can't make it ring by staring." It was Cal.

"Real funny."

"You aren't going gaga for this guy are you?"

"Cal, let's not go there."

"Whoa, touchy." Then Cal added, "You see the footage on the news last night, with Dad getting the Medal of Freedom?"

Deborah's heart sank. She'd been so absorbed with Ethan that she forgot about her dad.

Cal shook his head. "You didn't see it, did you? . . . So is Dad going to offer him a job?"

"Don't know. I hope so."

"Funny how he refused the request from his own son."

"What are you talking about?"

"I asked Dad to bring me into the Roundtable somehow and help him and Mom out. Nothing big."

"What'd he say?"

"Too much risk, which I find ridiculous after what he and I have gone through."

"I can understand his concern."

"Oh, really? How?"

"The Roundtable deals with some sensitive information. National security stuff. Highly controversial. There are people in Washington who don't like what he's doing. Besides —"

"What ..."

"Let's be honest. Until recently, you couldn't be bothered with the kind of issues Dad and Mom deal with: politics, national defense, freedom. You wanted to be an artist."

"So? I've changed my major — and my interests."

"I respect that. So do Mom and Dad. But this high-level intelligence stuff, you think you can just jump right into that?"

"Oh, so here we go. You're the almost-graduate from West Point, and I'm just a nerd at Liberty University. Is that it? Well, there's only one person in this room who's gone face-to-face with a terrorist. And you know exactly who that is."

"I'm not trying to downplay what you went through, but let's be objective. I'm majoring in defense and strategic studies at one of America's most prestigious military academies. I've studied military history, strategy, counterinsurgency. Up to now your biggest decision was whether to paint in watercolors or acrylics."

"Ooh, two points sis. Shot right to the heart."

"Forget it. This discussion is stupid. Besides I've got my own professional plans with Dad."

"Right. I'm sure. Like what?"

Deborah hesitated. There was a part of her that wanted to keep this to herself. But something made her say it. Maybe even flaunt it. "Before he and Mom took off for Washington, I overheard Dad on an international call. Defense guys in Israel are interested in his RTS system. And if he goes to the Middle East, I have every intention of going with him."

Cal laughed out loud. "Do you really think you can just tell him like that, that you've invited yourself along for the ride? This is a guy who won't even let his own son play fetch-and-carry for the Round-table, and you think he'll take you along to a weapons meeting?"

Deborah had had enough. She stood up and threw Cal her potent older-sister look and a final retort to match: "We'll see, won't we?"

TWENTY-SIX

Mall of America, Bloomington, Minnesota

Two grade-schoolers tagged along after their mom as she strolled through the mall. Having lived in the suburbs of the Twin Cities all of her life, she knew the mammoth, four-million-square-foot Mall of America pretty well.

She and her two daughters had just stepped off the escalator, and she was trying to locate the men's clothing store to pick up something for her husband's birthday. A fashion show was in progress farther down the mall; nearly a hundred shoppers had stopped to watch.

For a fleeting second the mom thought about wandering over herself. She craned her neck, and one of the outfits caught her eye. *Oh my gosh, I think that's a Lloyd Klein dress. I love that old Hollywood glamour look!*

"Mom, what are you smiling at?" her eight-year-old asked.

"Nothing honey. Just a dress."

Time was short. She only had forty minutes to pick something out for her husband and then renegotiate the labyrinth of the parking lot. She then had about thirty minutes to get the girls to soccer practice. They would have to change into their soccer duds in the girls' room at the park. They hated that. They preferred to change at home, but life rarely seems fair to an eight-year-old.

As she walked toward the men's store, something else caught her eye. Standing in the crowd in front of the runway stood a young woman in a scarf, hands on a baby carriage. But instead of a baby she just had packages piled in the carriage.

115

There was something unusual about the carriage and the woman pushing it, so the mom kept watching. The woman in the scarf was looking around. She took two cautious steps away from the carriage.

Several stores down, a white-shirted security cop in a bike helmet was riding a Segway in her direction. The woman in the scarf turned and began walking away, a little more quickly, leaving the carriage with her packages behind.

The mom had a sinking feeling of dread, fear. But it came and went quickly; she wasn't looking for something to be wrong.

Then there was an ear-shattering explosion. Instantly her body was punched into the air by the percussion, and sonic waves knocked other bystanders to the tile floor.

"Girls! Girls! Oh my God, where are you?"

The mom found her daughters sprawled on the ground, stunned but unhurt. They started shrieking. She gathered them into her arms and rocked them.

Her eyes drifted back to the fashion show. The world was off-kilter. As the smoke cleared, she could see the bodies by the runway, blown apart and strewn haphazardly. Blood was everywhere. A moment later, the screaming started.

Washington, D.C., National Security Council Meeting

President Corland had been going over the details of the statement he would make later in the day, to be broadcast to the nation over Internet TV and I-radio. The plan was to reveal the fact that the Chicago crash had been a terrorist attack, though he continued to struggle with how many details should be shared with the American public.

But then he'd been informed of the mall bombing. Forty-five dead. Twenty more in critical condition. Dozens injured. Once again, terror had reached the streets of America.

The president felt burdened, his face more drawn than usual, with even more grayish pallor. "I still plan to make the statement about the Chicago air disaster, but I'm not having any Q&A. No press conference. Right, Hank?"

Hank Strand nodded. A somber stillness pervaded the room, but the quiet didn't last.

Vice President Tulrude wanted to bring the Mall of America attack into the discussion, and quickly. "Excuse me, Mr. President, I think we need to raise the issue of today's bombing in Minnesota — "

"Thank you, Jessica. But no. Chicago first. Okay, folks. I plan to tell the American people that the Chicago crash was an act of terrorism."

Helen Brokested, director of the Department of Homeland Security, winced and twitched. "Just a reminder, Mr. President. Executive Order number 14,321 directed all executive branch communications to avoid using the words *terrorism*, *terrorist*, and particularly *Islamic terrorism* or any derivatives — "

"I ought to remember," Corland broke in. "I'm the one who issued that EO. But I've talked with White House Counsel. We're changing it."

Tulrude threw a lightning glance over at Hank Strand but quickly regained her composure. That was one she hadn't been told about. She'd give Strand a verbal smackdown later, in private, for his failure to sneak that political intel to her in advance of the meeting.

National Security Advisor, Admiral William Patch got back to the point. "In your press conference are you going to share any information about the JFK flight?"

"No, Bill, I'm not."

Patch continued, "How about the RTS aspect? I hope you're not intending to tell the people that the Return-to-Sender system failed during the Chicago flight. You know where I stand on that. The case isn't closed. It's still too early to condemn a pretty remarkable defense weapon — "

"I have something to say on that issue," Tulrude snapped.

Corland gave a weary hand wave for his VP to stand down. "I'm leading the band here, Jessica," he said. "If some of you dislike the tune I'm playing, so be it."

"Just a word," she said and struggled to smile.

The president was firm. "That's one word too many, at least on the Chicago flight. Now I want everyone to hear me. I will be saying *nothing* about RTS in my statement. Nothing. And it ought to be crystal clear why. National Security. The FAA, NTSB, and DOD investigations are still ongoing on the alleged failure of the RTS, and we've got the criminal investigation on some terror suspects still at large." Then he changed gears. "Okay, now, the Mall of America ... this sickens me, ladies and gentlemen. This should not have happened on my watch! Now we've got an airplane down in Chicago and people murdered in Minnesota. This has got to stop."

Jessica Tulrude was squirming.

Corland could see that she was about to come unglued. He finally gave her the nod to go ahead.

"Mr. President, it's time for us to change strategy. Rather than trying to stop the criminals from killing once they are within our borders ..."

National Security Advisor Patch shot out, "*Criminals*? You mean *terrorists*? Enemy combatants?"

"I don't want to argue over semantics. I mean all types of wrongdoers, Admiral," she barked back. "What I'm saying, Mr. President, is that we have to stop them at the borders."

Corland asked her to elaborate.

"The BIDTag idea."

"The Biological Identification Tag?"

"Exactly. For the last eighteen months, the EU has required every citizen in Europe to have one — and they haven't had a *single* incident. It's an effective way to screen out the bad apples. We can do long-distance targeting of every human almost anywhere. And if someone *doesn't* have a biotag tattoo, the screen will show that, and we know we have a suspicious individual right away. And when they *do* have a biotag imprint on their body, we can immediately tell who the person is, any arrest record, travel history, their home address, telephone numbers, social security number, blood type, marital status, religion, everything. All their pertinent data. Screening devices can be set up at the entrances of shopping malls, theaters, every soft target. We now know that the woman who detonated the bomb at the Mall of America had ties to a terror group. A screening device would have picked up her BIDTag — or her lack of one — and either way she would have been spotted. A terror matrix would have been instantly sent to the mall security office and local police. She'd have been stopped within minutes."

Corland said, "Civil-liberties groups like the ACLU have been screaming bloody murder about this, haven't they?"

Attorney General Cory Hamburg leaned forward. He had a neatly prepared defense for the vice president's proposal. "That was before the mall disaster and the Chicago shootdown. Mr. President, the polls are clear. Americans are feeling desperate. After all, there's a basic right not to be blown up. Because the BIDTag isn't inserted into the body, but is just imprinted on the skin, painless and invisible to the eye, and can only be illuminated by our government screening devices, there is really no Fourth Amendment unlawful search-or-seizure argument. Besides, we're close to a compromise with the civil-liberties groups. In the BIDTag bill we've got in Congress right now, federal agencies would still have to obtain a warrant before we targeted someone for the more enhanced screening that would reveal things like home address, religion, that kind of thing. But no warrant would be necessary for picking up terror-matrix information where there's a serious threat to personal safety or national security."

"Privacy?" Corland asked. "What about that?"

The attorney general grinned. "I think the probable-cause legal test we're proposing fully accounts for your concerns, Mr. President."

As the rest of the council debated the issue, Jessica Tulrude settled back in her chair. She had managed to get her bio-identification idea front and center. The international community loved her for actively promoting it in the U.S., and when the bombings stopped, and the terror level dropped, she would be the champion. Now all she had to do was get Hank Strand alone and hammer him good. No more holding out on her. He needed to tell her everything about his boss, Corland ... that is, if he ever wanted to serve in Jessica Tulrude's cabinet when she finally pushed Virgil Corland out of the White House.

But then something grabbed her attention like a slap in the face. After closing the BIDTag discussion by saying he wanted more time to think about it, Corland said, "One last item, not on the agenda. Last night I asked our intelligence agencies to round up the best information we have to date on any coordinated efforts between the Russian Federation, Iran, and North Korea in terms of an offensive against the United States."

The look on Hank Strand's face showed that this too was something he hadn't known about.

Corland steamed ahead. "They're getting me that assessment. Some of you may already know about my directive, some may not."

The attorney general put a finger in the air. "If I could ask, Mr. President, what's the source of this concern?"

"Someone who is now a little outside of the Beltway. But former U.S. military. Let's just say he is a fairly trustworthy source."

The assistant secretary of state shook his head, apparently sharing the attorney general's skepticism. He knew that he had his boss's proxy on this one. "Mr. President, I second Attorney General Hamburg's surprise that you are implicating Russia in some kind of operational plot against us. Obviously North Korea has been a high-risk state. That's nothing new. Iran, well, a perennial problem, though the risk is overstated. But the Russians? They sold us oil supplies when our strategic reserves dipped drastically low. We've got good trade relations. Our diplomatic relations have never been better."

Corland was about to respond when the director of the FBI jumped in. "We've heard this rumor before, Mr. President. We chased it down awhile back and were satisfied that it was nothing but a tall tale."

"I'll leave it at that. No more comments 'til I get the reports." Corland had effectively closed the meeting.

Jessica Tulrude glanced at her e-pad digital appointment calendar. Her next meeting was with Attorney General Hamburg. In the previous months she had managed to recruit him to her side. The year before, her control over him had fallen apart after she'd asked him to order a temporary stand-down on efforts to locate Algerian assassin Atta Zimler inside the U.S. Her request, which Hamburg reluctantly granted, was a favor to Tulrude's good friend Caesar Demas. It was a favor she quickly regretted. Zimler ended up slithering into the United States, murdering a few folks along the East Coast, and causing havoc at Grand Central Station. But in the end, Zimler's official connection to the murders was covered up, so no harm, no foul. Anyway, when Hamburg threatened to blame Tulrude for the Zimler debacle, Tulrude, red-faced, dressed him down.

"Hamburg, you're the attorney general," she had said. "It's probably an impeachable offense, maybe even criminal, for you to take your law-enforcement orders from the vice president. And if you cause problems, I'll make sure the media splatters that fact over every Internet news service in America."

Ever since, Hamburg had been a pussycat. Her appointment with him in forty minutes would be a good chance to remind him how much she still needed his support. She'd also remind him that if anyone challenged either of them on the Atta Zimler matter, they had a retort for that too: If America had had the BIDTag system in place back then, Zimler wouldn't have been able to enter the U.S. Problem solved.

After Hamburg, Tulrude was scheduled to have a long meeting with some of the president's economic advisors on the disastrous unemployment numbers to discuss how to stave off riots. Tulrude was trying to figure out exactly how quickly she could grab Hank Strand in between her meetings. She needed to know everything that Corland was up to.

TWENTY-SEVEN

Pack McHenry strolled at a leisurely pace between Joshua and Abigail as they walked around the Lincoln Memorial, keeping their distance from the tourists and cameras. Joshua had arranged the meeting on the fly, immediately after his conversation with President Corland. McHenry was in Rhode Island when he got the call and flew to D.C. the next day. He sounded skeptical about Joshua's meeting with the president.

"I don't mean to downplay your talk with Corland, but I should have been born in Missouri. Translated, *show me.*"

Joshua admitted that Corland hadn't made any promises. "I'm not naive. The commander in chief's not about to treat me like a cabinet member just because he gives me a medal during an election year."

"Who else was in the room?" McHenry asked.

"The president's chief of staff."

"Hank Strand?"

By the way McHenry spoke the name, Joshua could tell that McHenry knew something about Strand and that it wasn't good.

"Look, Josh, as I explained, we ran this through the right channels. We have pretty good evidence that our government is failing to treat this as an authentic threat. And nothing you've told me about your meeting with President Corland changes that."

Abigail chimed in. "What if you're wrong, Pack? What if your intel is from unreliable leads, misinterpreted data?"

"Like another Iraq WMD intelligence mistake? Abby, I wish we were wrong on this. It would make everything easier, wouldn't it? But we're not. We've triangulated it. We have multiple sources, and they all fit together. Just yesterday, before your call, I received an eDatFile showing a flurry of activity in Kyrgyzstan, at a museum that's been converted into an operations center. We've tracked communications between that command center and operatives in Russia, North Korea, and Iran."

"So you have surveillance?" Abby asked. "You know the content of those communications?"

"No. Just the fact that messages were sent, and there's some kind of tracking going on. It seems they're following an airplane or a ship, not sure which. My guess is a shipping vessel, probably commercial. They're easier to hide in the expanse of the ocean. And easier to disguise. You can change flags, captains, vessel names pretty easily."

Joshua was struck by Pack's candor. His friend was usually tight-lipped about details, but not now. As Joshua started to piece together the picture, Pack McHenry's real position suddenly became clear. He was not really retired from "the Company." It seemed clear that he was still employed as a private subcontractor for the CIA, which explained his access to this kind of intelligence. If that were the case, and federal officials were ignoring his pleas, what did that mean about the attitude of the government toward provable threats?

"What's going on here, Pack?" Joshua asked. "You're still connected, aren't you? You're still deep inside — and somebody isn't listening. Somehow the chain of command has been compromised."

Pack McHenry stopped in his tracks. At first he didn't say anything. His eyes searched the ground. "I'm not saying that the president is unconcerned. I'm saying ... that it just may not matter."

Joshua continued to push him. "So are you saying that the president is unable to use his executive powers? That Corland is blocked from executing certain commands ... orders having to do with national defense, intelligence?"

McHenry looked off toward the memorial. Then he took something out of his pocket and held it up. Joshua and Abigail were looking at the profile of Lincoln on a penny.

Pack asked, "A little quiz. What's on the flip side of this penny?"

Joshua hesitated but Abigail didn't. "The Lincoln Memorial."

"And the inscription above it?"

"*E Pluribus Unum.*"

Joshua smiled. "Now you know why I won't play Trivial Pursuit with her."

"So what are you telling us to do?" Abigail asked.

"To figure it out," he replied.

Pack McHenry began to walk away. When he was almost out of hearing, Abigail shouted out to him, "*E Pluribus Unum* ... 'out of many, one.'"

McHenry didn't turn around; he simply held his hand up and gave a sort of salute.

Abigail looked at Joshua. "Out of many, one. The need for American unity. That's his point. Things are unraveling at the top ..."

Then she had another thought, but it sickened her as she said it. "Josh, I think there may be a silent coup going on in our government."

TWENTY-EIGHT

The two containers had arrived in the Port of Philadelphia on the Danish-flagged ship, along with a hold full of other shipping goods, mostly boxes of machine parts from Germany. The radiation-detecting instruments installed by Homeland Security hadn't picked up the shipments. The newest generation of synthetic lead linings had done their job.

The two containers were loaded onto two trucks as planned, one corrugated steel container on each truck. The two truck drivers headed in opposite directions, each with a partner. One was driving to a warehouse outside of the little town of Clifton, New York, situated on Staten Island across the bay. The deadly container was buried beneath a load of crates containing medical supplies. Some of them had radioactive isotopes used for radiation therapy. The plan was that *if* the truck was stopped and the driver questioned, and *if* someone detected low-level radiation emissions in the shipment, the driver would have an easy explanation. He carried a forged trucking bill of lading showing that he was carrying radioactive isotopes for cancer treatments, destined for the Richmond Medical Center near Clifton.

The other trucker and his partner were driving south to Virginia. He had the same kind of load and the same answer prepared if a curious state patrol officer pulled him over. His papers showed he had medical supplies for the hospital complex in Winchester, in the northwest corner of Virginia.

The trucks disappeared into the slowly moving traffic as they traveled to their staging destinations. An army of drivers, coming home from work, were oblivious to the two trucks on the highway next to them. Just more traffic in the middle of congestion. Nothing more.

University of Hawaii, on the Big Island

"You talk about power? *I'll* tell you about power."

Dr. Robert Hamilton stood at the front of the lecture hall. He had momentarily forgotten about the phone call he'd received before class — from his oncologist. Instead, he was now in the happy oblivion of his favorite class: introduction to geology.

The students gazed numbly into the distance or doodled in their notebooks. Dr. Hamilton paced around the podium, his eyes glued to the floor, as if he were lecturing to no one but himself.

"And I'm not referring to nuclear fission. The physicists can tell you about that. I'm talking about something else altogether." He clicked a button on the video control. The big screen lit up behind him and showed a photo of Mount St. Helens exploding. "Look at that volcanic plume," he said, "that column of ash, gas, and pumice fragments reaching high into the atmosphere!"

After gazing at it for a moment, Hamilton wheeled around and continued, "The volcano in Iceland in 2010 paralyzed air travel around the world. And now consider this year's record number of eruptions, more than any time in recorded human history. I was at the Saudi Arabian site recently, just after an eruption at Harrat-Ithnayn out in the western desert, which reminds me ..."

He pulled out a sheet of paper and scanned it. "What number is that ... the map ... oh, yes, here it is." He pushed that number on his control. A world map appeared on the screen. Small colored circles dotted parts of Asia, India, and the Middle East. "Look at the circles — areas where it is estimated that the most volcanic activity, with the highest fatalities, is predicted to occur. Some of this data is from the Earth Institute at Columbia University. Now, here's something interesting ..." Hamilton took his laser pointer and put a red dot on the circles in the Middle East, running from Turkey in the north, through Syria, through Israel, and down to Cairo. "Look at this . . . this is ground zero for the most massive volcanic activity . . . right here."

He stopped and looked out at the class as if suddenly remembering where he was. "But I was talking about power, wasn't I?" His gaze was met by a sea of vacant stares, but something else caught his eye . . . an unfamiliar face, someone out of place. In the very last row sat a middle-aged man in a short-sleeve white shirt and a tie, which was loose at the neck.

Hamilton refocused on his lecture. "Power. Yes. Volcanoes and earthquakes are intimately related. They can cause tsunamis at sea . . ." He noticed a hand go up from a student. At last, he thought, someone was awake; Hamilton nodded for him to ask his question.

"Can a tsunami swallow up a ship out in the sea, like an ocean liner or something like that?"

"The simple answer is no," Hamilton replied. "Because of the geophysics of the tsunami wave. In open ocean the depth of the seafloor keeps the wave down to a short height but spreading it over a huge distance in its length so it's hardly noticeable. But when the surge of water hits a shallow sea floor, as you have when you approach the shallows of a harbor, that's when the top of the wave mounds up over the bottom part, and you have *wave shoaling*. Creating a wall of water. In fact, the word *tsumani* is a Japanese word, meaning 'harbor wave.'"

Another student's hand shot up. "The textbook showed pictures from the Japanese earthquake and Tsunami back in 2011. The waves didn't seem that tall."

Hamilton smiled at the sudden interest. "They didn't have to be, yet they created widespread damage. On the other hand, geological events can create colossal tidal waves. Volcanic eruptions. Earthquakes. And those in turn can cause monster walls of water. In 1958 in Lituya Bay in Alaska a landslide created a tidal wave that was seventeen hundred feet high."

The classroom exploded with a chorus of disbelief. Professor Hamilton was energized.

"Students, that's what I am talking about when I talk about the raw power of physical events in the earth. The 9.0 earthquake in Japan actually accelerated the earth's rotation slightly. Take another comparison. Take a mushroom cloud from a nuclear explosion. The bombs tested in the Nevada desert in the 1950s sent mushroom clouds about seven miles into the sky. Compare that with Mount St. Helens, whose plume reached fifteen miles high.

"Volcanoes can spit out pyroclastic flows at fifteen hundred degrees Fahrenheit, full of rock, hot ash, and gas. The movement of these flows has been clocked at a hundred and fifty miles per hour, mudslides at forty miles per hour, searing hot lava flows at thirty miles per hour. The effects of a volcano can cover up to eight hundred thousand square miles, like the one at Krakatoa, Indonesia, in 1883. And a volcano can fire off natural bombs called *tephra* — huge pieces of rock propelled outward in a diameter of up to fifty miles. Can you imagine one-ton boulders being flung into the air for miles? Then there are the other effects: disruption of electronic transmissions, clogging the jet engines of aircraft, jammed radio and television signals. When you're in the middle of one of these, it's the closest thing imaginable to the end of the world. That's what the survivors of the ancient eruption at Vesuvius must have thought. They must have wept and declared that their gods had betrayed them."

Having exhausted his tangent, Hamilton returned to his prepared lesson, about the basics of tectonic plates.

Soon the bell rang, and Hamilton gathered up his notes. That's when, in the quiet of the classroom, the phone call from the oncologist came rushing back into his mind. "Some spots lit up on your last scan," the doctor had said. "We need you to come in so we can discuss some options. I'm sorry, Dr. Hamilton."

As Hamilton was deep in thought, the man from the back of the room slowly sauntered down the aisle. He seemed to be timing his gait to give a few straggling students a chance to clear the room. When the lecture hall was empty, the man approached Dr. Hamilton. The middle-aged man had a tangle of uncombed hair and an intense look to him.

"Professor Hamilton," the man said, looking around as if he were afraid of being overheard. "I'm Curtis Belltether. Remember me?"

Hamilton gave a vague shake of the head.

"I'm the blog journalist. I called you about your studies ..."

"Oh, yes. Right. Were we supposed to meet?"

"Not really. I flew here on a bit of a whim. I thought we should talk face-to-face."

"Tell me about yourself again, Mr. Belltether. I'm afraid I've forgotten."

"I used to be a reporter for a couple of major print dailies. They went belly up, so I transferred over to some Internet publications. I kept a job, for a while. My specialty is investigative reporting, but with the changes in the electronic media, with foreign interests buying everything up, and then with the political controls that Washington has placed on the Internet, I found myself ... oh, you might say, rubbing the cat's fur the wrong way. I'm your all-purpose offender. So, finding myself out of work, I started my own Internet news source. My first site was called NewsJunk. That got shut down. Too controversial. Then I launched one called the Barn Door. That one apparently stepped on some toes as well. My Internet provider and the telecom company said my site was shut down because it had too many viruses. What a laugh. I had a cyber expert examine my site. Guess what? No viruses ... Am I boring you?"

Hamilton's expression brightened. "No, go on."

"So now my blog site is called Leak-o-paedia. I expose secret conspiracies and government corruption based on information that people ... like you ... give me."

"Like me?"

"Yeah. Just like you. Experts who've had some time in the belly of the beast and have a story to tell."

"What beast?"

"How about the International Conference on Climate and Global Warming at the United Nations?"

"They rejected my credentials. I wasn't allowed in."

"My point exactly."

"What is it you want, Mr. Belltether?"

"Your take on the recent spike in worldwide temperatures, the U.N. conference, and what you tried to tell Washington but what they didn't want to hear ... that sort of thing."

Dr. Hamilton was smiling. For a brief moment that phone call from his doctor had just been tucked away in the out basket.

TWENTY-NINE

Amman, Jordan

The palms of his hands were cold and sweaty. He felt that empty, roller-coaster feeling in the pit of his stomach.

Inside his tiny nondescript apartment in Jordan's capital city, Rafi could hear the last chanting echoes of the dwindling mob in the streets below. Thousands of Arab members of the Muslim Brotherhood had filled the streets, chanting and shouting, *"Mawt Israel! Mawt America!"* He'd heard it before. These displays were a regular occurrence in the streets of Amman. Calling for the death of those two nations was nothing new, but it seemed to Rafi that they came more frequently now.

As a member of the Mossad, Israel's spy agency, Rafi was also accustomed to blending in, looking relaxed and natural in hostile surroundings. But today he wasn't calm. He had to make a call on the customized sat-fone in his apartment. He didn't have any doubts about it being a secure line or that the encryption was less than perfect. The *yahalomin*, the Mossad communications technician who had installed it, was one of the best. No, it was the message he had to transmit that made him uneasy.

He tapped in the code, then waited. Three beeps. He gave the voice command to the recognition software on the other end. After a few seconds, he heard a tone. Then an automated voice asked him for today's password phrase.

He spoke it. "He caused the storm to be still."

"You have been authorized. Please hold."

Rafi waited. He glanced at the mini-cam monitor, which showed a view of the hallway outside of his apartment. It was clear.

He generally didn't give much thought to the pass-phrase, but he wondered who had picked the one for today. Rafi had gone to Yeshiva, and in his studies he had come across that verse from Psalm 107:

He caused the storm to be still.
So that the waves of the sea were hushed.

A voice came over the line. Rafi recognized it. It was General Shapiro, head of the IDF special operations.

"Number 8, good day."

"And to you, sir."

"News?"

"Yes."

Rafi had to give it in code. *Prince* meant Iran, and *king* meant Jordan. Nuclear weapons were referred to as *arrows*, and nonnuclear conventional missiles were *sticks*. A ground invasion was called *surfing*, and a terror attack *a game of badminton*.

"Sir, the Olympics are approaching."

"Sounds competitive."

"It will be."

"Tell me, what's the game exactly?"

"Archery, sir."

There was a pause. When he spoke next, General Shapiro's voice was punctuated, each word painfully clear and crisp. "How many arrows?"

Rafi replied, but as he did, he caught something on the monitor next to him. "Three arrows ..."

"Are you sure?"

"Yes."

"Who's playing?"

"The prince."

"Your source?"

"Friends close to the king. The king has been warned, assured by the prince of no harm to his land. Also so that they can prepare. Because the king and his people live next to the Olympic stadium."

"You are sure of this?"

"I am sure. One second, sir ..."

In the fish-eyed lens of the monitor, Rafi could see two men, one in a short-sleeve shirt and the other in a suit with no tie. Both had beards. They were walking toward his door.

"One second, sir —"

"Timeline? We must have the timeline —"

"Soon —"

"How soon?"

The men were at his door.

"Have to sign off."

The two men in the hallway pulled out their ZOAF 9mm handguns.

Rafi disconnected. He grouped the monitor and the sat-fone together on the table and then reached into a briefcase on the floor. He pulled out a block of plastic explosives, the size of a small brick, with a detonator already in place. He clicked on the Allfone wired to it. Then he sprinted to the window.

The door to his apartment burst open, the men rushed in, quickly scanned the room, and then started shooting. They emptied their magazines at the open window where they had just glimpsed Rafi's form jumping out.

Rafi landed twenty feet below on a metal awning. He hit his right shoulder and hand in the leap. The shoulder felt dislocated, and his hand was probably broken. With his left hand, he painfully opened his other Allfone and tried to hit the speed dial. His right arm wasn't moving well.

He looked up. The Iranian gunmen were bending out the window. They spotted him. As they tried to draw a bead on him with their weapons, Rafi clumsily hit the speed dial button again. The upstairs apartment roared with the blast of fire and smoke that shot out the window. The two gunmen were blown out of the apartment in a hail of debris and sent sailing across the narrow street where they slammed into a building opposite and dropped onto the sidewalk in a heap.

Rafi rolled off the awning and dumped himself in a pained heap on the street. People streamed out of the nearby shops and apartment buildings to see what had happened. Rafi ran and ducked into a nearby alley. He'd have to make it to the next safe house in Amman before the mob — or the police or more Iranian agents — caught up with him.

☐☐☐

At Mossad headquarters in Tel Aviv, General Shapiro, who had just finished his call with Rafi, looked at the six men around the table.

"When is the meeting scheduled with the American colonel?"

"Soon, but it hasn't been finalized."

"We need him here immediately. How about the NATO protocols? Any problems there?"

One of the men said, "All set."

"How about the U.S. Department of Defense?"

"We've got the sign-off from the U.S. Missile Defense Agency. We're ready to go."

General Shapiro knew the answer to his next question but asked it anyway. "We're looking at the question of notifying the Department of Defense before we actually hit the On button for our RTS systems. But there's a bigger problem: do we tell the Corland administration directly what we now know about an impending attack against our nation?"

He didn't wait for an answer. "Probably not. There are those close to the president who will jam a wrench into this thing. We'll end up waiting for support that will never come, and Israel will be bombed into a patch of scorched sand." Then he added. "Get Joshua Jordan over here. *Now*. We need the best eyes there are on this RTS antimissile system. It's his design. Let's get his eyes."

But the director of Mossad had another question. It would have seemed absurd if it were not so ominous: "What exactly do we tell him? Do we warn him? Do we say, by the way, Colonel Jordan, we thought you ought to know … we're having a nuclear war over here, and you're invited."

THIRTY

Abigail and Joshua were in their hotel room in D.C. after meeting with Pack McHenry. Abigail clicked off her Allfone and said, "That was Pack's wife, Victoria. She's made reservations for brunch tomorrow, just the two of us. Great, huh?"

Joshua was irritated. "So what do I do? Stay here in the hotel twiddling my thumbs? Abby, excuse me, but the world's falling apart and you're doing lunch!"

"Brunch actually," she said with a look that said she would not be moved. "And about your thumb twiddling, well, I have a message on my Allfone that concerns you, Josh. I've got a suggestion ..."

"A message from whom?"

"Pastor Campbell. He's here in D.C. He had a meeting with the Senate Chaplain but said he would like to take you out for lunch. Sort of a way to congratulate you on getting the Medal of Freedom. He was very impressed."

Joshua had become an occasional golf partner with Campbell from time to time when the two would meet up at some of the upscale golf courses outside of New York City. The pastor wasn't a half-bad golfer, and he was good company, although he would inevitably introduce the topic of his wife's faith, and Joshua's own lack of it. For Joshua, that was always the sticking point.

He gave his wife a doubtful look and complained that he needed to get back to his work on Israel's request for advice on their RTS system.

She walked over and gave him a lingering kiss. "I'm not going to coerce you or badger you, but I'm looking forward to a great time with Victoria. What you do on your own time tomorrow is your business." She slipped him a piece of paper. "Here's Pastor Campbell's number." Then she added, "And on the Israel issue that you're working on … that may be more important in the big picture than you think. Just my little thought."

"Big picture?"

"Yes, and you know what picture I'm talking about."

He did. Abigail's Christian faith, which had proved to be a fully operational lifestyle for her, had also made her a keen student of the Bible. She talked a lot about the theological significance of the Holy Land and Israel's role in the wrapping up of all human history. It came up more and more recently, ever since Joshua was invited to work with the Israeli defense officials. Yes, he knew about her "big picture."

Joshua called Campbell. He figured he owed him that.

The next day they met for lunch at a pricey place with a grand view of the Capitol Dome and a menu that included some great Maryland crab cakes. Joshua tried to tell himself that he had done it for Abby. But then, he knew that wasn't exactly the truth.

As usual, the two of them led off with some golfing stories. Campbell was relating his last defeat on the links. "I couldn't concentrate," Campbell admitted. "Every time I got that putter in my hand, I felt distracted."

Joshua knew the feeling. "People don't appreciate the mental aspect of golf." Then he remembered something. "I saw the blurb on your press conference in New York. Looks like a riot broke out. And here I thought I was the public instigator."

Campbell chuckled. "Oh, it wasn't that bad. You know how cameras can make a small group of protestors look like a major revolution."

For Joshua it seemed evident. "Well, pastor, you tell people that the world's coming to an end — that the earth is going to blow up, which I gather is what you were saying — then you're bound to get a reaction. On the other hand, you know my approach: if I know an explosion is coming, then I'll try to stop the timer on the bomb."

"Some explosions can't be stopped," Campbell said. He was pushing himself away from the table a little to stretch out.

"I don't believe that."

"Josh, if God's directing the cataclysm, you're going to be sorely disappointed if you think you can stop it."

"That's a big *if.*"

"Fair enough."

Campbell thought about it for a few moments. "Okay, so we need to resolve your 'big if' issue. Now here is how I do it. I search the Scriptures and I read the news. Put the two together. My group of fellow 'searchers of the times,' the prophecy scholars I meet with regularly, agrees with me about one thing — that the signs of the times, foretold thousands of years ago, are starting to unfold. Right now. Right here on planet Earth. God is about to make a miraculous showing. Awesome. Fearful. Mighty. The human vocabulary fails us when we try to describe the importance of what is coming."

Campbell tossed his napkin on the table. "The thing is to recognize that it is unstoppable. You can't pull the pin out of the preordained providence of God. The first order of business has to be to prepare to meet Him."

Joshua resisted the urge to challenge Campbell, so he let it drop. But he sometimes felt that the pastor and Abby, and yes, even his own son and daughter, were visitors from a distant world. They saw things he couldn't see and felt things he wished he could experience but didn't: a spiritual awakening. He had seen the change in Abby over the years. That much was undeniable.

As they were strolling out of the restaurant, Campbell stopped him, "Keep your eyes on Israel," he said. "That's how you can read the time on God's clock."

That startled Joshua, particularly in light of the call he'd received two days before from the commander of Israel's IDF, requesting a meeting eventually in Tel Aviv about the RTS system.

Campbell said something else. And when he did, it struck Joshua as both odd and strangely pointed: "But Josh, you can't be prepared for those great events, for God's imminent revealing, His apocalypse, until you make a very personal decision. To open the door of your heart to His Son, Jesus, the Christ. The coming King. Listen, the return to this world of Christ the King of Kings is a fact. One that is absolutely certain, more certain than you can possibly comprehend."

TH1RTY-ONE

Abby was waiting for Joshua in their hotel room. As he came through the door, he expected her to start grilling him about his time with Pastor Campbell, but she didn't. Nor did she expound on her chick lunch with Victoria McHenry. Instead, with an urgency in her voice, she said, "Josh, your office has been trying to reach you. It's about Israel. They said you need to check your encrypted DOD Allfone right away."

Joshua grabbed his deep blue Allfone, the one he used only for top secret Department of Defense business. He pulled up an email that had been routed through the Pentagon and cleared through the Technology Transfer Office. It had originated from the office of General Jacob Shapiro, chief of the general staff of the Israeli defense forces. It read,

Col. (Ret.) Joshua Jordan

We had previously extended an invitation to you to meet with our U.S. representative from our Antimissile Research & Development branch, to be followed up with a visit here in Israel at an unspecified time in the future. However, our operational timeline has shortened, and we would greatly appreciate a joint testing conference with you and our team here in Tel Aviv as soon as you can make travel arrangements. If at all possible, we would like to convene the session the day after tomorrow at our headquarters at the Kirya compound. I have spoken personally with Lt. Gen. Michael Wooling, the director of the U.S. Missile

Defense Agency, and he has kindly concurred with our request for an expedited meeting and has verified Pentagon approval.

We hope to receive your confirmation soon.

Best regards,

For General J. Shapiro,
Lt. Gen. Gavi Havrel,
Deputy Chief of Staff

The email had an attachment. He clicked it and read the certification document. Then he looked at Abigail and explained, "The Israelis want me over there in twenty-four hours."

"So soon?"

"Yes."

"What's the rush?"

"They didn't give me the specifics."

Abigail waited for her husband to process the news and then said, "Josh, don't these defense-technology transfers take a long time to iron out? Approvals from DOD and everything?"

"Usually. I knew they were testing the Return-to-Sender system with DOD approval, but this is different. They want me to consult with them personally in order to make it operational. That usually requires a whole additional level of Pentagon sign-offs, tons of red tape. But this time it's all been done in advance. It's right here in this attachment. The Pentagon certifies compliance with NATO mandates, approval obtained from our four-star regional commander and from the Missile Defense Agency. This thing's been put on a fast track, triple time."

"I hear the wheels churning in your head. Talk to me."

"I'm thinking about the Roundtable, the threats that Pack McHenry told us about, the White House paralyzed. Maybe, as you put it, there's some kind of silent coup going on. And a plot to bring hostile nukes into our borders."

"I think you've got to ask yourself where you can do the most good."

"I don't know. I founded the Roundtable. I can't walk out on everybody now. This is a crisis moment."

Abigail placed her hand softly on his back. "I'll do whatever needs to be done. How can I help?"

"The attached document says that Michael Wooling, director of the MDA, apparently wants me over there stat. He's a rock-steady guy, so if he thinks this is an emergency, sees smoke, it's not just from a burned pot roast ... he must believe the house is on fire. He's also close to Admiral Patch, the national security advisor. The two are clones on the need for strong national defense. I'm wondering ..."

"Maybe they know something we don't."

"Remember the intel that Pack McHenry gave us a year ago?"

"That the United States and Israel were both at risk?"

"Yes. And our briefing a few days ago. Evidence that Iran is closing in on a nuclear strike against Israel, just as Russia and North Korea are moving toward a nuke attack against us."

Joshua was thinking out loud, his head bobbing as he dissected the problem. "So where does that leave us? Abby, you could run the Roundtable for me, of course. But is it really a defense-system question that the Roundtable has to answer? Or could it be something else? Something like — "

"A critical failure in the executive branch?"

Joshua nodded, his face showing a granite resolve. "Exactly. The fact that the attack might be successful is really secondary to a constitutional implosion that's preventing the Feds from intervening to protect us. I guess it's really more a political crisis, which is where you come in. That's your skill set." Joshua looked up. The decision was made. "Okay. I go to Israel. Abby, you stay here and lead the Roundtable discussions about what we can do here on the home front."

They looked at each other, and as they did they recognized the familiar expression. The silent acknowledgment that they were not only lovers and friends but also partners. And they were facing once again a crisis that was so titanic that it dwarfed who they were even when they were together.

Abby spoke it, but Josh felt it too. "Josh, we'll do what we have to do, what we're called to do. But I'm heartsick that we have to be away from each other, separated by thousands of miles, an ocean, and by whatever danger is out there, pulling us apart."

For a moment, Abby looked as though she was about to say more but didn't. As Joshua gazed at his wife he couldn't get his mind off the deadly gravity of their mission. As Abby kissed him on his square jaw, she noticed that he'd rushed out without shaving that morning. She half smiled, then kissed him on the lips. She pulled back to look him in the eye, to remember his face and everything about him and quietly whispered.

"God help us."

THIRTY-TWO

John Gallagher had returned to Hawk's Nest on Sunday night so he could make the meeting the next morning at 10:30. Some of the members would be joining in by conference call. Others, like him, had decided to make the trip to the Jordans' Rocky Mountain retreat.

That night, by phone, Joshua had directed Gallagher and the others to make themselves at home in the guest wing; while he had urgent business overseas, Abigail would act as the group's temporary chair. Of course, no one objected. Joshua also gave Gallagher a briefing of what the "Patriot" would reveal to the Roundtable the next day.

Each of the guestrooms at Hawks' Nest had a name. Gallagher laughed when he saw the plaque over the door of his room: The Roy Rogers Room.

He smiled. "This is great." The retired FBI agent had always been accused by his stiff-necked, rule-book supervisor of "playing cowboy" in his pursuit of bad guys. So for John Gallagher this was the perfect room.

Hungry, he wandered down the spiral staircase at the west end of the lodge, past a row of antelope antlers over doorways. He caught a glimpse of himself in a full-length mirror, his belly hanging slightly over his belt. *Boy, I've got to get to the gym.*

He recalled that the Jordans had a full-size Nautilus workout room, including a treadmill and a stair climber. *Maybe I'll work out a little ... man-up with a good sweat.* Then the next thought. *But only after I feed my face.*

He sauntered into the restaurant-sized kitchen. Carletta, the Jordans' chef, had been working on the food for the Roundtable meeting the next day. She was cleaning up.

"Señor Gallagher, can I fix something for you?"

"I don't suppose you have any chili dogs?"

She shook her head.

"Just a sandwich would be fine. Just point me in the right direction. I'll fix it."

A moment later Cal walked into the kitchen and greeted him as "Agent Gallagher."

"Come on, Cal, you know I've retired from the Bureau. I'm just plain John now." Cal gave a hearty nod. "After all," said Gallagher, "you and I were partners in battling evil last year, fighting for truth, justice, and the American way. Right?"

Cal grinned at Gallagher's loose, good-buddy approach.

As Gallagher threw a club sandwich together, he got serious. "You know, you were the one in the closet with duct tape over your mouth and a bomb around your neck. And where was I? In a surveillance truck on the street eating donuts. Who had the tougher job that day?"

"Yeah, well, you saved my life."

"Naw. Your dad did that. I was strictly an FBI bystander, trying hard not to screw things up."

"You're still one of my heroes."

Gallagher gave a half smile and felt a little embarrassed. As he crunched on a dill pickle, a jolting thought occurred to him.

Cal noticed the change in Gallagher's face and gambled that he and the former special agent were thinking the same thing. "You ever get any news on Atta Zimler after he slipped away from Grand Central Station?"

Gallagher chewed slowly and swallowed. "Listen, kid, now that I'm sort of officially part of your family, if that scumbag ever comes within a hundred miles of you, I'll take care of business." Gallagher wondered aloud about an unrelated thought. "Shouldn't you be at college?"

"Got a few days off. No classes for a while."

"So then why aren't you going off on a date with some pretty coed?"

"I wanted to be here. I'm interested in this Roundtable stuff. Would love to be involved."

Gallagher sat down and hunched over the table, taking a huge bite of his sandwich. With a full mouth he managed to say, "Youth ... man, it's wasted on the young. So what's your interest in the Roundtable?"

"I just want to be part of what my dad and mom are doing."

John Gallagher sat up a little straighter. "Boy, to have my son say that ... that'd be great."

"You have a son?"

"Yup. I'm not sure where he is right now. Maybe with his mom."

"So ...," but Cal didn't finish the thought.

"That's okay. You can ask. Yes. I'm divorced. My wife says I was a jerk to live with. One of the few things she ever said that was absolutely accurate. The divorce was finalized years ago. Water under the bridge." Then he added. "Though now that I think of it, my wife got the bridge in the divorce settlement too."

Cal tried not to laugh, but he couldn't help it.

"A good laugh is a healthy thing now and then."

Cal smiled.

Gallagher added, "Especially for you guys. Man, you have *one intense family.*"

"Copy that." Now Gallagher was laughing.

"So you want to be involved in the Roundtable, huh?"

"Yeah. Anything, really. Doesn't have to be big."

"What's your expertise? Everybody in the group's got a specialty."

"Well, I've changed majors to poli-sci. Up to now I've got straight A's in all my classes, dean's list."

"Gee, with two genius parents, I'm shocked. I guess you could do research."

"Sure. Certainly."

Gallagher paused and looked Cal in the eye. "And your dad is okay with this?"

Cal was caught. He knew his father didn't want him involved, but on the other hand, just doing some research, that wasn't really being involved, was it?

"I'm sure it won't be a problem."

"Okay. So here's a hypothetical. Let's see what you come up with. Pretend that one day the Russians sit down and decide to bring some small nuclear weapons into the United States ..."

Cal blurted out, "You're kidding! That's what you guys are dealing with?"

"Whoa, hold your horses. I said this was a story, a hypothetical. Got it? Not real life, just a mental exercise. A pop quiz."

Cal nodded.

"So go along with the assumption. Now do some research on that. Ask yourself, where would they bring portable nukes, what would their targets be? Show me what you can do."

"Where do I start?"

Gallagher grinned. "You figure it out. You're the straight-A student, aren't you?"

The former special agent settled back in to his sandwich. He figured that he'd placated Joshua's son sufficiently. He liked Cal, but he also knew that Josh probably wanted to keep him out of too much of the sensitive stuff. The assignment he had just given him — the hypothetical — should do the trick. By his estimate it would keep the kid busy for the next year.

THIRTY-THREE

Dr. Korstikoff was driving a midsized loaner. It had been rented by a third party with an absolutely clean background check who then handed over the keys to the Russian physicist. Korstikoff had flown into Richmond International Airport to avoid Reagan National as well as Dulles, where security was usually ramped up.

He was now heading north on Interstate 81, up the western edge of Virginia. The rounded peaks of West Virginia were on his left, and in the distance to his right were the Blue Ridge Mountains of Virginia. In between, straight up the valley where he was cruising in his Ford sedan, was the Shenandoah Valley. The land was green and rolling, dotted with farms, small towns, and horses grazing along wooden fences.

It was perfect in its bucolic isolation. The whole county had less than fifty thousand inhabitants in its five hundred square miles of woods and meadows — minimizing the risk of nosey neighbors. And there were only small local police forces. The state patrol would stick to the interstate and wouldn't be likely to venture into the countryside.

Perfect for the final phase of the deadly operation.

Korstikoff flipped his turn signal and moved onto an exit ramp. After making a careful stop at the traffic sign, he clicked his stopwatch and drove till he came to a small county road. He turned left and drove two and a half miles until he saw a sign that read "Mountain Pass Machine Parts Co." hanging from a post. He turned onto the dirt and gravel drive. A quarter mile down the road, he came to a security fence. He reached out the window and tapped in the security code on the pad; the gate opened. Korstikoff drove through a wooded area for a hundred yards until he came to a metal barn in the middle of a clearing. Several cars and a rental truck were parked outside. Off to the side were two long trailers with sleeping quarters. When Korstikoff slowed his rental car to a stop at the barn, he clicked his stopwatch off. He read the elapsed time. *Eight minutes and forty seconds from Interstate 81 to the place of assembly. Perfect.*

He smiled and walked into the barn that housed the assembly shop.

They were all there waiting. The Muslim Pakistani scientist who had worked on his own country's nuclear weapons program and had been apprenticed to the notorious A. Q. Khan, the dreaded arms dealer. There was the Canadian transplant from Iraq who had once been in charge of an electrometallurgical plant, which had been a useful cover for Saddam's fledgling WMD program. Also several technicians who were the "nuts, bolts, and wrenches" guys who would finally clamp together the updated version of the RA-115 portable nuclear bomb and help load it onto the truck.

Last but not least, there were four Middle Eastern men with automatic weapons assigned to drive the completed weapon to its final destination.

The team broke into applause when Korstikoff entered.

He smiled and shook hands all around. He stepped over to the empty metal shell that would soon contain the nuke. He placed his hand on the titanium steel casing.

In his deep Russian baritone, he began singing loudly and mockingly, in celebration of their deadly project and the quiet valley where it would be prepared:

Oh, Shenandoah,
I long to see you,
And hear your rolling river ...

The room erupted in coarse laughter. When it subsided, everyone found themselves looking with excitement at the mechanical nightmare that lay on the floor — the nuclear weapon that was awaiting final assembly.

□□□

In her office in the West Wing, Vice President Tulrude was reading the recent fed-secure-telex message from the secretary of energy. It read:

> Jessica: Heard that you, and not POTUS, are meeting with Ambassador Portleva from the Russian Federation. I heard POTUS had a "scheduling conflict" today. Have you seen the news today? A truck driver in Indianapolis couldn't get gas because of the oil rationing, so he opened fire on the gas station owner and bystanders. Three dead. This makes the third incident like this in the last forty days. Hope you can make headway with Portleva to help us out.

Within the hour, Ambassador Andrea Portleva was escorted into the Yellow Oval Room of the White House where Tulrude had decided to entertain her guest. It was a classy room, beautifully historic.

When the Russian ambassador entered, she flashed a gracious smile and shook Tulrude's hand. She took a sweeping look around at the gold-tinted china on display and the graceful, arching walls. "Such a wonderful room," she said with a smile. "And it was, I believe, first used by your president John Adams, correct? Whose own son was an ambassador to Russia!"

"You're an astute historian!"

Inwardly Tulrude was muzzling some mild resentment. The younger, glamorous Portleva was even more beautiful than her pictures. Tulrude didn't spend much time dwelling on her own looks, except to take the advice of Teddy, her dresser, so she could look "both competent and feminine," in his words. She knew she'd never win a beauty contest. But there was another contest she planned on winning, and Portleva was going to help her win it.

After some chitchat and a cup of tea, Tulrude suggested that they meander over to the Treaty Room. "Let's discuss," she said, "the possibility of increased shipments of oil from Russia to the United States."

As they walked in, Portleva pointed out the obvious, that Russia had already been generous in diverting certain increased petroleum allotments to help the beleaguered U.S.

"Certainly," Tulrude acknowledged, "but not enough. Unlike your country, we've been unable to expand offshore drilling platforms."

Portleva nodded. She understood all too well. "Yes, ever since your British Petroleum disaster in the Gulf so many years ago, followed by all of those most unfortunate political squabbles, and another oil spill ..."

Tulrude had calculated that the Treaty Room would send a message to her visitor, since it was the president's private study. Clearly Virgil Corland wouldn't be meeting with Portleva that day. Tulrude would meet with her instead. Corland had no "scheduling problem." He was having another one of his attacks and had blacked out. When Tulrude first heard about the president's illness, and that she'd have to meet with Portleva that day, she looked up at the sky and uttered a pronouncement: "There *is* a God!"

Of course, she didn't really believe that, but she did feel as if some supernatural force was putting the wind to her back and aiding her advancement. Now, if she could wrangle enough oil from Russia to lift the rationing order on American consumption, she'd be on her way to becoming a national hero.

And all that would make her earlier conversation with Attorney General Hamburg even more important. She'd asked him at the time about Corland's absurd order to investigate a possible Russian conspiracy against the U.S.

Hamburg had asked her, "Where did Corland's order come from? His fear about the Russians, I mean?"

Tulrude didn't waste time spitting it out. "It came from that nutcase defense contractor, Joshua Jordan. He met with Corland personally, filled his head with some crazy scenario."

"How'd you find out?"

Tulrude was not about to share the fact that she was using the president's own chief of staff as a spy. "Reliable source, Cory. Trust me."

"On the other hand," said Hamburg, "I don't want to be accused of countermanding the president ..."

"You aren't. You can just say that the supposed Russian plot has been looked into and found totally wanting in substance. Period."

Now, as Tulrude sat in the president's chair in the Treaty Room, with Portleva in the armchair across the antique oak table from her, she was proud of herself, that she had defused any embarrassing investigation into the Russians. She was free now to really push the oil issue.

"Ambassador, we need a substantial increase in oil imports. We need evidence of further goodwill from Russia."

Portleva smiled. They talked some more, and when the meeting ended, they shook hands, with the ambassador promising to recommend to Moscow that Tulrude's demands be "fully met." All the while, Tulrude was thinking about her political future. It was bright and beautiful.

At that moment, Jessica Tulrude certainly wasn't thinking about history. If she had, she might have realized that this was the very same room where, in 1941, President Roosevelt had received an urgent bulletin.

Telling him Pearl Harbor had just been attacked.

TH1RTY-FOUR

While Abby traveled back to Hawk's Nest, Joshua had flown to their New York penthouse to get ready for his international trip. He had just finished packing. He wondered where his passport was, but he dug around and finally found it. That was the last detail.

He had thanked the Pentagon for offering to fly him to Israel but had decided to use his personal pilot, Billy, and Jeff, his copilot, instead. They had wrapped up the checks on Joshua's own private jet; it was fueled and ready to go. Maybe it was a sign of getting older, but Joshua found his own jet more comfortable than even the cushy ones the top brass used.

The doorbell rang. When he swung it open, his daughter stood in the doorway, bag in hand.

"Greetings, Daddy!" Deborah gave him an enthusiastic hug and marched inside.

He was about to explain that he needed to leave in a few minutes for his private hanger at JFK, but Deborah jumped in first. "Look, I know all about the Israel trip."

"Oh?"

"A few days ago Mom said you might have to fly overseas. Then I just happened to overhear the phone call you got from the Israeli military folks. And last night she called me and said you were staying in New York getting ready for an overseas trip. I put it all together."

"So ..."

"So now that I'll be graduating at the end of this term, I have some time off, two weeks before classes start, and ..."

"And?"

"You know my interests, Daddy. You're doing the kind of work I want to be involved in: national defense, counterintelligence. I couldn't have a better professional mentor than my own father."

"I'm flattered, honey, really, but let's talk about this when I get back."

"I have a better idea. Let's talk about it on the flight over to Israel ..."

Joshua couldn't hold back a smile. "Well, at least you've got moxie."

"No, listen. This isn't a stretch. It's perfectly logical. It's an opportunity for me to watch and learn while you confer about weapons with a friendly nation. It's the ultimate military practicum. That'll put me heads and shoulders above my classmates."

Joshua pushed back gently. "Deb, you don't have a security clearance."

"I don't need one. Obviously, I'll be excluded from anything top secret. That's okay with me."

Her father's back straightened, and his jaw flexed. "Well, I'm certainly glad it's okay with *you* ..."

"I didn't mean it that way. I know I can only attend the nonclearance stuff. Then you can tell me to get lost when the confidential discussions begin. Whatever I can be part of, whatever that means, this would be an unbelievable chance for me."

She took his hand and squeezed it. "Please, Dad. I really want this ..."

"I'm not sure it's safe, darling."

"I've chosen life in the military. I assume the risk. Just like you did."

Joshua took a deep breath. He could take risks for himself, but not for his kids. He looked hard at his daughter. A grown woman. That look of resolve in her eyes. Yes, he recognized that look. It was one of the things he loved about Abby. The soft exterior that covered an iron will. Deb had it too. So here he was, standing in front of a daughter who was third in her class at West Point and the youngest cadet ever allowed in the program. It suddenly became clear. She was part of the proud tradition. She had earned it.

"Deb, have you talked to your mother?"

She shook her head no.

Now Joshua had one more thought. *There'll be hell to pay from Abby.*

After a few seconds, he looked Deborah in the eye. "You're sure about this?"

She snapped back, "One hundred percent, sir."

For Joshua, there was only one more question to ask.

"You have your passport?"

Tehran, Iran

Yoseff Abbas was Iranian — but he was also something else, which meant he had reason to be scared.

He glanced over his shoulder as he walked. He looked again and again. He checked the plate-glass windows of the stores he passed, to see if anyone was following him. What he feared was the MOIS, Iran's Ministry of Intelligence and Security, the dreaded secret police. He'd gone to the food market near the Vali-E Asr, with its pricey shops and little boutiques, to pick up some groceries, but the store was packed with customers, and the lines were awful. Abbas knew how the U.N. sanctions had made life harder for the average citizen — but it hadn't stopped Iran's plans for a nuclear showdown with Israel.

And of all people he ought to know.

Back at his upscale apartment, he sent yet another urgent encrypted email to Rafi, his counterpart in the Israeli Mossad. The last he'd heard, Rafi was in Amman, Jordan, but in the last twenty four hours, he'd dropped off the radar. Yoseff's orders were not to send anything directly to Tel Aviv ... too easy for the Iranians to trace. Instead he was to use Rafi. But the intel that Yoseff had gathered simply couldn't wait. He was toying with blowing protocol completely, contacting IDF headquarters at the Kirya compound in Israel and letting them know what he knew.

Yet for Yoseff, this whole thing felt like a bitter act of betrayal. As a proud Iranian, he hated what he was doing. He felt like a traitor — even though he despised that crazy man, Mahmoud Ahmadinejad, and the Ayatollahs and their ilk. Thinking back, he wished he'd been left alone to study Persian literature and Sufi poetry and teach at the university. That was his passion. But then his brother and sister were captured by the Israelis up in the Golan, spying for Iran, and placed in indefinite detention. Yes, he told them, he would give the IDF what they wanted in return for the release of his siblings and their safe passage back to Iran. What choice did he have? He also cursed the fact that he had accepted a lucrative job as a documents researcher in the Atomic Energy Organization of Iran, the AEOI. This made him a useful pawn for Israel.

Suddenly he received a secure text message from Rafi. It was terse: "Send pictures immediately using HD encrypt code."

Yoseff jumped into the chair at his computer and uploaded an array of digital pictures that showed Iran's nuclear refinement facility at Natanz. The photos proved that the site contained missile silos. It seemed grotesquely audacious for Iran to weaponize the very facility that Israel and the Western nations had complained about and Americans had put under surveillance with a spy plane so many years before.

But now Iran's program was complete, the nuclear warheads were armed, and the missiles were being readied for launch. Yoseff needed to get his siblings out of Israel before death rained down from the sky. He even thought that maybe, if he prevented Iran's missiles from leaving the silos, just maybe he could save not only his brother and sister, but also millions of innocent Iranians who would be caught in the horrors of a full-fledged war when Israel retaliated.

Yoseff put his index finger down on his computer keyboard and hit Send.

It was done. For good measure he double-checked his Sent folder. Delivery and receipt were verified.

Suddenly, Yoseff felt sick with fear. He knew he needed to vacate his apartment and go into hiding. At least for a while. Or maybe longer.

TH1RTY-F1VE

Hawk's Nest, Colorado

Abigail kicked off the meeting.

"Everybody's here. Thank you for coming. And those of you on speakerphone too. You all know that Joshua had emergency business out of the country. He's not free to discuss the details, but he suggested I stand in as chair. No one objected, so here I am. Okay. Let's start."

Abigail was seated at the head of the long table in the conference room at Hawk's Nest. A few members, like John Gallagher, were there in person.

She quickly cranked the meeting into high gear. "The question before us is whether to take action on the possible nuclear threat that our contact, the Patriot, has explained to us. He's available to be hooked into this meeting. He's standing by."

Senator Alvin Leander, who was there in person, led off. No one was surprised at that since they all expected opposition from him. "So, what verification do we have that our government is standing down on this? I'm skeptical."

Abigail suggested that they loop the Patriot into the meeting by Allfone. The group agreed. After a minute, he announced that he was on. Leander asked his question again.

Pack McHenry said, "I have it on good authority that Attorney General Hamburg has downplayed the risk."

Fort Rice, the retired state supreme court judge, was usually the most cautious member of the Roundtable. He had flown in from his home in Idaho. "What do you mean 'downplayed'? Define that for me."

McHenry explained. "The AG has officially informed all U.S. intelligence and investigative agencies that Joshua Jordan was the source of the information about this possible Russian – North Korean – Iranian plot, and that Joshua is an unreliable source."

Beverly Rose Cortez, a Fortune 500 business exec, sputtered through her speakerphone connection, "Josh is a national hero. The president hung a medal around his neck just this week."

But McHenry reminded her of the lay of the land in Washington. "Of course you're right. We all see that, and many Americans do too. But Josh also refused to obey a congressional subpoena last year regarding his RTS design, and then he disobeyed a federal court order. On Capitol Hill that can make even a hero look like damaged goods, particularly among the top brass in the DOJ whom he thumbed his nose at."

Cortez followed up. "What does this mean in practical terms?"

"It means," Gallagher interjected, "that the federal agencies are all going to drop this whole nuclear threat issue into the nearest hole in the nearest outhouse, excuse my French."

Phil Rankowitz, the former TV-network executive, was also on speakerphone. "What about our running a major media piece on the government's failure to protect Americans? Use our AmeriNews service to break the story over the Internet? It's worked before. Our readership is on a tremendous growth curve."

"Forget that," General Rocky Bridger growled. "We're talking about funding some black-ops-type paramilitary action here to stop some bad guys who want to blow us up, right? That's not the kind of thing you blast all over the media."

Abigail said, "Let's focus. First question: do we agree there's a credible threat to American security and American lives?"

No dissents were voiced.

"Okay, next. Should the Roundtable fund and support an effort to counter that threat? Are there any objections?"

Leander spoke up. "I have no objection, but I do have an extreme caution. I'm feeling incredibly uneasy about this."

Rocky Bridger shot out, "The question isn't who feels warm and fuzzy ..."

Silence for a few moments. Then Abigail said. "Then hearing no formal objections—"

John Gallagher jumped in. "Then we're talking about direct action, tracking down the scum and hitting them hard, inviting the Feds to join us ... but don't hold your breath. Remember, I saw the change-over at the FBI in the last few years. I was there. From the top down everything was injected with a big dose of politics, like everybody got formaldehyde pumped into their veins."

Abigail addressed Pack McHenry. "Mr. Patriot, what would you need?"

"My group is effective, but small. We need additional investigative staff, and we need it yesterday. And we need people who are willing to shoot to kill if necessary. And we're also talking a million and a half, maybe two."

"Dollars?" Cortez asked.

"Right."

Gallagher said, "I say we get ready to rumble."

Judge Rice wrinkled his brow; he scratched his eyebrow, then lifted his hand to speak. "I'm not sure we are about ... what this group is about ... is hiring private paramilitary operatives within our own country. That sounds like vigilantism. We could be in deep trouble for that. Abby, you're not just the temporary chair here; you're also the head of the legal section. What's your take on the ramifications here? I'm already convinced we have criminal exposure ..."

Abigail leaned forward. "You're right, Fort. A skilled, motivated federal prosecutor could put together a case against the Roundtable, against all of us, alleging a conspiracy, using the seditious conspiracy statute."

Fort Rice turned to face the big star-shaped speakerphone in the middle of the table. He addressed his next question to the Patriot. "Sir, whoever you are … one more question. Do you have any information regarding whether the attorney general's office knows about us?"

"Yes. They do."

"Anything else?"

"Yeah. There are prosecutors in Attorney General Hamburg's office who want to bring a grand jury investigation into your activities."

Alvin Leander pounced on that. "See? This is exactly what I was afraid of — "

Gallagher shot back. "Senator, with all due respect, you knew our group wasn't the Rotary Club — "

"Let me clarify something," Abigail cut in. "We will not — I repeat — will *not* obstruct or interfere with any lawful action of the United States government. What we are talking about here — "

"What we're talking about," Phil Rankowitz jumped in, "is filling in where the federal government has failed. When they don't show up, and evil is going to happen — "

"Sort of like the legion of superheroes," Gallagher said with a grin. "Batman, Superman, flying into disaster scenes to save the citizens when the local constables can't get their act together."

Leander was shaking his head. "Not for me. I didn't join to be some kind of covert strike force. I want change, I want my country back, but — "

"You're not going to have a country to save," Rocky Bridger shot out, his seventy-year-old face purple with emotion, "if we drag our heels."

For another four hours they debated the issue. The final decision was a compromise. The Patriot was only authorized to investigate the matter further and to make a detailed "wish list" of what he needed and how much it would cost. John Gallagher said the compromise was a "cop-out." Rocky Bridger was also visibly upset.

Abigail adjourned the meeting and asked Pack McHenry to call her back separately. When he did, only Abigail and Gallagher were in the room. The rest had left.

"I want you to know," Gallagher said, that I'm not waiting for the

Mickey Mouse Club here to give me the go-ahead. I'm going to figure out something on my own."

"Stick with us, John," Abigail pleaded. "There's strength is unity. Hang with us."

"Speaking of hanging," Pack McHenry said from the speakerphone. "Wasn't it Ben Franklin, on signing the Declaration of Independence, who said, 'We must all hang together or assuredly we'll all hang separately'?"

"And I'm just trying," Abigail said with a struggling smile, "to keep every one of us off the gallows."

Gallagher said he had an early flight the next morning so he'd catch some dinner and retire early to the guest wing with a few of the other members of the Roundtable.

Abigail checked her Allfone voicemail when she was alone. There was only one message. It was from Joshua.

Honey, we are about to take off. First, want to remind you how much I love you. Thanks for being you. For leading things with the group while I'm out of pocket. Also ... how lucky am I? To be married to a brainy beauty like you. Not only that, but somebody who's on speaking terms with the Almighty.

Abigail laughed and then teared up a little. She loved the guy something fierce. There was still only one real thing left undone between them — and she shouted it at her Allfone: "Oh, Josh, I love you so. But for crying out loud, why don't you just give in to the Lord? Open your heart to Jesus and get yourself radically saved!"

But the rest of Josh's message took a strange turn.

Also, I have a surprising twist to my trip. A passenger with your same last name. I've decided to let Deborah come along. Thought this would be a great practicum for her. I'm taking responsibility for this. And for her. I'll talk this over with you when I can. Sorry to break it this way. It came up suddenly. Love you like crazy, Abby. You know I'll miss you. Bye.

Abigail had just taken the roller coaster. Now she was dumbfounded. She marched upstairs looking for Cal. She found him in his bedroom hunched over his computer. He was scribbling notes on a pad.

She had that look of fiery determination on her face, and her son saw it. "Cal, did you know anything about Deb going to Israel with Dad?"

He looked up, his eyes wide open. "You're kidding. So she really did it?"

"You knew?"

"No, not really. She just said something about how she was going to ask Dad."

Abigail turned away, talking out loud to the air. "And why am I the last one to hear this?"

"Sorry," Cal said. "I thought she was just blowing smoke."

Abigail was wordless for a second, then muttered, "Lord, give me patience with that man. And with that girl."

Abigail gestured to Cal's computer. "What are you working on?"

"Just some research."

Abigail was still reeling from Joshua's message. So she didn't notice the secretive smile on Cal's face just before he turned back to his project.

TH1RTY-S1X

Union Beach, New Jersey

"We had to move. Very dangerous to stay in Clifton. Everything had to go."

The Indonesian armed with an automatic weapon was trying to explain the change of plans to Dr. Kush Mahikindrani, the team leader for the New York attack. The Muslim nuclear physicist from India, whom everybody called "Dr. Kush Mahi," was not happy.

"How do I know that the components weren't damaged when you moved our operations?"

The Indonesian tried to assure him. "Don't worry. We were very careful. With everything. Promise."

Dr. Kush Mahi looked around the large machine shop. When he had driven to the new location, he scouted out the area. The shop was in Union Beach, New Jersey, not far from the sewage treatment plant. Suitable but not ideal. The original plan had been to assemble the small nuclear weapon in a much more remote area in Clifton, just a short drive from New York City. But not now. Union Beach was more than twenty miles from Manhattan as the crow flies. Driving the bomb into the city would be double or triple that distance. And the trip would be across state lines, and the route more complicated.

On the other hand, Dr. Kush Mahi wasn't responsible to deliver the bomb. Only to put it together. The "thugs," as he called the armed members of the terror cell, would drive it into the city and detonate it.

"I just don't understand the need for the change," he complained.

The nuclear engineer from Kenya spoke up in his thick British accent. "I can explain. There was some kind of dispute with the owner of the other building, a problem at the last minute. So they moved here." After looking around, he added, "I think this will do. When I worked on the nuclear missiles for the British submarines, we had a space just about like this. More elaborate machining tools, but we don't need those. Assembly should be fairly simple."

Dr. Kush Mahi was not impressed. "Arming a nuclear device is never simple." But then he stripped off his suit coat and added, "Let's get to work."

They walked over to the crates containing the nuclear components. They inspected the wooden boxes to see if they had been damaged in shipment. The containers were lined with high-grade titanium and synthetic lead, so any real damage would most likely occur if the containers had been dropped and the fragile contents disrupted.

Dr. Kush Mahi, satisfied that the boxes were not damaged, stood up after his inspection. No reason not to make himself at home, he thought.

"Is there any place to get good Indian food?"

□□□

The last address John Gallagher had for Ken Leary, his old buddy at the CIA, was an office in Washington, D.C., just off Capitol Hill. Gallagher wanted to catch up with him, so he flew into Reagan National Airport and headed into the city.

An hour later, as he sat in the back of the cab, he found himself in a traffic nightmare. Some kind of huge rally was taking place on the long grassy National Mall leading to the White House.

"What's the deal?" Gallagher asked the driver.

The cabbie shook his head. "Always something going on at the Mall."

Gallagher saw rows of banners. One said, "One Planet — One God — One Climate Mission." Other banners showed a picture of Romanian ambassador Alexander Coliquin, along with his now-famous quote from his U.N. address: "The only earth we shall ever have."

When they slowed to a stop, a young man in a blaze yellow vest came up to the cab armed with a stack of fliers. He tried to hand one to Gallagher through the cab window. Gallagher said no thanks, but he did ask the young man what was going on.

"We're rallying to support the World Religious Coalition for Climate Control meeting here in D.C."

Gallagher, never one to miss an opportunity, smirked and said, "Tell them to set the weather at seventy degrees and clear, with a slight breeze. That's my favorite."

The man in the vest gave him a funny look. "You really don't know about this?"

"Naw, that's why I asked."

"This is the United Nations initiative on the climate crisis."

"Crisis? Give me a break."

"Man, where have you been? It's all over the news. The figures just came out. We're on the verge of a catastrophe."

Gallagher gave a sardonic chuckle. "Yeah, little do you know."

The man kept pitching. "Religious leaders from around the world are here: Hindus, Buddhists, Muslims, some High Church dude from England, an emissary from the pope. They're all here, man, and for once they're all singing from the same hymnbook. You know what they're saying? Save the planet. *Save the planet!*"

"Funny," Gallagher quipped, "that's exactly what I'm trying to do."

When Gallagher arrived at Leary's office, it was empty. No sign of life. So he made a couple of phone calls and then a house call to CIA headquarters in Langley. He discovered that Leary had been transferred to Richmond, Virginia.

So Gallagher rented a car and headed south on I-95, crawling through traffic until he was closer to Fredericksburg and the pace picked up. Leary's new office was inside an import-export shop called International Trading Cooperative. He recognized the faux setup and asked the pretend receptionist about meeting with Ken Leary. No, he admitted, he didn't have an appointment. "But Ken Leary knows me, and this is absolutely urgent."

After a few minutes, Ken walked out, took one look at Gallagher, and scowled, but out of professional courtesy he invited him into his office.

When the door closed, Leary explained, "I got transferred here. I used to be in the New York field office chasing terrorists and managing clandestine offshore operations. Now look at me! They got me working with Homeland Security monitoring things like international flights at the Richmond airport." Leary pointed his finger at Gallagher. "And why am I talking to you anyway? You're poison. Slipping you information when you were at the Bureau is probably what got me stuck down here in the first place."

"Sorry."

"That doesn't cut it."

"How about this. I'm *really* sorry — and if it weren't about a suitcase nuke coming into the U.S. within your jurisdiction ... hey, I wouldn't be bothering you."

Leary was looking at his wall clock and then shot back, "Oh, so you're *really* sorry?" Then Leary stopped. He looked up and added, "*What* did you say?"

Gallagher said, "I mean I'm genuinely bummed about what happened to you —"

"No, no," Leary said, "not that." He titled his head closer. "The other part ... about a suitcase nuke ..."

TH1RTY-5EVEN

Ethan March had tried to connect with Deborah several times, but he only reached her voicemail. He left two messages. They weren't returned. Then he took a chance and called the unlisted number at Hawk's Nest that Deborah had given him. Abigail Jordan answered. She simply said, "Deb's traveling with her father ..." and didn't elaborate.

After he hung up, Ethan thought back to his sense that Deborah's mother had some doubts about him. He thought that was interesting, since her husband was the one who had known about Ethan's screwups at McGill, and yet Joshua seemed to be willing to consider hiring him. Ethan had even come clean with Deborah about some of his dumber moves. In spite of that, Abigail was the cautious one.

Maybe it had something to do with the superreligious atmosphere that permeated the Jordan household — except for Joshua. They prayed before meals; Mrs. Jordan quoted the Bible; even Cal talked about his "spiritual journey" at the dinner table. Maybe Deborah's mom only approved of Christian crusaders for her daughter.

Things started to add up when Ethan thought back to their picnic. They had traveled by horseback to Deborah's favorite spot. After tying up the horses, they chatted as they ate lunch. Ethan could see that Deborah was different from the girls he flirted with in singles bars. Solid. Real depth. A great sense of humor. And beautiful. Oh, yeah.

Then the discussion got serious. Deborah looked him straight on. "So, you told me about flying that experimental F-35, getting the kinks out — when everything went wrong and you thought you were going to crash."

"Yeah. I had my hand on the handle, ready to blow the ejection seat."

"And if you did?"

"Then I'd have been in for an interesting ride. We simulated it in flight school, but when you're up there going Mach two and things go south, man, it's really different."

"But what I mean is, so you eject ... and then your chute doesn't open. What then?"

"Well, first there's the smaller one, the drogue that opens. Then the main chute."

"And if neither one opens?"

"You die."

"That's it?"

"What do you mean?"

"Don't you think about dying?"

"Of course."

"Anything else? Thoughts about heaven? About God?"

"Sure, I guess, but not like you guys. Deb, you call yourself a Christian. You've obviously got a tight set of beliefs; you're really strapped into that. But that's not where I'm at." Then he changed the subject. "Got any more fried chicken?"

Maybe that was a stupid dodge, but the more Ethan thought about it, the more he figured he was who he was. Why change?

Now, Ethan was driving to the unemployment office in Waltham, Massachusetts, the city he'd called home while he worked for Raytheon. As he drove, a sickening despair overcame him, a feeling of complete mission flameout. The thought of going on the public dole because he was unemployed made him want to vomit. That was for other guys. Not him.

He passed the office with the sign out front that said "Division of Unemployment Assistance." He looked for a parking spot. But then he was shocked by what he saw. The line stretched outside and wrapped around the building. A patrol cop was in the middle of the line, trying to separate two men who were arguing with each other.

Ethan slowed down. He eyed the dismal scene of out-of-work America and then drove away. *Forget this*, he thought. *I've got my pension. Some savings. Besides, Joshua Jordan said I might talk to him about working with his company.*

Of course, Ethan knew the downside too. He didn't want the job just because he'd helped Jordan's daughter in a crisis. That would make him a charity case. Besides, even if he did get the job, would Jordan, remembering Ethan's wilder days, ever take his eye off him? Would he ever really trust him?

Then the image of Deb's face, her smile, flooded back, overshadowing everything. He wanted to be with her, and he wondered what she was doing right now. According to her mother, Deborah was traveling with her father. Okay, did that mean they were on defense business? Had she forgotten about him?

Ethan's feelings for Deb were pushing him back into a familiar pattern, a dangerous one. He found himself wanting to take risks, possibly doing something stupid, just to be with her, wherever she was.

□□□

Joshua and Deborah, squinting in the glare of the blazing Israeli sun, reached into their pockets for their sunglasses. Standing on the tarmac, they looked around and stretched.

Now that the Citation X jet was parked, Billy told his copilot to pull the bags out of the storage deck.

Joshua glanced at the sign on the edge of the runway. The top half was written in Hebrew, the bottom half in English: "Welcome to Ramat David Air Force Base." A host of F-16 fighter jets were lined up at the far end of the field.

Across the tarmac, two IDF officers were striding quickly to their location, the younger one carrying a briefcase. Joshua recognized the older one, an officer with stars on his uniform and gray at his temples. He broke into a grin.

"*Aluf mishne*, Colonel Kinney!" Joshua called out, and the two gave each other a hearty handshake.

Colonel Kinney then turned to Deborah with a wry smile. "You must be Joshua's daughter? Great to meet you. Never mind your father, by the way ... he's just trying to impress us with his linguistic skills. He was using the Hebrew term for my rank." Then he turned to Joshua. "How much Hebrew do you still remember, my friend?"

"Not much," Joshua said with a chuckle. "*Shalom*. And *boker tov*. That's about it ..."

Kinney waved the group toward a large military helicopter that was farther down the tarmac and had just started its rotors. As they walked, he said to Deborah, "Your dad might be downplaying his role, but when he was here a decade ago, we worked together on Iranian reconnaissance — his clandestine flyover of one of their nuclear facilities. He spent so much time with us that he started speaking the language pretty well. That's when I first met him."

They ducked and climbed into the chopper. Kinney instructed Joshua to sit up front next to the younger officer with the briefcase. "This is Major Tikva. He's the operations liaison from General Shapiro's command. He'll brief you on the situation."

Joshua responded to the last name of the officer seated next to him. "*Tikva*. Good name."

"Yes," Kinney said with a nod. "Especially for this mission." Kinney reached forward and closed the metal doors.

"So," Kinney said to Deborah as they sat in the rear seats, "you'll be graduating from West Point soon ... with honors, I bet."

"I hope so, Colonel."

"Must be interesting to pursue a military career in the Army when your father's a bona fide Air Force hero."

"Well, sir," she said with a smile, "you know what we say in the Army: What do you have when you have an Air Force hero?" She paused for comic effect. "The bottom half of a real Army hero ..."

Kinney roared with laughter. "Josh! Your daughter's all right."

The big CH-53 transport helicopter took off and started winging its way toward the Negev desert. Deborah studied the dry, tan profile of the Israeli landscape; arid and harsh in places, yet studded here and there with lush fields of green.

She turned to Kinney and asked, "What part of Israel is the Ramat David Air Force Base in?"

"Southeast of Haifa, not far from Megiddo."

Deborah's face brightened. She knew about that place. "The Jezreel Valley?"

"Exactly. We'll be flying over it shortly," Kinney said, then added, "As a Christian you recognize that place, I'm sure ... the book of Revelation chapter sixteen."

Deborah was dumbfounded. Deborah tried to hide her surprise, but Kinney saw it in her face. "Surprised that a good Jewish fella like me knows the New Testament? And the prophecies of the apostle John about the final battle of Armageddon, or more literally, *Har Megiddo*?"

She nodded.

"There's a story there. I'll share it with you sometime."

Deborah went silent. It was almost more than she could process. As she gazed out the window, she remembered something she had wanted to ask. "Major Tikva's name ... my dad said it was a good name, and you said, 'Especially for this mission.' What'd you mean?"

"*Tikva*," Kinney said, looking ahead without expression, "means 'hope.' "

Suddenly Deborah realized the sheer size of this adventure and wondered what she had really signed up for. She looked down to the valley floor below, with rocky outcroppings here and there and its trimmed agricultural fields spreading like a greenish tan tabletop all the way to the mountains at the horizon, occasionally studded by slender pines and bunches of date trees and palms.

This valley ... yes, she had read all about it. She had been taught about it in Sunday school and at her mother's knee.

A place of foreboding ... but where Heaven would finally triumph.

Where this world would have its last, most horrific war.

TH1RTY-E1GHT

Krasnodar Krai, Russia

In the grand palace of the Russian Federation overlooking the Black Sea, Andrea Portleva, Russia's ambassador to the U.S., was walking down the marble steps to greet Caesar Demas. He had met her before. The long-legged beauty had always caught his eye. As she greeted Demas and led him to their meeting room, he toyed in his mind with the idea of beginning an affair with her, especially now that they would be doing business together. Of course, he was still married to his wheelchair-bound wife who, when she wasn't wheeling herself endlessly around their villa outside of Rome, would have the servants drive her to their vineyards in the north. But such a marriage had never slowed his appetite for sexual trysts over the years, including a long parade of expensive call girls. The billionaire's wallet could pay for anything he wanted, whenever he wanted it.

When they were settled in the small sitting room full of black oak chairs upholstered in leather, she ordered drinks. She was drinking vodka. He wanted gin.

After some pleasantries, Caesar Demas asked directly, "When?"

She replied, "A week. Maybe less."

Demas wanted assurances. "Since I will have Russia's backing, I need your guarantee that when it happens, it can't be traced back to Moscow. That would taint everything I have been trying to do."

"We have been playing this game with the United States in some form for almost a hundred years. We've perfected discretion and subterfuge. Be assured, we have an even greater need to keep our hands clean than you do."

Demas smiled and gazed into her face. "On the other hand, I can also appreciate a beautiful woman who has ... well, less than clean hands."

Portleva laughed. A good sign, Demas thought. He didn't want to negotiate with a prude.

He redirected the conversation. "And the new international coalition, the one I have been building ..."

"Yes, we still want you at the head. You've earned that, and you have shown a particular ability to forge a solid front made out of divergent nation groups. The European Union, well that didn't surprise me, but bringing the Islamic nations, the Arab League along with the Asians ... and key nations in the African continent and South America. Good work. You've been a busy boy ..."

She sipped her drink, and he laughed.

He wanted to know more about the United States. "Jessica Tulrude. We still need her ..."

"Of course ..."

"I have pledged many millions to her presidential campaign."

"She will be an important component, but we are concerned about President Corland."

"His health is failing," Demas said, dismissing Corland with a wave of his hand. "He's a dead man walking. I don't know why he hangs on. There is some conversation about his having a change of heart. In any case, it's good that he won't last. We can't do business with Corland, now that he's *gotten religion*. But Jessica Tulrude we can deal with. She still thinks she is going to have a dominant role in the coming global coalition. I have been working her from my end. She's salivating to expand her power, not satisfied to be just the American president. She wants to be historic ... the first U.S. head of a world government. Behind the scenes, I've promised her that."

Portleva wondered, "After the great unpleasantness happens in the United States — irradiated populations, leveled cities — won't she be forced by her own political party and her own people to fight back, clawing and scratching like a caged animal against the aggressors?"

"By then, the United States will be so weakened, so declawed, that it will be worried about survival, not dominance. Tulrude will be at our mercy. I can play her, believe me. Besides, I think you have done a good job of hiding the identity of their true enemies. The only ones the Americans will be able to identify will be a handful of dead Islamic martyrs."

"And the American media? What will happen there?"

Demas had already calculated that. "Remember 9/11. The American press bent over backward not to be condemning. Editors told their staffs not to use the phrase *Islamic terrorist*. There's a sizable connection between Russia and the United States. Many folks from Russia and the Baltic republics live in America. The U.S. would not want to be politically incorrect toward Russians, now would they? The same 9/11 media backlash will happen again, but perhaps even more so now. Why, some of the media people may even intimate that it was American foreign policy that caused the attacks against them."

That was a wonderful thought, and Portleva laughed. She reached over to grip his hand. "I think we are going to work well together."

Then she raised her glass. He followed suit. She said, "Here's to what is coming... the setting of the sun for America's arrogance. And the bright sunrise for the new world order."

○○○

Gallagher convinced Ken Leary, which was a major task in itself. What had finally turned Leary's head is when Gallagher mentioned one name that, as it turned out, they both knew in common: *Pack McHenry.* "He's the source," Gallagher explained, "of all my information."

They knew that McHenry was doing "way out there" surveillance for the CIA, along with his Patriot group, strictly as a black-ops subcontractor. Much of their work had tendrils into the American homeland, but always with international implications and usually because they had located a foreign source of aggression that directly threatened American citizens. Was it legal? Not if Jessica Tulrude and her ilk had their way. But the FBI had been gutted by politics and hog-tied by insane regulations, many of them now the result of international treaties that the United States had been roped into.

Leary was now so concerned that he even violated one of the big commandments: he took his CIA laptop home. He knew he could be fired for that, but what did that matter in the face of this threat?

Gallagher and Leary ordered Chinese food and worked late into the night in Leary's apartment along the James River on the Shockoe Slip.

Leary said, "Look, all I have is the suspicious names on inbound and outbound flights at Richmond International Airport. That's all, John. They won't grant me even a look-see at any of the bigger airports. I've been cordoned off from the rest of the Agency."

They ran down the thousands of names on Leary's computer. About 3:00 in the morning, they had narrowed the list to three names that fit Gallagher's profile of Russian, North Korea, or Iranian involvement. One was a South Korean journalist with possible sympathies to China. He had flown into the U.S. three months before to cover some political news in Washington. But he had left the country for Venezuela.

The second was an Iranian diplomat suspected of spying for Tehran, but it couldn't be proven. He had an apartment near Embassy Row in Washington.

Gallagher squinted at the last name. He stuck his finger on the laptop screen. "Who's that?"

"Russian engineer. Taught at a technical institute over there. Now he's a visiting professor here. Supposedly."

"Is that his last name?"

"Right," Leary said.

Gallagher said the name slowly. "K-o-r-s-t-i-k-o-f-f ..." Then he asked, "What kind of engineering?"

Leary typed a search into his computer, then another. After about forty minutes, he started nodding his head. Then he nodded more vigorously.

"Okay, what's the scoop?" Gallagher asked.

"It says here he also spent time disarming old Soviet nuclear missiles so they could comply with the nonproliferation treaties."

Gallagher stood up straight. "I say we start working this guy Korstikoff—and I mean right *now*."

Leary was tired. "How about a few hours of shut-eye?"

"You go ahead. I saw an all-night coffee shop down the street. I'll grab a triple espresso. No time for sleep. I got work to do."

"Like what?"

"Superhero type stuff ... you wouldn't understand ..."

TH1RTY-N1NE

Cairo, Egypt

Atta Zimler watched the ceiling fan in the little gem shop. He was killing time while waiting for Donkor, the diamond dealer. Donkor was in the back room examining three of the diamonds that Zimler had brought with him. Zimler noticed that the fan was wobbling slightly off-balance.

Donkor reappeared through the faded curtain and swept around to the other side of the counter. He laid a soft cloth on the counter with the three diamonds.

"Do you want to know how to fix that ceiling fan?" Zimler asked, pointing up.

Donkor rolled his eyes and shook his head.

"Just get a clothespin. Do you have one? I will show you."

"Atta, you know something? You're always trying to remind people how smart you are ... I mean ... smarter than they are." The words came out too fast. The gem dealer swallowed.

Atta leaned forward, a little too close, and Donkor took a step back.

"Was that meant to be funny? I'm sure you meant it as a joke."

Donkor struggled to flash a quick smile, but his lips, suddenly dry, stuck together. "Of course. You know me. Always joking."

Zimler said, "I want to talk business, Donkor. What will you pay me for all these diamonds?"

Donkor swallowed again. He shrugged. "One million ... Egyptian pounds."

"I said I wanted to talk business. No more of your stupid jokes."

"Atta, I'm sorry, but that is all that I can pay for these ..."

The offer was only a third of what Zimler was expecting, but cash was drying up. Things had become complicated. He could make a clean exit from Dubai with the diamonds, with no trail behind. But the pretty girl at the bank window at the Desert Palm Bank gave him an idea. He had wrangled a dinner date with her. Then another, this time on his rented yacht. Zimler had figured she knew the bank codes so he could get to the bearer bonds he knew would be stored there. But she didn't have the codes. And even under torture, he couldn't get what he was after. So he ended up killing her and dumping the body.

It turned out that the Dubai police were quicker to investigate a missing bank teller than he had anticipated. Once more he was on the run. Now he was forced to return to this jewel fence he had worked with for years. A small-time dealer but sufficiently black market and extremely well-connected in the Middle East.

Donkor stood there, shifting on his feet. He erratically reached out to sweep some dust off one of the shelves behind him. Then he brushed his hands and cleared his throat.

"I don't think you understand the market for these diamonds," Zimler said in a casual tone.

"Oh, no, but I do," Donkor replied. "Diamond market is very different now. All of this blood-diamond fuss. Dealers can't afford to just buy and sell. Now there is a big problem because of conflict gems. People want to know where you got them."

"You're not the only dealer ..."

"Any dealer will tell you the same. Really, Atta, I'm telling you the truth. And in Zimbabwe, Côte d'Ivoire, places like that, it's even worse."

Zimler smiled playfully and took a step back, thrusting his hands in his pockets. He was fishing. "Okay, so you tell me why I ought to take your lowball price, you scoundrel."

Donkor grinned and loosened up. "Because I'm telling you the truth, my friend. Look, I'm willing to buy the diamonds. You need the money. Let's call it a deal ..."

That was what Zimler was waiting for. He leaned forward on the counter and picked up one of the diamonds. He then set it apart from the others. "How about this one ..."

Donkor leaned toward the counter to inspect it. That is when Zimler struck. His right hand flashed out toward Donkor's throat and gripped it. The gem dealer gagged and struggled to breathe as Zimler's powerful fingers closed slowly like an industrial press.

Just when Donkor thought he would pass out, Zimler eased up, but only slightly, keeping his fingers locked around his throat.

"Why do you say I 'need' the money?"

The diamond dealer was coughing and gagging. When he could finally speak, he simply said, "Didn't mean anything by it."

"I don't believe you ..."

"I know ... you ... can kill me ... very strong ... but please don't ..."

"Why did you say that? Tell me, and I won't kill you ..."

"Just something I heard —"

"What?"

"You had some kind of problem ... in Dubai —"

"What else?"

"I don't remember ..."

He squeezed a little tighter. "What else?"

"Just the Caesar Demas thing."

"What about it?"

"He didn't pay you for some job in the States."

"What else?"

"That's all."

He was now satisfied that Donkor knew enough to be valuable. He released his grip. "I'm removing my hand now. Don't you move. Just stand there."

Donkor did as he was told, rubbing his neck and panting for air. Then he said meekly, "Atta, I want to do business with you. But not like this. Let's deal with each other, please, like businessmen."

"Is this your final offer?"

Donkor rotated his head a little back and forth and massaged his neck. He was thinking. Then he said, "In cash, yes. I can pay with Egyptian pounds, or euros, or the new international CReDO. Anything you want."

Zimler countered. "How about other than cash?"

"What do you mean?"

Zimler was feeling pressed. The Dubai thing hadn't worked according to plan, and he still had several law-enforcement agencies looking for him as a result of the Grand Central Station fiasco. Things were closing in on him. Cash was good to have, but information might be just as good. Maybe better. "You are a man with information, Donkor. How about your cash offer, plus some information I can use. But it better be good."

Donkor shrugged and gave it a few moments of thought. Then his face lit up. "Well, I just might have some information."

"Tell me." Zimler was expecting to get something about the local cops being alerted to his presence in Cairo or Interpol agents nosing around. But what he heard was something different altogether.

"Well," Donkor said, "that American guy is not far from here right now. He's up in Israel, supposedly. Don't know why. Just that he is meeting with the Israelis."

Zimler looked into Donkor's eyes. He stared him down. "What American guy?"

"You know," Donkor said cautiously, "the guy you were chasing down on the Demas job. The American ..."

"Joshua Jordan?"

"Yeah. That's him."

Zimler's mind lit up like a kaleidoscope. A whole spectrum of possibilities lay before him.

"Donkor, do you think you can get some more information on Jordan? Where he is right now?"

Donkor nodded. "I think so, maybe. Yes. So, do we have a deal? For the diamonds?"

Atta Zimler smiled and held out his hand to shake. "Of course. It's a pleasure doing business with you."

FORTY

At Hawk's Nest, Abigail Jordan was sitting with Victoria, Pack McHenry's wife, on the big wraparound porch. The perfectly quaffed platinum blonde in her late fifties said she was flying through Denver on the way to Los Angeles. She had an urgent message that she needed to deliver to Abigail in person, something from her husband Pack that had surfaced just after their recent visit together in Washington.

Abigail had brought out some tea, but neither was drinking it yet.

Abigail and Victoria had hit it off fabulously in D.C. when they had brunch together. Though Victoria never said it out loud, Abigail had assumed that she had experience in the clandestine services herself, just like her husband. It was implied in the way she talked — her knowledge of national security issues and the "agency" lingo she used so proficiently. Just a hunch. But Abigail was sure she was right.

Victoria asked, "You're running things in the Roundtable for the time being?"

"Until Josh gets back."

"Pack speaks very highly of you, and of Josh too."

"Funny. Josh thinks the same about you and Pack. It's too bad our talks are always so crisis driven. So little time for real conversation. That's why I enjoyed our lunch together."

When Victoria spoke next, there was regret in her voice, "Well, Abby I'm afraid we need to get down to brass tacks."

"I understand. So, speaking of crises, you said you had a message?"

Victoria's expression changed. It was all business. "Here it is. Pack says the most recent intel — and I am talking within the last twelve hours — is that we now know the targets and the general staging areas."

Abigail felt a nervous fluttering in her stomach. "For the attacks?"

"Yes. Pack has filtered this information down the line to the right people in the federal agencies, but he wants to scream bloody murder because no one is listening, or if they are, then their hands are tied." Victoria paused before she delivered her caveat. "This information is arguably classified. I emphasize *arguably*. Do you want to hear it? You know the repercussions."

"I know the consequences if we do nothing. Josh and I don't believe in sitting on the sidelines. So tell me what you can."

"The targets are New York and Washington, D.C. The staging areas are lower New York State, or possibly New Jersey, and Virginia, respectively. The nuclear devices are small enough to be transported by a medium-sized truck, much smaller than a semi. And we're just a matter of days away. Pack is over in Paris right now, coordinating this information. He's getting this from one of the Russian republics. So that's what I know. What can your people do?"

"John Gallagher, a former special agent for the FBI, is out on his own right now trying to turn up leads. We couldn't get a consensus from the Roundtable for any specific funding."

"Did Pack's budget summary come through?"

"It did, and I sent it immediately to each member of the group. Josh and I are willing to put up some money. Beverly Rose Cortez has personally pledged a boatload. But everybody's jittery. The Department of Justice is looking into our operations ... you know what that means."

Victoria gave a look that let Abigail know they were on the same track. Victoria pushed her teacup away. "Before I go, I'll give you the account information and routing numbers to wire the money. Pack has lined up men, equipment, as much as he can, you know, to try to interdict these mass murderers, just in case the Feds really do stand down on this. But this whole operation is off ledger. So it has to be privately funded." Then Victoria added, "And one more piece of data. According to Pack, the Russians said that the staging site for the Washington attack was — and this is a direct quote from surveillance — 'a blast from the past,' whatever that means."

Abigail leaned back in her chair. She took a deep breath. This was no time for hand-wringing. Action needed to be taken. She said, "I'm going to contact John Gallagher immediately and give him this information. This is frightening, like a bad dream ... We've got to stop this horror from happening, but everybody, everything is moving in slow motion."

"Do you have any family in D.C. or New York? You may want to get them out right now."

"No, thank goodness. We have a penthouse. No one's there. But ... oh no, our housekeeper's still in New York. I'll need to find a reason to get her out of town. Cal is here with me and has a few more days before classes start up. And Deborah should be back at West Point by now ..." Abigail knew she was missing something in her thinking about her daughter, but she kept talking. "How close is West Point to D.C.? Dear Lord, it's only about forty miles. I have to get her out immediately."

"We have a condo in Manhattan too. I'm out of town now until we find out what's happening. And Pack of course is over in France ..."

Abigail looked off to the mountains and drifted away for a second. Then she said, "You and Pack must spend a lot of time apart."

"Part of the deal, I guess. It gets a little easier with time. But it's never really easy. You try to manage, try not to become strangers; you work at loving each other, to keep it together. And the pressure, of course, of what he does ..."

There was a catch in Victoria's voice. Abigail heard it. She reached over and squeezed her hand and then found herself getting teary eyed. "I do wish Josh was here. All this is overwhelming."

Victoria glanced at her watch. "Abby, dear, I have to go. Don't want to but I must."

Abigail nodded and got up with her.

"So," Victoria said, "with Josh overseas you're holding down the fort here?"

"I guess so. But I feel like the hostiles are closing in, surrounding the fort."

"That doesn't sound like the person I've heard so much about ... the woman with an invincible faith in God."

"God's the invincible one. I wish my faith was unshakable. When I feel weak, vulnerable, that's when I just drop down before the Lord and claim His grace. I figure if He loves me enough to send His Son to *save* me then He's more than able to direct me."

"I was raised a churchgoer, but Pack and I ... that hasn't been part of our life. Some of his Patriot group, they're like you, really into the born-again Jesus thing. Makes me think ..."

Victoria paused, as if she wanted to say more, but she didn't. Instead she gave Abigail a warm hug, a kiss on the cheek, and then headed to her rental car.

Abigail ran inside to call Deborah, then stopped in her tracks. In the stress of the moment, she had completely forgotten that Deb wasn't at West Point. A momentary rush of relief washed over her as she remembered that Josh had taken her to Israel with him.

But just as quickly she had another thought. Was her daughter any safer in Israel?

FORTY-ONE

Gallagher was like a hunting dog listening for the whistle. He was straining to hear Abigail's voice on the phone over the sound of traffic. "'Blast from the past'? Somebody in the Russian camp used that phrase?"

"Yes," Abigail said. "Victoria was very precise about it. Maybe it means nothing, but I thought you ought to know."

Gallagher was still in Richmond. He had tried a few of his local FBI contacts, fishing for information, but came up dry. He'd been standing in line at an espresso shop, with coffee and baked goods in hand, when Abigail's call came. So he had to set the cup and bear claw down on a table and headed outside.

To Gallagher, the assignments were clear. "Okay, I'm in Virginia now Abby. I need to know that Pack McHenry's folks can handle New York while I work the Washington angle from here."

"I'll call Victoria. I don't think she's boarded yet."

"Oh, and for what it's worth, ask Cal if he's got any brilliant information for me."

"Cal?"

"Yeah. Hope it's okay, but I threw him a little research bone. He wanted something to do. So I had him look up some stuff for me."

"John, I think Josh wanted to keep him out of this ..."

Gallagher smelled a family feud. "Sorry, Abby, hope I didn't interfere."

"No, it's okay." Abigail sounded upbeat. "Bless you, John, for wanting to include him. I'll talk to Cal."

After they hung up, Gallagher called Ken Leary, who was back at his office. He was put on hold. Finally Ken picked up.

"Ken, I need everything you've got on the plans of the old Soviet guard and their plans for nuking the United States."

"Gee, thanks. You got a warehouse or two? I'll need 'em so I can fill them with everything we've got on that. Really, John …"

"I don't want the entire history of the Cold War. We're talking the suitcase-nuke scenario."

"I'm not an expert on Soviet stuff. But I'll see what I can do."

Just then Gallagher's call-wait light flashed on his Allfone. He put Ken on hold and took the call.

"John, this is Cal."

"Right. Hey, I've got a call going here. Can this wait?"

"I don't know. I've got something interesting —"

"Interesting is not what I need. We're up against it here, Cal."

"Well, you wanted research on Soviet plans for portable nukes inside the U.S. Well, this thing popped up …"

"Quickly …"

"Well, a former KGB agent wrote a book years ago about Soviet plans to hide nukes in Virginia — "

"Whoa, hold up, cowboy; I'm going to loop someone in." Gallagher clicked back to Ken Leary and said he'd patch him into a three-way but reminded Ken that this would be a young civilian doing the talking.

"Okay, Cal, keep going."

"Well, the former KGB guy's name is Stanislav Lunev. He defected to the U.S. in '92. His book was published by Regnery in '98. He says the Kremlin had plans to plant nuclear weapons within driving distance of the Capitol, in a remote area of Virginia."

"Like where?"

"Shenandoah Valley."

"Okay. Good work, Cal. You passed the test. Thanks. Now I got to go. Good talking with you. Bye."

After clicking off with Cal, Gallagher went into his jackhammer routine with Leary. "Ken, get everything on this Lunev. See about the backstory. Get the debriefings."

"I vaguely remember this guy."

"Me too. Some of my compatriots at the Bureau thought he might be a master exaggerator, but this Shenandoah Valley stuff is news to me. Maybe this is the 'blast from the past' that the Russians are talking about."

Ken Leary's voice went up an octave. "I think the debriefing interviews would be in the archives at the Counterproliferation Center at the Agency. I'll need information about the places where the Russians scouted out nuclear hiding spots."

"Exactly. Now, go, go, go." Gallagher clicked off and fished in his pocket for a prescription bottle. He popped a pill in his mouth. He'd finally given in to the doctor's orders to deal with his acid reflux. His chest was burning like a bucket of molten steel.

Negev Desert, Israel

It was blistering hot in the rocky desert plains in southern Israel, not far from the border with Egypt. Joshua Jordan was with a team of Israeli ballistic experts and weapons physicists. Earlier in the day they had arrived at an area marked by a tall stone obelisk with a warning in Hebrew and English: "ENTRANCE FORBIDDEN." This was the IDF weapons-testing range. Joshua and the missile-defense team had just run through some tests for the Return-to-Sender system.

One of the Israeli physicists approached Joshua. "Colonel Jordan, I have a concern about the ability of RTS to handle multiple warheads, and there's also that matter of the RTS failure in the Chicago flight — "

"Doctor," Joshua answered, "about the commercial jet ... we've repeatedly requested the accident data from the NTSB so we can evaluate it ourselves. They've refused to cooperate. So was there an RTS failure? Or was it compromised by the pilot? By the airlines? Disengaged by a mechanic? We simply don't know. As for the multiple warheads, the North Korean episode last year should answer that. RTS performed perfectly."

One of the weapons engineers shook his head. "We know you are required by the Pentagon to deliver a lower-quality weapon to us. So what *aren't* we getting in this package? Will it compromise our ability to stop Iranian missiles?"

Joshua dabbed the sweat from his neck. He took off his sunglasses and wiped his eyes. "Pentagon protocol requires a *slightly different* weapons version for our international partners. Same capabilities, but the engineering guts are a bit different, for obvious reasons. We don't want anyone out there to be able to reverse engineer our exact design. Rest assured that the RTS system will protect Israel. As we saw today, we're ten out of ten on the scorecard for the tests out here in ... what desert is this, Clint?"

Colonel Clinton Kinney reminded him. "Paran ... where God brought Moses and the children of Israel after rescuing them from bondage in Egypt. He brought them here with a pillar of cloud to lead them. This became the staging area for their entrance into Canaan."

One of the military officers chuckled. "You're forgetting something, *Rabbi* Kinney. A small matter of their wandering for forty years in the wilderness."

"Sure," Kinney said. "Because of their cowardice and disobedience. Gentlemen, I think we have to believe that God is able and will do what He has promised to protect Israel. When the flood comes, He will part the sea. When the missiles come, God will deflect them. When the armies roll toward us, He will shake the ground with thunder and scatter them."

"Let's hope," another IDF officer quipped, "that God will make the RTS system work, because we all know that our nuclear capacity has been — "

"Circumcised?" said another officer, evoking laughter from the group. But beneath the laughter was the sobering realization that Israel, under crippling international pressure, had been forced to dismantle its own nuclear weapons system. Now the RTS system had an even higher value to this tiny nation surrounded by enemies.

Just then, several Israeli F-16s roared overhead, swooping into the valley and leaving their white contrails behind.

Kinney stepped up to Joshua. He said in a low voice, "They're getting ready. Israel is not going to sit back and wait for Iran to make its final gambit. We'll strike first."

That realization hit Joshua like a ton of bricks. He thought about Deborah and whether it had been wise to bring her here. "Thanks for having your wife, Esther, spend the day with Deborah. Much appreciated."

"She'll show her the sites in Jerusalem. They're having a great time, I'm sure."

With their work done for the day, Joshua, Kinney, and the rest headed toward their vehicles.

Just a few miles outside the testing perimeter, a small group of hikers was sitting in front of a small portable satellite monitor, watching the picture. Even though it was a little scrambled, they could make out the image of Joshua Jordan climbing into a Jeep next to Colonel Kinney.

One of the hikers, speaking in perfect Persian, said to his fellow Iranians, "There he is. Jordan is the civilian. See him?"

Then he added. "Give the command."

FORTY-TWO

Iranian Airspace

Joel was at the head of the formation of Israeli F-16 fighter bombers. They were flanked by a protection squadron of F-15s. They were flying low, perilously low, at ninety feet above the desert floor. In the valley between the Karkas Mountains, they were hoping to avoid any ground radar within a twenty-mile radius. At the speed they were traveling, they would reach Iran's Natanz nuclear launch facility and drop their bombs before Iran's antiaircraft missiles were ready to launch. They would have loved to have the new American F-35 jets, but the U.S. government balked at giving Israel the new fighters.

David, flying on Joel's starboard, noticed something and laughed. Below, a goat herder, who had heard the roar of the low-flying jets and must have thought the sky was falling, was sprawling spread-eagle on the hardscrabble ground, surrounded by his herd. "Let's hope he doesn't have a cell phone," David quipped.

"Okay, final checkpoint approaching," Joel radioed back to the formation behind him.

So far the flight had been uneventful, which was surprising. Maybe this would be a repeat of the Israel's bombing of Saddam Hussein's nuclear facility in Iraq in 1981. They had used a similar flight plan back then. The IAF launched a surprise attack and swept over the location, bombed it, and got out without a scratch.

"Check your radar-detection receivers, and keep your eye on the circle on your screen for the incoming missiles nearest you ..." Joel checked his flight-deck clock. "Right about now they're probably scrambling their jets." He knew that the Iranians had the newest generation of Russian MiG fighters. But the F-15s would be able to handle them. Command had calculated the time that would be needed for the Iranians to prepare their antiaircraft-missile controls and then hone in on the incoming jets. If they were lucky …

"Okay, everybody, let's get into welded wing formation; tighten up folks."

The jets pulled into a near wing-tip-to-wing-tip position. Just a matter of moments now until the strike.

The large buildings of the Natanz facility came into sight in the distance. Since most of the centrifuges and uranium-enrichment equipment were underground, the F-16s were carrying super bunker-busters that would crack the ground wide open and blow down deep enough to destroy everything, including the nuclear-launch missiles they were told were in the adjacent silos.

Joel only knew what IDF command had told him. Those in charge of the operation, like General Shapiro, had to rely on intelligence, information from people like Rafi, their own clandestine agent in Jordan, and Yoseff, the Iranian insider whose motivation was unimpeachable: he needed to rescue his brother and sister from an Israeli prison.

But there was something the pilots did not know, any of them.

As each of the bomber pilots hit their Drop buttons to let loose their deadly payload, their flight-deck radar-detection screens lit up. One circle. Two circles. Three circles.

"We've been painted!" Joel cried out. "Drop and get out …"

Now the sky was filled with antiaircraft missiles. Dozens of them. Maybe hundreds.

Joel dropped his bombs and pulled his F-16 skyward. But something — a red flash — caught his eye to the starboard. It was from the ball of fire from the missile strike that had just decimated David's F-16. No parachute. No escape.

"I'm hit," another F-15 pilot screamed over the radio.

Below, Joel saw bright explosions from the fighter jets of his team being destroyed, one after another. His radar showed three Iranian MiGs fast on his tail.

Everything had gone wrong.

□□□

Miles away, in another part of Iran, at the nuclear launch site at Bushehr, the facility that the U.N. and the IAEA had declared to be safe and used only for public-energy purposes, the chief of operations and his officers were cheering wildly. *"Allah Ackbar!"*

The plan had worked. Yoseff and Rafi had been deliberately duped. The site at Natanz had been abandoned, and the equipment moved to tunnels in the mountains. The empty facility was a piece of dramatic stage dressing. Military theater. The real nuclear-launch command and the silos loaded with nuclear warheads at Bushehr were untouched. When Iranian intelligence grew suspicious that some of the local citizens in Bushehr might try to filter information to the West about the nuclear missile site, they evacuated the entire city, forcing the residents to move out. Iranian nuclear command would take no chances. The Bushehr facility was too valuable.

The Iranian chief of operations smiled now as he thought of the gift of good fortune concerning the useless Israeli strike against Natanz. *Thank you, Israel. Now we can launch our nuclear warheads at you and can claim to the whole world that it was self-defense.*

Old City, Jerusalem

Deborah Jordan couldn't take it in fast enough: the narrow cobblestone streets, the women in head coverings peaking out of small windows, the crowds of pilgrims and tourists, and merchants selling leather goods or dates laid out in trays.

"I've always wanted to come here," she said. "Especially this, the Via Dolorosa. This is unbelievable. This route, the way of the cross. The path taken by Jesus on the way to the crucifixion ... almost ..." Deborah stammered and couldn't finish.

Esther McKinney, the colonel's wife, was bright-eyed and smiling at her young visitor. "We thought you'd appreciate it."

Esther stopped in the middle of the narrow street. "Now, turn around and look up."

When she did, Deborah recognized an ancient, graceful stone arch connecting the buildings on either side.

"Now imagine," Esther said, "you are here two thousand years ago. Make the stores and buildings disappear. Tradition says that this Roman arch is the place — or at least near the place — where Pilate appeared with Jesus. The gospel of John makes it clear. The Roman governor had allowed Jesus to be found guilty, though he admitted there was no evidence for it. Then he ordered him to be scourged. The Roman guards mocked Jesus and rammed a crown of thorns down on his head, beat him, and laid a purple robe on his back, which had been torn open by the whip and was bleeding. Then Pontius Pilate said to those in attendance, 'Behold the Man.'"

Deborah was silent. Her face showed her astonishment.

Esther said, "But Pilate was only half right. He forgot the other part."

"Which part?"

"He should have said, 'Behold the Son of God' ..."

Deborah smiled. "It's interesting I'm here now. This place ... at this point in my life. I've been a Christian for a while, received Christ as a teenager, but lately I've been wondering about things. My life, plans, people ..."

"People?"

"Well, there's this guy ..."

Esther laughed loudly. "Yes, there's always a guy, isn't there!"

"So, I've got some things to work out. I need to take things to the Lord. I need some guidance." Then she looked at Esther. "It must be hard on you, being Jewish here in Israel, as deeply involved in the government as your husband is, yet both of you also being ..."

"... Also being messianic Christians too? Believing that Jesus, Yeshua, is the promised One? The once-and-for-all sacrificial Lamb, offered up to take away the sins of the world for all who trust in Him? Yes. It's not been easy. But who says any of this is supposed to be easy? It's supposed to be true and right. Yes. It's a sensitive issue. We handle it with discretion. Clint doesn't wear 'Jesus Saves' T-shirts to work, if you know what I mean!"

Esther looked at her watch. Then she checked her cell phone. "Deborah, have you received a call from your father in the last hour?"

"No. Why?"

"Oh, probably nothing. Clint usually calls about this time each day. It's a routine we have because of the way things are here. Clint and I have a joke: we say living in Israel is like the thorn trees, lovely from a distance but painful at close quarters. Life in Israel is beautiful but precarious. Clint and Josh were at a remote testing site today but should have been back by now."

Deborah pulled out her Allfone and dialed her father's private number. It rang ten times and then went to voicemail. "No answer," she said.

Deborah thought she caught something in Esther's expression, a vague look of apprehension. The next moment Esther said, "Let's keep walking. So much to see. I know a great place for lunch."

FORTY-THREE

Tehran, Iran

Joshua cried out. Somewhere in his numbness and confusion he felt searing pain. He couldn't locate it at first. His body was not on the ground. He thought he was flying ... no ... that wasn't it. *I'm hanging.*

Joshua Jordan struggled to see where he was. As he did, he located the source of his torturing pain. In each of his shoulders. They were pinned behind him, in hog-tie fashion. He was hanging from a wall. The tips of his feet were barely touching the concrete floor. His chest had been stripped bare, and his shoes and socks were off.

He blinked and shook his head, trying to clear the cobwebs. *Think back, think back. What happened ... ?*

It started coming back.

He had been climbing into the Jeep with Colonel Kinney. The other members of the IDF team had already left the testing site. He remembered seeing the dust from their trucks ahead.

Then, from somewhere behind them, an Israeli Apache helicopter came swooping down. It landed fifty feet away. A man wearing an IDF uniform came striding out with two other soldiers. He said, "Colonel Jordan, urgent message ..."

The man in the IDF uniform held out a piece of paper. Joshua climbed out of the Jeep as Kinney yelled to him to stop. Then, one of the soldiers dropped to a kneeling position, close enough that Joshua could see the soldier was aiming a strange-looking handgun at him. Joshua turned back to the Jeep. Then something struck Joshua in the back of the thigh. He grasped for it. A dart protruded from his skin. He tried to run, but the dizziness stopped him. He dragged his feet as if they were cinder blocks. Gunshots, a lot of them, were being fired. He saw Clint Kinney firing back fiercely from the ground next to the Jeep, and then Kinney was hit and went down. Joshua fell into the vehicle and found the other handgun with the clip already in. He turned clumsily and started firing toward the helicopter, emptying the clip. Someone yelped in pain. But Joshua couldn't hold on. The pistol dropped from his hand. He was blacking out. The last thing he remembered was a bearded man bending over him and laughing.

Now Joshua was in a concrete room hanging from a hook. There was enough light for him to get an idea of where he was. There was a drain in the middle of the floor. And blood stains. This place of cruelty had been used recently.

Then he heard voices outside. One guy asked, *"Hale shoma chetor ast?"* Another man answered something about being okay, but his wife was sick. They were making small talk. Joshua recognized the language. Persian Farsi, the language of Iran. Years before, when he'd been running spy plane flyovers to document Iran's nuclear facilities, the Pentagon had taught him some Farsi in case he was shot down and captured.

That never happened, though there was a story behind that too. Although Josh was feeling light-headed and woozy with pain, he found himself floating back to that distant point in time, to that last time he'd flown his newest generation U-2. He'd been alone in the bubble, thousands of feet above Iran, with only the sound of his breathing in his mask. Inhale. Exhale. Then he spotted the site. He clicked on the high-speed cameras in the belly of the aircraft. They had crystal clear photo acuity, so that when the digital photos were downloaded, you'd practically be able to measure the size of the bolts on the girders of the nuclear plant.

Then the call came in, "Hollywood One, Hollywood One, you've been made! Abort ... get out of there ..."

But he didn't abort. He wanted to finish the mission. He shouldn't have made it out alive, but only later did he find out why he had.

A noise snapped him out of his reverie. The metal door to the room swung open. Three men strode in. The guy in the front had a neatly trimmed beard and wore the uniform of an officer in Iran's Islamic Revolutionary Guard. It was the military unit that controlled Iran's nuclear-weapons program. Next to him was a large soldier.

"I am Captain Ackbar," the officer announced. "You are our prisoner. We need some information."

Another man, dressed as a civilian in a suit, stepped forward. "Colonel Jordan, the Iranian Atomic Energy Organization simply wishes to supply safe energy, electricity, modern conveniences to our people. But today, Israel bombed one of our facilities at Natanz — a ruthless act of aggression. We have the sovereign right to protect ourselves. If you can answer some simple questions, then we will let you go. You will be safely returned to your family."

Joshua tried to lift his head to see the man.

The civilian from the IAEO continued. "We just want some data so we can protect ourselves. Nothing more. We mean no harm."

Joshua growled in a hoarse voice, "Then why's there blood on the floor?"

The soldier standing guard off to the side had a metal rod in his hand, and he stepped forward, but the officer stopped him. "There's plenty of time for that ..."

The civilian asked, "Have you supplied Israel with your Return-to-Sender technology?"

No answer.

"I will ask it again ..."

Again, Joshua did not answer.

Now the big soldier was given the go-ahead. He stepped forward and lifted Joshua's head so he could stare him in the face. Then, smiling a wide grin, the soldier took his stick and rammed it up, butt end, into Joshua's solar plexus.

Joshua gasped for air, unable to breathe or scream in pain. Spittle ran down his mouth as he convulsed.

The civilian said to the officer, "We have a tight schedule. We need this information immediately, you understand ..."

The officer nodded. "Don't worry. We'll get it."

Hawk's Nest, Colorado

When Abigail received the call from General Shapiro in Tel Aviv, it was early afternoon, mountain standard time. She vaguely knew who General Shapiro was, but her heart dropped like a brick when she heard his voice. After all these years expecting a call or a knock on the door, while Josh had run dangerous missions or tested new aircraft, a call never came. But today it did.

"I regret to inform you, Mrs. Jordan, that your husband has gone missing in the Negev desert."

"Missing ... I don't understand ..."

"His convoy was attacked. The attackers were dressed like Israeli soldiers. We believe he has been taken hostage."

"By who? Where is he now?"

"Our best intelligence is that he is now somewhere inside Iran. We believe the Iranian government is behind this."

"The American embassy ... have you contacted them ... or the Pentagon?"

"We have contacted the U.S. Defense Intelligence Agency and the Pentagon."

"What are they doing about it?"

"We have every confidence that they will assist us in trying to locate and extract your husband."

Her words were trembling. "Oh, dear God, please protect my husband ..." Then in the next breath she asked General Shapiro, "Deborah, my daughter ..."

"She's safe. She's with Colonel Kinney's wife, Esther."

"I have to get over there, General, to Israel ..."

"I wouldn't advise that, Mrs. Jordan — "

"A rescue plan. We need one immediately."

"We're working on that. I promise we will keep you informed minute by minute."

Shapiro had no more information. When Abigail hung up, she stood in the middle of the big family room and shrieked Cal's name.

He had been working close by outside, repairing a section of broken railing on the big wraparound porch. Now that his father was overseas, he was taking care of a few repairs that his dad had planned on doing.

Cal sprinted through the front door. He found his mother with her hands over her face, shaking as she sobbed. Abigail blurted through her tears, "Your dad's in trouble. He's been grabbed by terrorists. They think he's being held hostage in Iran ..."

Cal reeled and his face drained. When he caught his breath he asked, "Who's going to get him out?"

"The Israelis are working on it ... waiting to hear from Washington."

Abigail wiped her eyes and tried to take a deep breath. She and Cal locked eyes. Instinctively, they had the same thought.

Cal voiced it first. "No way, Mom ... we can't wait for the politicians or the White House. They've been gunning for Dad. They'll let him twist in the wind ..."

"Exactly. I'm calling Rocky Bridger. He was invaluable during your crisis at Grand Central Station."

"How about John Gallagher?"

"Can't afford to take him off task. What he's doing for us right now is critical to American security."

"So it's true then ... what Gallagher had me researching, about Russia, a nuclear threat?"

For Abigail it all fell together. Cal's working on his computer. His desire to contribute to the Roundtable effort. She offered him a simple reply to his question. "Yes. It's true."

As she looked at her son, she knew that a convergence of circumstances had now brought him into the inner sanctum. She also knew that there were no accidents, not in a universe governed by a God who directed the destinies of people as well as nations.

"Welcome to the Roundtable," she said.

FORTY-FOUR

John Gallagher gunned his rental car toward Virginia's Shenandoah Valley. After getting off I-64, he streaked up Interstate 81 at eighty-five miles an hour. He hoped the state police were busy stopping everyone else.

Ken Leary called. "Okay, I got into the archives . . . read the reports. Several spots in the Valley were mentioned."

"Go down the list . . . geez, oh geez, I hope we're not too late."

The key was to isolate the one that the Russians thought was truly a "blast from the past." Gallagher and Leary agreed on one, which seemed to be the best from a strategic standpoint. It was just off of I-81, about ten minutes by car from I-66, which led directly to downtown Washington.

But Gallagher also knew that if he placed all his eggs in one basket, and lost the bet on which basket, he was about to lose hundreds of thousands of lives, the U.S. Capitol, and most of the American government in the bargain.

To make matters worse, Gallagher felt like he was doing that balancing act while running a gunnysack race.

"Thanks, Ken," he said. "Gotta go."

Gallagher fished through his private book of phone numbers, until he came across a retired FBI guy by the name of Frank Treumeth. Gallagher remembered that Frank had bought a place in the Shenandoah when he left the Bureau and was doing something "folksy," like being a fishing guide or something. The last case they had worked together was in North Carolina, busting up a terror cell that was smuggling drugs to finance their plans to then bomb bridges in major cities during rush hour.

He voice called the number into his Allfone while driving. It rang at the other end. It kept ringing. Then he heard a voicemail. "Hi, this is Doris and Frank. We wanna talk, and so do you. So leave a message."

"Frank, hey, John Gallagher here. Retired from the Bureau just like you; you may have heard. How's the fishing? Say, got an emergency here. Don't want to overplay my hand, but I really, *really* need to talk to you ASAP. Please, buddy. Give me a ring, pronto. Okay?"

As Gallagher flew up the interstate, he knew that Frank Treumeth was the only play he had left. Sure, Gallagher had some other backup plans if Frank was unavailable, but in the light of day they all looked tragically stupid.

For a fleeting second he thought, *I left the FBI ... so why am I still trying to save the world?*

But as quickly as he asked that question, he answered it.

Because it's worth saving.

Tehran, Iran

Yoseff Abbas was running for his life. He'd abandoned his apartment as soon as he heard about the Israeli attack on the Natanz facility and how the whole thing had been a setup. He realized he'd been played for a pawn by the Iranian leadership. That meant that Iran's ruthless MOIS agents were on to him and would be looking for him at that very moment.

He stuck to the back alleys of Tehran as he walked, trying to figure out where he could go. He had received several calls from his Israeli Mossad contact, but he didn't pick up. Of course, no messages were left. He never trusted the Israelis completely, and now he couldn't trust anyone in the Iranian government.

That left him only one option. He needed a safe house. He only knew of one place, even though he knew all the reasons why this place might spell death for him too.

He walked to an entryway off the alley, opened the blue-painted door, and climbed the stairs. At the top, he knocked three times, then twice more.

The door opened. A familiar face from his university days was in the doorway.

"So, Yoseff Abbas," the other man said, smiling, "you've finally decided to join the CDCI?"

Yoseff shrugged as he entered the apartment. On the wall was a poster that read: "The CDCI — Agents of Change." Underneath that it read: "Committee for Democratic Change in Iran."

□□□

A few miles from that apartment was a nondescript, two-story building that had once been a warehouse. The government of Iran had converted it into a secret prison, a place for the forgotten, the forlorn, and the brutalized enemies of Iran.

That was where Joshua Jordan was being held. In the third cell from the end on the second floor. His innards had been punched in with a metal rod, the bottoms of his feet beaten, and finally he had been strapped in a crude electric chair and shocked repeatedly.

When they tossed him back into his cell, he was out cold for several hours.

When he regained consciousness, he thought he'd been roused by someone talking to him. He was slowly aware of several voices. Some talking. Others yelling. All in Farsi.

Except one.

"Colonel Jordan," the voice said, cutting through the din, and in the English of an educated Iranian. The voice had a strange nasal quality to it. "There is a bowl of water in your cell. You should take it. Be sure and hydrate. You must avoid dehydration."

Joshua dragged himself slowly and painfully over to the clay bowl that had some putrid water in it. He tried to use only his hands and wrists to pull himself along because his arms felt as if they may have been dislocated. But he couldn't pick up the bowl. He lapped the stale water like a dog.

The voice went on. "It seems they want you to drink water like a dog. They're trying to reduce you to a dog."

With great effort, Joshua rolled over onto his side to check out his cell. It was concrete, with bars on one wall facing the hallway and a solid metal door with some kind of small window in it. He rolled onto his back and stared at the ceiling.

"You speak English?"

"A lot of educated Iranians do," said the voice, which Joshua now realized was coming from a nearby cell.

"Who are you?"

"Dr. Hermoz Abdu."

"I wish you were in my cell. I need a medical doctor."

"No," the man said, "I'm not that kind of doctor; sorry."

Joshua collected his strength. "How do you know who I am?"

"I hear things."

"Why are you here?"

"I am what you might call an enemy of the state but a friend of the Iranian people."

Joshua knew he couldn't afford to trust anyone. They had tried to break him in a short amount of time, using a rapid torrent of pain. No chance for something like waterboarding. When he was flying for the Air Force they had taught him how to endure that. But he had figured out the reason for the quick, dirty, maximum pain routine they were using. Iran was obviously planning a retaliatory strike against Israel. They needed to know the specifics of the RTS missile-defense system that was in place — and they needed it quick. Joshua figured he just needed to hold on through the torture for a short period of time.

On the other hand, once the attack was launched, what reason would the Iranians have to keep him alive? He thought about that. And he had already made up his mind. *I don't want to die.*

He had so much to live for. Now, it seemed, more than ever. And so much left undone. Not just his "official" business with the Roundtable or even his defensive-weapon designs that he sincerely believed could protect innocent life. More than that. His wife, his precious Abby. And his son, Cal, ever seeking to please a father who regrettably was so hard to please. And his headstrong Deb.

Yet he knew there was something even beyond all of those things that he would have to deal with, a force that had been pursuing him, making him choose his course as if he were in the middle of a crossroads in a strange land. He felt he had become a kind of fugitive. But from what? His life seemed to be closing in on him like the walls of his filthy cell.

So he needed to survive this. But Joshua had a tactical worry. What if the Iranian Revolutionary Guard had planted this friendly prisoner, this Dr. Abdu, just to gain his confidence?

Time was short. He had to take a chance.

Joshua asked, "Why should I trust you?"

The other man laughed, but it really wasn't from amusement. More from irony perhaps.

"If you could see me," Dr. Abdu said, "then you would understand. Besides, Colonel Jordan, I have a secret. And it can save you."

FORTY-FIVE

U.S. Secretary of Defense Roland Allenworth had traveled to the White House to discuss the Joshua Jordan hostage situation. He had been unable to meet with President Corland, so he was led to the Situation Room. When he walked in, the only people there were Vice President Tulrude and Corland's chief of staff, Hank Strand.

Allenworth was not pleased. "Where's the president?"

"There's been an incident," Tulrude said. Then she nodded to Strand.

The chief of staff said, "As you know, the president has been in poor health ..."

"That's nothing new. Where is he? When can I talk to him? This can't wait."

"I'm afraid that won't be possible," Strand said. "He's in a coma. It happened very suddenly. He passed out again. This time he didn't wake up."

The look on Allenworth's face said it all. He never liked Tulrude, but she'd been a nonissue at first, particularly because Allenworth worked directly with Corland as a member of his cabinet. He had wondered, sometimes, why Corland had picked him. In the beginning Allenworth had been a staunch advocate for the Pentagon, and many of his positions diverged from Corland's internationalist tendencies. But things had changed over the last year. Corland and he had begun to work well together.

Allenworth had always feared Tulrude's politics, her lust for power, and her constant deference to the "international community of nations." Now his worst fears were being realized.

Allenworth asked the obvious question. "Do I call you Madam President?"

Tulrude said, "We will be executing the constitutional transfer of power shortly."

"Excuse my bluntness, but this needs to be done quickly … if what you are telling me is true."

Tulrude's eyes glinted with an inner explosion. "Are you questioning my honesty, Mr. Secretary of Defense?"

"No, only the medical judgment of those who say the president is unable to execute the duties of the presidency."

"Well," she snapped back, "that's not your call to make, is it?"

"I suppose not —"

"What is your question, Roland?"

"It's about Joshua Jordan. The Israeli government has indicated that during a test run of the RTS missile-defense system, Jordan was taken hostage and is presently inside Iran. I don't have to tell you how sensitive this situation is. Jordan possesses vital American-defense information."

"You mean vital *if* we continue to use his RTS technology?"

"Of course."

"But not vital if we discontinue using the RTS?"

"That would be a reversal of policy —"

"Maybe yes, maybe no, but that is my call to make now that I will be assuming executive powers."

"But if our enemies acquire the RTS design, they could create their own Return-to-Sender laser shields."

"Well, if we don't lob missiles at them, then the RTS formula won't do them much good."

"If you'll excuse me for saying so, that would represent a preposterous approach to national defense —"

"Well," Tulrude blew back, "to answer your first point, no, I won't excuse you, and secondly, I will not authorize any participation in any attempt to rescue Mr. Jordan. At least not at present. Things are much too delicate in our negotiations with Iran and Iran's partners among the Arab League to jeopardize things with some harebrained scheme to try to get Jordan out."

"What about Israel's interests?"

"What about America's interests? We both know about that Israel air strike against Iran's installations. Iran fended them off. The entire Middle East is destabilized thanks to the decisions made in Tel Aviv. And you want me to worry about Israel?" She picked up a stack of news releases. "You see what the Internet dailies are saying? 'Israel Provokes Mid-East War' ... 'Naked Israeli Aggression — Massive Strike against Iran.' You want more?"

After that, Allenworth had stormed out of the White House. Now he was back at his office. He assigned his assistant secretary the distasteful task of advising the Israeli government that the United States would be unable "at present" to participate in any "direct action to accomplish the immediate rescue of Joshua Jordan. However, the United States will work through the Department of State to open up a dialogue with Iran and hopefully effect his release in the future ..."

In Tel Aviv, General Shapiro received the message from the U.S. Defense Department. He could only shake his head in disgust.

Israel was in a state of high alert. The mission to proactively prevent Iran from launching a nuclear attack against Israel had been a disastrous failure. Now Israel had only one option: to brace for Iran's brutal counterattack on the Israeli homeland. Israel was busy marshaling all of its military assets in hopes of stopping the inevitable.

Shapiro delivered the news to the chief of staff for the Israeli Defense Forces. The chief, in turn, pulled together his strategic team for an emergency briefing.

"It appears," the chief announced, "that the Return-to-Sender system may now have an even greater significance for the defense of Israel. Which is interesting, considering the fact that its designer is now being held hostage in a jail cell somewhere in Tehran, according to our intelligence. Should we divert our attention from the task at hand, which is the defense of our very lives, homes, and families, to rescue him? What information will he be forced to divulge if we do not? And yet, even now, the Iranians may have already extracted strategic design plans from Jordan, including the details of Israel's own version of RTS — "

"Don't bank on that, General," a voice came from the speakerphone. It was Clinton Kinney, from his hospital bed, recuperating from the two bullets that had pierced his chest, one lodging in a rib and another in his lung. "Jordan's only been in custody for a day and a half. I don't care what they've done to him up to now ..."

The group around the table at IDF command considered what they just heard.

Then Kinney added, "The plain fact is that Joshua Jordan hasn't spilled his guts to the Iranians. At least not yet. I'd bet my life on it."

ㅁㅁㅁ

The last thing Abigail asked Victoria at Hawk's Nest was to relay a desperate request to her husband, Pack, to get a group of trained men to New York City to stop the portable nuke attack.

Victoria had called Abigail back to relay her husband's response: "Abby, it's in the works. Pack has deployed a small force of operatives to New York State as we speak. We received the expense money wired to the operations account. Thanks for that. One thing you need to know. Pack will not be considered a part of this. The Patriots are not part of this. Our men on the ground know only that you, as de facto leader of the Roundtable, are the one directing and authorizing this offensive. If things go bad ..."

Victoria didn't have to finish the sentence. Abigail knew only too well the nightmare in store for her if this privately funded strike force of paramilitary agents was unsuccessful, or if innocent lives were lost in the attempt, or if they were just plain wrong about the threat to begin with. She was walking the outer line of treason in a desperate attempt to save her country.

Now Abigail was on the phone with retired Army general Rocky Bridger. She had explained Josh's desperate situation as a captive of the Iranians. She knew this wasn't the first hostage situation Bridger had encountered.

"Abigail, have you tried to reach your friend in the Patriot's group about Joshua being captured?"

"Yes, and I can't get through."

Abigail knew, of course, that Pack McHenry was at some unnamed location in Paris, knee-deep in surveillance of the Russian offensive.

When Abigail told Rocky Bridger that the Patriots were out of the mix, Bridger had only one plan for the rescue of Joshua.

"Abby, I'm going to call together some special-ops guys I know. They're all out of active service now, but well trained. Good men. If I ask them, they might just lend a hand. But I need some pretty powerful intel about where they're keeping Joshua — maps of the area, scouting reports, structural details about the building itself..."

Abigail understood. "I'm going to give you General Shapiro's international number in Israel. He's my contact. If anyone would know that information, it would be him."

Cal had been sitting next to his mother during the call. When she clicked off the phone, he opened up. "Okay, Mom. First things first. We need to pray."

FORTY-SIX

Inside the metal barn in the Shenandoah Valley, Korstikoff stood over the portable nuclear weapon. It was close to completion. The delicate operations involving the neutron initiator and the use of uranium deuteride as the neutron source still needed to be dealt with, but he had personally supervised Iran's development of those components. Once the initiator had been connected to the bomb, Korstikoff felt satisfied it would be a work of perfection. Now they were only hours away.

The only other thing that needed to be done was to make the encrypted sat-fone calls to the collaborators to the north who were simultaneously preparing their bomb for New York City. The two teams would confirm final assembly and then coordinate the strikes so they would be only minutes apart. Even though the call should be very secure, they were taking no chances. Each had a method of making sure that no other telecommunications took place within a fifteen-mile radius of their positions. Their special devices would ensure absolute secrecy.

When all of that was done, they would delicately load the bomb onto the truck, which would head up I-81 toward I-66, then into Washington, down Constitution Boulevard, and straight for the Capitol.

The route would take the truck to a cul-de-sac at the bottom of the hill under the Capitol building, in the shadow of the Washington Monument, which was only a few blocks away.

When detonated, this bomb, the bigger of the two, would send out a blast-furnace shock wave with the heat intensity of the sun. It would obliterate the Capitol and all of the members of the Senate and the House of Representatives. The White House would be blown clear off the surface of the earth. All the Senate and House offices and their staffs would be incinerated instantly. The Supreme Court, the Library of Congress, the Smithsonian, and the central offices of the entire federal government would be vaporized.

Much of the Pentagon, farther from Capitol Hill and closer to the Beltway, would be devastated, though there would be survivors. But America's ability to make immediate military decisions would be paralyzed.

The rest of Washington, D.C. — the apartment buildings, condos, shops, the glass commercial towers housing lobbying organizations, law firms, trade associations — all would be shattered and in flames.

The marble monuments, Lincoln, Jefferson, Washington, would be blown into rubble.

Korstikoff looked at his watch. He needed to check his flight out of Dulles to make sure it was still on time. He wanted to avoid Reagan National. He had no intention of being anywhere near the blast.

□□□

John Gallagher was twenty miles from the exit off of I-81 that led to the spot where he was betting the nuclear terror cell might have set up shop. He was gambling on a location designated by the KGB decades before.

His Allfone rang. He clicked it on. A familiar voice from the past said, "John, Frank Treumeth here. Long time —"

"You said it," said Gallagher.

"You sound like you're in a rush —"

"That's putting it mildly. I gotta crisis. I'm working freelance now."

"Gee, John, that kinda language makes me nervous. I'm running an outdoors shop now; fishing gear, kayak tours —"

"You still own guns?"

"You kidding?"

"Still know how to shoot 'em?"

"Okay, what's up?"

"A portable nuke has been located here in the valley."

"What!"

"I'm not kidding. Excellent intelligence on this. The Feds are in total denial."

"Why?"

"Don't get me started. I just need to know if you can help ..."

"Who you working for?"

"Does the name Joshua Jordan mean anything?"

"The Air Force laser guy?"

"Right. Washington doesn't trust him, but I do. He's received credible evidence of a suitcase-type nuclear device being assembled not far from you. The clock's ticking. This may have to be a citizen's arrest ..."

"Okay, listen, John. You're a good guy, did some pretty gutsy stuff in your career. But here's what I heard ... you were ordered into some kind of counseling cause you didn't cooperate. You got pushed out of the Bureau. I'm sorry buddy, but this whole thing sounds crazy — "

"I don't beg well. I can't get down on my knees 'cause I've got arthritis. But if could, I would. I'm on my knees, crying like a little girl for you to help me."

"What is it you want?"

"I know you're connected here. I don't think the Feds will get involved, or if they do, it'll be too late. I'm sure you got street cred out here in Petticoat Junction, you know, with officer Barney Fife or whoever's the local constable. You need to round them up and get some firepower to join me at the site."

"What site?"

"I have reason to believe — "

"So you don't know for sure?"

"Not absolutely."

Frank Treumeth groaned on the other end.

"How do I get through to you, Frank?"

Then someone, a woman in the background, was yelling something to Frank, who yelled back, "Honey, it's John Gallagher. He's on the phone."

Then Gallagher could hear Frank's wife groaning too.

"Look, John," said Frank, "I think I need to talk this over with Sandra first. This is really way out there."

"Fine," Gallagher said, "go ahead and talk it over, but I'm telling you, it's time to cross the Delaware. You know? We gotta stop the Hessians and save the Republic. You with me or not?"

Pause.

"Okay," Frank said. "Whatever ..." Then he hung up.

Minutes later Gallagher saw a sign saying that his exit was ten miles away. His esophagus was burning again. Stress.

He started calculating the ludicrous stand he was about to make. One man against ... how many? He had his clip-loaded Berretta with him and a permit to carry. He also had his 357 Magnum Short Barrel with him. But these guys, if he knew anything about terror cells, would have armed guards packing automatic weapons, maybe shoulder-mounted grenade launchers.

If they really had a small nuke destined to turn Washington into a big landfill, they weren't going down easy.

More acid searing his chest.

His Allfone rang. He snapped it on. He hit the Video button this time; if Frank was going to turn him down, he was going to do it to his face.

Frank Treumeth's face flickered on the screen.

"Okay, I talked to my wife." Frank didn't look happy. "You know, John, she remembers you from the Bureau. Never liked you. Didn't know if you were aware of that."

"So you're going to let your country be destroyed because your wife thinks I'm a jerk ..."

"Not exactly."

Gallagher was listening.

"Despite all that ... I told her I didn't feel I had enough to go on to stick my neck out for you ..."

Gallagher kept listening.

"And Sandra said, and I quote, 'Then you're gutless, Frank.' So," Frank continued, "I put in a call to Corby Colwin, the deputy sheriff.

He's on his way over here. I didn't tell him much, for obvious reasons, but Corby and I will meet you in his cruiser. Where will you be?"

Gallagher gave him the exit number, which was right in front of him at the moment, and clicked off the cell. He turned onto the exit ramp and pulled over on the shoulder by the stop sign to wait.

He leaned back in the driver's seat and whispered, "Thank You, God."

FORTY-SEVEN

Deputy Corby Colwin, Frank Treumeth, and John Gallagher stood in front of the security gate a quarter of a mile down the gravel road from the sign that read "Mountain Pass Machine Parts Co." The electronic gate was locked.

Deputy Colwin scrunched up his face, as if he was about to be slapped. "Okay ... this is a problem."

Gallagher said, "We can't afford to announce ourselves. I say we take a trek through the woods."

Frank said, "Okay, but if those people really are in there, won't they have sensors out in the woods too?"

"Yeah, but they might just attribute that to a false signal, some animal or something. Our options are limited here."

"Okay, hear me out," the deputy said. "I know you say this could be serious — "

"Right," Gallagher snapped. "Nuclear weapons ... mass destruction ... somewhat serious, I'd say, yeah ..."

The deputy said, "And I don't have a warrant."

"You've got exigent circumstances."

"Sorry, Mr. Gallagher. I've only got your word on this nuclear business."

Frank said, "Corby, how about zoning? The sign said this is a light industrial shop here. But isn't this all zoned A-1 agricultural?"

"I suppose you're right. But only technically."

"Great. Then you've got probable cause to enter their property.

You've got Gallagher's report and a possible violation of zoning restrictions. That'll do, won't it?"

Deputy Colwin was squinting and fidgeting.

"All we're asking," Frank said, almost pleading, "is that you take a walk with us onto their property and take a look-see. No big deal, right? I mean really, Corby, you've gone onto property to catch wildlife poachers for crying out loud. You think we just might have something here more serious than illegal shooting of coyotes?"

Five minutes later the three of them were stomping through the thick woodland brush outside the perimeter of the barn. They came to the edge of a clearing. It was a large metal barn with a few cars and a truck in front. But no signs of life. Colwin took out a pair of binoculars. They got down to kneeling positions as Colwin studied the scene.

"Nothing happening that I can see."

Then a swarthy-skinned man exited the building and walked to the truck. He entered the cab, fished out some papers, and went back inside the barn.

"That doesn't tell me anything," Deputy Colwin said.

A few minutes later, two other men walked out of the barn, carrying automatic weapons.

"Okay," the deputy said, "now that does tell me something..."

The three of them crawled backward until they could safely stand up without being seen. They made their way through the underbrush back to their cars.

Deputy Colwin said, "I'm willing to bet what we're actually dealing with here is some heavy-duty drug trafficking."

"Or a bomb," Gallagher said stiffly, "something right out of your worst nightmares."

Frank Treumeth was beginning to think that Gallagher might be on to something.

Just then, they heard a quick electronic screech. Gallagher pulled out his Allfone. It was dead. He pulled out the battery, booted it back up. Nothing. It was still dead. Frank and Deputy Colwin did the same, and their Allfones were also dead.

Colwin swiped his face with his hand. "I gotta get to the squad car, call for major backup. I need more deputies, state police, anything." He sprinted to his cruiser and jumped in. He grabbed his police radio and tried to call dispatch. But it was dead too. "What's going on here?"

"EMP?" Frank looked over at Gallagher.

Colwin opened his eyes wide. "What?"

Gallagher explained, "Electromagnetic pulse. Knocks out all electronics within a certain radius. The new generation EMPs can zero in on communications transmissions."

"That kind of equipment," Frank added, "is exactly what I'd expect from the kind of folks you've described, John. High-tech terrorists. Whoever's planning this doesn't hang out in caves. This is major technological apparatus."

Gallagher bent down and looked into the squad car, right into Colwin's eyes. "These guys look like they're ready to take a ride. We've got to stop them. You know any deputies who live within a mile or two, anyone we can round up in a hurry?"

Colwin shook his head and thought hard. Then he looked up. His eyes lit up. "No deputies. But I've got another idea. Almost as good. Follow me."

ㅁㅁㅁ

Joshua was bracing himself for the next wave of torture. "Any idea when they're coming back?" he asked the prisoner in the next cell.

"No," Dr. Abdu replied. "Haven't heard anything. They usually beat me on alternate days ... today is my day off."

Joshua hadn't seen Dr. Abdu yet; he only knew him by his voice, but there was a kind of lightness to the tone in Dr. Abdu's conversation that Joshua found remarkable, a calmness when he spoke of his beatings. Of course, Joshua still wondered whether his prison mate was telling him the truth. Joshua knew there were other prisoners too. He could hear them speaking in Farsi on his floor, though he couldn't remember enough of the language to figure out what they were saying. Just a few words and phrases, mostly complaints about the food and thoughts about the safety of their friends and family.

"Pssst," Abdu whispered. "Colonel Jordan. Can you stand up?"

Joshua moved his arms a little. No, his shoulders were not dislocated, though still incredibly painful. Maybe the rotator cuffs were torn though. He sat up. His legs felt wobbly, and the bottoms of his feet were beaten black and blue, but he figured he could stand for a few seconds.

Dr. Abdu said, "Poke your head out the food window."

Joshua looked up at the square window in the solid metal door to his cell. A little wooden door on hinges swung open from the outside, just large enough to pass one's head through.

Joshua struggled to his feet. His knees buckled because of the pain in his feet, but he clamped his jaw down tight in a wild grimace and took two excruciating steps to the door. He hung on to the doorframe.

He pushed his head through the opening. Looking to the left, he saw the head of Dr. Hermoz Abdu hanging out of the opening in his cell door. Abdu was wearing a kind of bandit's bandana, which hid his face between his eyes and chin. His right ear had been cut off.

"Oh, yes, I forget," Abdu said, almost apologetically. Then he reached his fingers into the space left in the door window and yanked on the bandana. Now Joshua could see. Dr. Hermoz Abdu's nose had been cut off as well. Joshua was starting to understand.

"I used to prize my looks," Abdu said with a laugh. "I had many lady friends. They used to say how handsome I was. I enjoyed that. I was what you call a playboy. But everything has changed. That's okay, you know. Tell me, what do you prize, Colonel Jordan?"

Joshua was feeling queasy, sick to his stomach from the roller coaster of pain he was feeling. But he held on. "Wife. Family. My country."

"Ah, yes. Is there anything else, Colonel Jordan?"

Gripping the doorframe with shaking fists, Joshua was astonished how quickly the answer flashed into his brain. Pain had not obscured it. Fears about his own death had not diminished it. "Yes, there is something else."

Dr. Abdu fell silent.

Joshua said, "My freedom."

"Oh?"

"Yeah. My control ... of my life ... important ..."

"Interesting," Abdu said.

Joshua stared back at this man who had been thrust into his life. He studied the horribly disfigured face that was looking back at him, the slashed, ugly orifice that used to be a nose. But there was a smile on Dr. Abdu's face.

Then Abdu added, "Interesting how some men in the outside world, powerful, rich, independent, are still prisoners, while other men, confined in prison cells, laying in their own urine, are the ones who are truly free."

Joshua said, "The other men in this prison, what did they do?"

"Different things. Some wrote against the ruling imams, against the tyrants who run the government. Others formed political groups."

"And you?"

"I did something even more revolutionary. I left Islam and became a Christian. I follow Jesus now. I'm a preacher of the Gospel."

"That's why they cut you up?"

"First they cut off my ear, and they said it was to teach me not to listen to the words of the Christian infidels on the radio and TV. But I kept listening. I embraced the Savior, and my eyes were opened. I began speaking out, teaching others. I obtained a Bible and started reading it and memorizing it. I started a small underground church."

"And they caught you?"

"Yes. Then they cut off my nose. They said that I should keep my nose out of the business of Islam. No more teaching other Muslims about the love of Jesus Christ. But you see that's what drew me, like the powerful tide of the sea, the amazing love of Christ, his love for me. How could I be silent about that?"

Now the pain was too much. Joshua could stand no longer. He collapsed at the foot of the cell door.

Dr. Abdu said, "We need to talk, you and I, about how you can escape your prison."

FORTY-EIGHT

In Union Beach, New Jersey, the nuclear team had completed the assembly of their weapon. At the appointed time, they blasted their massive EMP signal over a ten-mile area, blocking all other telecommunications in that radius — further insurance of security for their sat-fone conference call. Their call linked them with both the terror cell in the Shenandoah Valley and the Russian special-operations headquarters along the northern Kyrgyzstan border. Radinovad, the brilliant Russian chief of clandestine activities, led the brief discussion from his office in the former museum building in the city of Taraz.

"*Metropolis*, are you ready?" he asked the New Jersey group.

"We are" was the reply.

"And *Marble Lady* are you ready?"

"Yes sir. Affirmative," answered the terror cell in the Shenandoah Valley.

"Any evidence of being compromised?"

Both groups said no.

"Let's all check our atomic clocks."

They were all coordinated, down to the second.

"Gentlemen, I must remind you that precision is key. Observe your schedules scrupulously. Thank you."

When Radinovad clicked off, he turned to several big satellite video screens in his office. He saw a host of blips on his electronic map. Each represented a naval warship from Russian-bloc nations heading to the Mediterranean.

He glanced over at the landmass comprising Mother Russia and the nations surrounding it: Kyrgyzstan, Kazakhstan, Uzbekistan, Turkmenistan, Tajikistan. Many dots within Russia, and several dots in the other countries, each representing the mobilization of troops. Then over in Turkey, more dots. Libya, Sudan, more dots.

He sipped his espresso and was satisfied. The Russian commander wished for the day when he could take a few days off with his mistress, go to the secret resort along the Black Sea reserved for only high-ranking officials of the Russian republic and members of the FSB like him, go sailing and sunbathing. *Pretty soon*, he told himself.

Until then, he had a front-row seat to a historic re-creation, like the Phoenix rising from the ashes. He put in an e-alert message to the rest of his team, telling them to come into his office for a briefing.

Then he entertained an aggrandizing thought once again while he took another sip of the black, grainy espresso: *The stage is dressed. The iron curtain is ready to rise again. Our global drama will be greater than anything Tolstoy could have imagined. It will rewrite everything.*

□□□

Deputy Colwin was in the lead. His squad car roared down a dirt lane a half mile from the site of the terror cell. Gallagher and Treumeth were behind him in Gallagher's rental, trying to keep up. They wondered what kind of wild-goose chase they were on because the sheriff's deputy had not bothered to tell them where they were going.

The two cars pulled up in front of a farmhouse. A few chickens wandered aimlessly on the lawn and clucked.

Colwin sprinted up the steps and banged frantically on the door. "Ruby," he called through the door. "Hurry it up!" It was a full minute before a big woman came to the door, wiping her hands.

She said, "Corby, sorry. I was out back, cleanin' chickens."

"Where's Blackie?"

"Inside. Trying to make a call. Says his cell phone went out when he was out on the tractor."

"How about Dumpster?"

"He's inside with him."

Colwin dodged inside with Ruby. There was a flurry of activity, and Colwin came flying out with Ruby, a man in his fifties, and a very large guy about six-four and three hundred pounds. They were carrying rifles and shotguns and a large plastic container that looked like a fishing tackle box. It had Remington and Winchester stickers on it.

Colwin pointed to the older man. "This is Blackie Horvath, part-time volunteer emergency-services coordinator. He's a gun permit instructor. This is Ruby, his wife. She won the ladies' shotgun competition last year."

Ruby turned to Blackie and pointed to one of his shotguns. "Hon, give me that Remington over-and-under will you? She's my favorite ..."

Gallagher turned to the huge man holding two hunting rifles with scopes attached.

"Let me guess, you're Dumpster?"

The huge guy smiled wide and nodded.

Ruby said, "My boy Dumpster here won the state wrestling championship in high school for his weight division."

Gallagher shot back, "You don't have Sumo wrestling here, do you, Mrs. Horvath?"

She bulleted back, squinting her eyes at Gallagher, "Dumpster did two tours in Iraq. Sharpshooter. Can shoot the head off a chicken at a thousand yards."

Gallagher stepped up and shook the man's hand. "Dumpster, you're my new best friend."

Colwin, already standing by his squad car, shouted that the Horvath family would ride with him, and he'd finish briefing them on the ride back to the site.

The two cars spit gravel and raced back up the driveway.

The whole thing seemed ridiculously surreal to Gallagher. Then again, that would describe most of his experience at the FBI. Gallagher looked at the squad car ahead. Dumpster's huge head bobbed with each bump in the dirt road. Gallagher tried to put a label on the whole thing, and he succeeded: *Special-ops unit of the Beverly Hillbillies versus some very scary terrorists.*

Or maybe it was more like a picture Gallagher remembered from his childhood, a picture of ordinary farmers running with muskets — on their way to Lexington and Concord.

Gallagher nodded at the squad car ahead of them and said, "Frank, we could do a whole lot worse ..."

FORTY-NINE

Four miles outside of Union Beach, New Jersey, three men from Pack McHenry's team sat in a black SUV in a McDonald's parking lot. They were waiting for the "go" authorization from their contact. All three were former special-operations agents from the U.S. Coast Guard. A fourth, Jim Yaniky, another reserve member of the Coast Guard special ops, was coming separately but had been delayed. He was still several miles away. They told him to pull over and wait. If the truck with the nuke got past them for some reason, then Yaniky could intercept it, like a "goalie" at the end line, though they all knew that was a pretty lousy Plan B. The main objective was to stop the truck before it left its assembly location, because once it was on the road, the dice became dangerously loaded against them. The team knew that the delivery vehicle would probably be rigged with a detonator that could be activated from the cab of the truck, so that if the terrorists felt themselves threatened, they could simply do a rolling detonation.

All of these civilians had been tasked by a simple call and a code number, which they knew was from McHenry's Patriot group. They also knew they were to consider themselves working only at the behest of one person. If stopped and detained, they would deny any connection to Pack McHenry or his Patriots.

The call was placed by Jim Yaniky, who had been designated team coordinator.

ᗡᗡᗡ

At Hawk's Nest, the phone rang. Abigail Jordan had been on a round-the-clock vigil, trying to work with Rocky Bridger to rescue her husband. Abigail picked up.

"Mrs. Jordan," said the voice, "my name is Jim Yaniky. I'm one of four former members of the U.S. Coast Guard strike force, retired but on reserve. We understand you'd like us to perform a citizens' action to halt suspected criminal behavior in or around Union Beach, New Jersey, namely, the transport of a truck thought to be carrying a nuclear weapon?"

"Yes, Mr. Yaniky, that's correct." She thought for a moment. "As former members of the U.S. Coast Guard, then you're all exempt from the restrictions of the federal Posse Comitatus Act, which prohibits members of the other branches of the military from performing law-enforcement duties?"

"That's pretty much it, yes."

Abigail now understood why Pack McHenry had selected these men. If things went bad, federal prosecutors would not be able to argue that this law had been violated at least. Now she only had a dozen other federal laws to worry about.

"You understand, Mrs. Jordan, we consider you to be our principal in this action. May we proceed under your direction and advice?"

She didn't hesitate. "I understand my responsibility, Mr. Yaniky, for this mission." Abigail was now fully committed. She knew she was way past second-guessing, but there was still a critical part of the plan she needed to know. She couldn't launch an armed campaign unless her soldiers knew where the enemy was.

"Have you located the cell group?"

"They're in Union Beach, ma'am, south of New York City."

"How'd you find them?"

"They used an electromagnetic pulse to blow out the local electronics. We figured they were doing covert communications and didn't want to risk being picked up. We've got special Allfones to resist that. They were designed, by the way, by your husband's company, Jordan Technologies, ma'am."

Abigail felt a lump in her throat. Joshua's work had come full circle.

Yaniky finished, "We have an EMP tracker. We pinpointed the source. We're pretty sure they're at that spot. Uh ... one moment." He put her on hold. Ten seconds later he came back. "Sorry ma'am, it's go time!"

"God go with you."

"Thanks."

Only when Abigail clicked off her Allfone did the immensity of the challenge hit her. During his military career, her husband had been the one responsible for the lives of those ordered into harm's way. Now she was the one shouldering that responsibility. She uttered a quivering prayer. Then she went back to her other task, waiting for Rocky Bridger's call, which she was expecting shortly.

ㅁㅁㅁ

Before leaving the machine shop in Union Beach, Dr. Kush Mahi confirmed that the bomb was ready to load. He was now on his way to Newark Airport to catch an international flight out of the country before the nukes were detonated. The gunmen had gingerly packed the nuke into a shipping crate and had carefully lifted it onto the truck. Painted on the sides of the truck was an advertisement for Mexican food. With a large Hispanic festival going on in downtown Manhattan, the truck would blend in perfectly.

ㅁㅁㅁ

The torture team had come back for Joshua. They dragged him to the windowless cement room and strapped him down. Again they shocked him with electricity. Again and again and again. Each time the voltage got higher. Joshua groaned and whimpered with pain. He wondered how long he could withstand the excruciating jolts before he began spilling his guts about the RTS units he'd provided to Israel.

But one thought helped him keep it together: one of the last conversations he had with Abigail. He tried to conjure up her beautiful face, but he couldn't. Was he losing his mind? Was his memory deteriorating? But he could remember what she'd said. She had told him that Israel would play a critically important part in the global scheme of things, in God's vast plan, more than perhaps Joshua ever imagined.

That was what he was hanging on to, though he wasn't sure why. Maybe it was just a rope to grab, to keep from giving up, to keep his focus off the pain, to help him tough it out just one more time...

When it was over, Joshua's tormentors dumped his nearly lifeless body back into his cell.

After the Iranian guards left, Dr. Abdu waited over an hour for sounds from Joshua's cell. Then he called out, "Joshua, my friend, are you awake? Can you hear me?"

There was no response.

"Joshua?"

The rest of the prisoners were quiet too, listening. But there was no reply.

ㅁㅁㅁ

Rocky Bridger had to do everything remotely. He didn't like that. As a four-star general in the U.S. Army, he had always preferred to be in the presence of as many of the men whom he would send into harm's way as possible. But the present desperate timeline didn't allow that.

Four heavily armed men, two former Army Rangers and two retired Navy SEALs, were on a private jet heading for Baghdad, Iraq. That was the closest staging point to Iran. Rocky pulled some strings with his former Army colleagues in the Pentagon for their landing. They were cleared for entrance into Iraq as "private VIP security contractors."

Though the mission was expensive, all the costs were covered by the Roundtable through Abigail's quick work.

Rocky was on a video Allfone call with the team, mapping out the strategy. He had just finished a conversation with Israeli general Shapiro.

Shapiro had sounded unusually calm. "General Bridger, good to talk to you again. It's been a long time." No hint in Shapiro's voice of the coming attack from Iran that they were preparing for.

Rocky reciprocated the greeting and then told Shapiro that he already knew about the White House shooting down an organized attempt to rescue Joshua. "General," Rocky said, "I'm putting together a private team to get Joshua Jordan out of there. What can you give us in the way of support?"

"I can share our intelligence," Shapiro said. "I'd like to promise more. Too early to say right now."

"Anything, General Shapiro ..."

"I will send you an encrypted e-file with some photos of the building in Tehran where he is being held captive. A map of the area. It's a special prison for dissidents, that sort of thing. They have probably tortured Colonel Jordan, I'm afraid ..."

"I'd assumed that," Rocky said.

"But it's also heavily guarded."

"I also figured that."

"But one additional possibility ..."

"I'm listening."

"We have an Iranian inside Tehran. He's been cooperating with us. We are trying to regain contact with him. I'll send you the e-file on him. Name is Yoseff Abbas. Maybe he can help, don't know for sure. We're also looking into air support for your team."

Rocky thanked the general, but after he hung up, his sense of history took over. So when Rocky Bridger connected by video Allfone with his strike force of four men who were winging their way across the Atlantic, he brought it up. "You fellas are all former special ops, I know, but you're probably too young to remember another rescue plan. Like ours, it was privately organized, and like ours, it was to save some Americans held hostage in a prison inside Tehran. They happened to be employees of Ross Perot's company over there. So Perot hired 'Bull' Simmons, retired Army colonel. Simmons put together a plan."

"What are you thinking, sir?" one of the men asked.

"I am thinking about repeating history ..."

FIFTY

Ethan March stood in baggage claim at the airport. He was leaving a voicemail for Deborah: "All right, Deb, I know what I'm about to tell you sounds crazy, but your voicemail said you were in Israel with your father. Then I happened to meet up with a friend of mine in the Air Force, active duty, detailed to the Pentagon. Without going into specifics, he hinted that Israel is digging in for a tough stand against an attack, probably from Iran. So ... well, I really appreciated the chance to protect you on that flight out of JFK. Deborah ... okay, I'm sorry, I haven't been more up front about how I feel. But the truth is ... I haven't been able to get you off my mind. I know this is all very fast, but maybe our being on the same flight was fate or something. Not that your father can't protect you. Please don't think I would ever say that. I just want the privilege of looking after you myself. I guess that's what I'm saying."

He took a deep breath, then finished his message. "Anyway, Deb, I'm here in Tel Aviv. I flew to Rome, then caught the last flight into Israel. I don't think Israel is letting any more flights in. Now I hear that Israel bombed Iran's nuclear site. So the ... well, chicken feathers are going to start flying ... I guess that's the polite way of saying it. I'd like to see you and make sure you're safe. Call me. Okay? Thanks."

Ethan clicked off his Allfone and watched the baggage conveyor. After a while, his bag came by and he snatched it. Through the glass doors he could see that it was early evening in Israel and darkness was falling. While he waited for Deborah to return his call, he had one question.

Okay smart guy, now what?

ⵔⵔⵔ

In the presidential palace in Tehran, an aging Mahmoud Ahmadinejad, Iran's long-reigning leader, was seated behind his ornate gilded desk. His hands rested comfortably on it, next to the special high-command Allfone. He was thinking.

Behind him, on either side of the floor-to-ceiling golden silk curtains, was a portrait of the grey-bearded Ayatollah Khomeini, the founder of the modern Islamic republic of Iran. Ahmadinejad had managed to hang on to power over the years, despite the sniping and complaining from the ruling imams. He had even been able to suppress the ever growing prodemocracy movement, though to his infernal rage, the "addicts of freedom," as he called them privately, would still surge onto the streets of Tehran with banners calling for reform, free elections, and an end to his own push for the nuclear destruction of Israel. Yes, he had been able to hang on to power. But barely. The people in the street protests were swelling in number. He could arrest, imprison, or torture only so many per day.

Often Iran's president would wonder to himself: *How did Saddam Hussein do it so effectively for so long?*

But now it was decision time. He would give the order to launch Iran's three nuclear warheads on the newest version of their Qiam — "Uprising" — missiles. Two of the targets within Israel were easy to choose: Tel Aviv and the harbor at Haifa. Some of his advisors wanted to destroy Jerusalem, but that posed several problems. The mosques on the Temple Mount in the heart of the Old City were Islamic holy sites. "That," Ahmadinejad told them, "would be very bad public relations." Then there were the Sunnis to be placated. That was critical in his attempt to unite the Arab Islamic world in preparation for his war against Israel and the West. As a Shiite, he didn't share their view about the location where the future Islamic messiah, the Mahdi, the "twelfth imam" long awaited and prophesied in Islam, would end up appearing. But the Sunnis envisioned it taking place on the Temple Mount.

He didn't mind preserving Jerusalem. It belonged to Allah anyway. So Ahmadinejad had decided that the third site would be Galilee. The city of Tiberias on the sea. It was a popular tourist site. Christians would cross the sea of Galilee in their tourist boats and sing to their Jesus, about His Godlike powers and His being their savior, the suffering Son of God. Ahmadinejad and his fellow Muslims considered them infidels. Yes, Islam considered Jesus a prophet, but when the twelfth imam, their true savior, appeared — and his appearing was very close now — Jesus would step back and bow to his authority. So the nuclear incineration of Tiberias along with Tel Aviv and Haifa would be a good choice.

Iran's president savored the moment. Decades of dreaming about the decimation of Israel, reducing its major cities to smoldering garbage dumps, was about to bear fruit. Still, there were lingering questions about Israel's Return-to-Sender systems. He had received word from the interrogators that the American inventor of RTS had given them no information. What a pity. Effective torture was an art form. Apparently, Iran's secret police were losing their touch.

But he wasn't worried. According to media accounts, RTS had failed to protect the American airliner that was blasted from the sky after departing O'Hare airport. Also, there was credible intelligence that Israel had obtained a less-than-reliable system. Although the Iranian secret police disagreed among themselves on whether that intelligence was credible, even if it were not, there was a new component in the guidance system of Iran's Qiam missile. The Russians had provided an antilaser shield in the nose cone to protect it from the RTS laser intrusion.

Most important of all, surely, Allah would be with them. Ahmadinejad was certain of that.

He picked up the receiver. A voice on the other end, from Iran's nuclear launch site at Bushehr, said, "Yes, Mr. President."

"Commence the attack, General."

□□□

"Joshua? Talk to me ..."

Dr. Abdu was still trying to raise a response, but so far nothing. Then he thought he heard some stirring in the cell next to his. More rustling. Then the sound of something shuffling on the floor. Dr. Abdu had poked his head out of the window in the door to his cell, craning his neck to see Joshua's cell.

Then something appeared in the food window of Joshua's cell. Joshua's head slowly emerged. He turned toward Dr. Abdu, who could see that both of Joshua's eyes were blackened, and he had blood running from his ears and nose. Dr. Abdu gave a start and jerked his head slightly when he saw it.

Joshua noticed it. He mustered the strength for a weak attempt at humor: "Who's ... worse looking now?"

Shaking his head and beaming with a wide grin, Dr. Abdu said, "So happy to see you alive my friend. So very good to see you again."

"Have you ... heard anything ... about war ... with Israel?"

"No, Joshua. Nothing."

"Think I'll rest now ... then we'll talk ..."

With that Joshua drew his head back into his cell and collapsed onto the floor.

FIFTY-ONE

John Gallagher's counterterrorism team consisted of him, a fellow former FBI agent, a local sheriff's deputy, and three farmers. That's all he had to work with. But they were all in position.

Frank Treumeth, Deputy Colwin, and Blackie Horvath were situated on the left side of the clearing, spread out in cross-fire fashion along the flank of the metal barn. Blackie had the high-powered deer rifle with a scope, since Frank and Colwin figured he had kept up with his distance shooting more than they had. Frank had his own handgun and a Western-style Winchester rifle. When Blackie saw it, he kidded Frank and called him "the Rifleman," after the old black-and-white television western. Colwin was holding the riot-quelling shotgun that he had snatched from his squad car.

Gallagher and Dumpster were on the other side of the clearing, scanning the metal barn. Their angle of aim was forty-five degrees to the front of the barn, the same as Frank's team on the other side. That way the two teams wouldn't inadvertently fire at each other.

Dumpster lay behind a bush at the edge of the woods, about twenty yards from Gallagher. He was sighting through the scope of his big .45-caliber rifle. According to the plan, when the armed men appeared, Deputy Colwin would use his bullhorn to shout a warning for them to drop their weapons. After a full two seconds, when they didn't obey, Dumpster would fire first. He'd try to hit the first gunman in the nearest shoulder. Then he'd fire off a second shot, aiming at whichever man was closest.

Then Blackie would fire, aiming for either the gunman nearest him or any of the men that Dumpster missed, though Blackie said matter-of-factly, "Dumpster doesn't miss."

Ruby Horvath with her Remington over-and-under pump-action shotgun was positioned about an eighth of a mile down the long gravel drive that led to the metal barn. That way if the truck got through somehow, she would stop it, though Gallagher was also hoping that Ruby would be clear of any fireworks.

"Call me old-fashioned," Gallagher cracked, "but I like to keep the womenfolk protected."

They waited. Ten minutes went by. Twenty minutes. Forty-five. Gallagher started getting restless. He looked at the cars parked in front of the barn. They were empty. And no one was in the white panel truck, which had a sign for a plumbing service painted on its side. He wondered if the bomb had even been loaded yet. What if it had? What if it hadn't? Each scenario carried its own catastrophic risk, but Gallagher resigned himself to the fact that they would have to play the ball where it lay — wherever that happened to be.

He kept asking himself one question, and it was starting to drive him crazy:

What are they waiting for?

□□□

Near Union Beach, New Jersey, the three commandos waited in their SUV, parked near the side of the sewage treatment plant bordering the machine shop. The engine was running. The curved dish of their long-range listening device was pointed at the machine shop, and they were relaying all of the audio to Jim Yaniky who was still positioned miles away. He, in turn, was feeding it to a translation service so that the translation could be bulleted back upstream to the three commandos. The voices were saying:

"The engineers should be ready to board by now."

"What does the gas gauge on the truck say?"

To that someone answered, "Don't worry. Filled it yesterday."

Several references to "Allah."

Someone asked about the GPS on the truck. Another man said he had checked it out and it worked.

But nothing about a bomb ... or their departure time.

The commandos would have to wait.

In his position in a neighboring town, Jim Yaniky tapped his hands on the steering wheel of his Hummer. He gazed out the window at a colored wind sock atop a local deli shop across the street. The wind had picked up. He worried about the quality of the audio feed of the listening device being affected.

Jim looked at the wind sock again. The wind was gusting to the east, in the direction of the ocean.

ⵔⵔⵔ

"Ethan you have no idea ... your timing ... oh, I don't know how to describe this ..."

"Just start talking, Deb."

"So are you really in Israel right now? This exact minute?"

"One hundred percent in Tel Aviv. Sitting at the airport. What's going on? You sound — "

"Thank You, God," she whispered, "that Ethan's here ..."

"Deb, talk to me."

"Dad's been taken ..."

"What do you mean? Taken where?"

"No, *taken*. Captured. They think by some terror group. Possibly Iranian. I've been pleading for more information, but the IDF won't tell me any more than that ... I've spoken to my mom, and she doesn't know anything more either. You know my mom. She just said, 'Stay put. Stay safe. Let the IDF take care of it.'"

Ethan March was stunned. He tried to sort it all out.

Deborah's voice cracked. "Please come down here."

"Where?"

"Jerusalem. I'm staying at the King David Hotel. I wanted to head up to IDF headquarters in Tel Aviv to see if I can get more informa-tion, but Esther Kinney ... a friend ... says it's too dangerous. Tel Aviv and most of Israel is under some kind of alert. Nobody seems to know why. Esther's husband was wounded in the same attack involving my dad. He's in a hospital in southern Israel."

"That explains the chaos I see going on up here in the Tel Aviv airport."

"Can you get down here?"

"I'll be there. I'm leaving right now. I'll meet you at the hotel."

Ethan grabbed his bag and rushed out to the ground-transportation area outside of baggage claim. There was a line of horn-honking cabs and minibuses, all filled, all trying to get out of Ben Gurion Airport and the greater Tel Aviv area. He pleaded with several cabbies, but they all turned him down. Every one of them was crowded to capacity.

Across the boulevard Ethan saw an older man leaning on a car, talking on a cell phone. The car had a sign that said something in Hebrew, but in English it read, "All Israel Tours."

Ethan threaded his way through the traffic and over to the car.

The man finished his call, clicked it shut, and waved to Ethan. "Sorry, no tours today ..."

"No, you don't understand. I don't want a tour. I need a ride — "

"You and the rest of Israel."

"I'll pay you whatever you want."

"My friend, I have a wife down at the Kibbutz at Kiryat Anavim and I need to join her. She heard the news, and she's going crazy. Our country is under an alert."

"I need to get to Jerusalem."

The tour guide lifted an eyebrow. "What's the rush ... other than staying alive?"

"My girlfriend is down there in Jerusalem. It's a long story."

"If it's about a woman, the story is always long."

"Can you take me?"

"I can take you, my friend, as far as Kiryat Anavim, where my home is. It's right outside Jerusalem."

"Please, I need to get *into* Jerusalem, to the King David Hotel ..."

Ethan didn't wait; he tossed his bag into the car, ran around to the passenger side, and hopped in.

The tour guide shook his head at the sky. Then he climbed in behind the wheel and pulled into the traffic.

"You look too young to have hearing problems. I said I could take you to the *outskirts* of Jerusalem …"

As they slowly snaked through the traffic, Ethan said, "The long story is not about the girl. I'm falling in love with her. That's just the short story. Haven't known her for long. But I don't need to …"

"I've heard that one before."

"The real story is that her father is an American military hero … Air Force colonel. He came over here to help Israel. Now he's in deep trouble; he's being held by the Iranians. So I need to get to his daughter, to look after her … she's the woman I'm in love with. There. That's the long story."

"And you? Your story?"

"I was in the Air Force with this colonel. He's true blue. He's my personal hero."

"So, this colonel … what kind of 'help' was he giving to Israel, exactly?"

"He invents defensive weapons."

The man drummed his index fingers on the steering wheel and bobbed his head. Then he said, "My name is Nony." He reached over to shake Ethan's hand.

"Good to meet you, Nony. My name's Ethan."

Nony said, "Okay. So, I think we can make a little side trip into Jerusalem, to the King David Hotel … drop you off before I hightail it back to my condo and my wife. I'll call her and tell her right now."

When they finally left the airport and were on Highway 1 southeast to Jerusalem, they looked ahead. Stretching as far as the eye could see was a line of slow-moving cars, also heading to Jerusalem.

"They tell us," Nony said, " when we have these air-raid drills to put on our gas masks. But you know what? This won't be gas. That madman Ahmadinejad has nuclear bombs. Forget about the gas masks …"

FIFTY-TWO

The four bearded men were lying on the floor of an Israeli Apache helicopter. According to plan, the next stop would be Iran and their attempt to rescue Joshua Jordan. The drop-off point was approaching.

Phase one of the operation had already been successful — the rendezvous between the four members of the rescue team and the IDF helicopter at a U.S. base in Baghdad. The two former Army Rangers and two retired Navy SEALs had arrived in Baghdad on a private jet that Rocky Bridger had booked for them. The Israeli Apache chopper had arrived a short time later; the arrival times were staggered to make them look coincidental.

The IDF had asked permission of the U.S. military transition team in Baghdad to land their helicopter. The stopover allowed the new long-range Apache to get refueled. The pilots said they were running a recon mission over Turkish airspace and had encountered mechanical difficulties. Turkey, they said, had refused to allow them to land. The U.S. peacekeeping command met the whole thing with skepticism. The U.S. troops had been ordered to refrain from engaging in military operations, essentially prohibited from returning fire without specific orders. They were to avoid anything that looked like choosing sides or picking fights. It was also part of something bigger. The unofficial word in the American command posts in that part of the world was that United States foreign policy toward the Middle East was changing. America would edge away from its traditional support of Israel and toward more friendly partnerships with Arab nations.

Conventional wisdom was that if all-out war broke out between Israel and the Arab League, the United States would ditch its longtime ally Israel.

When the two IDF helicopter pilots had lifted off from the U.S. air base in Baghdad they kept eyeballing the radio receiver, waiting for something to go wrong, like someone back in Iraq or from the U.S. command center ordering them to return to base.

But the order never came. That's when one of the pilots gave the thumbs up to the four special-ops contract warriors who then climbed up to their seats and buckled in for the long flight.

Now the chopper was approaching phase two, the drop-off point for the rescue team just off the Iranian coast. The pilots, on cue, radioed back to Israeli headquarters to report their status. That is when they received a message from Tel Aviv—in Hebrew and encrypted.

After deciphering the communiqué, the pilot turned to the special-ops guys in the back. The tightened muscles in his face gave a hint that something was up. "HQ's just informed us that Iran may be planning an imminent launch of several long-range missiles. Iran's official explanation is that they're only testing their defensive capability in light of Israel's strike against Iran's nuclear facility at Natanz."

The pilot then gave a gesture of disgust with his lips, as if he were ready to spit. "We know better."

In the back, Jack, the SEAL leader, turned to the guy sitting next to him, the lead Ranger, named Tom Cannonberry, though everyone called him "Cannon." Jack said, "Sounds like the Israelis may be hunkering down for war. We all know what that means."

"Yeah," Cannon spit back. "We may have just bought ourselves a one-way ticket to Iran."

A third rescue warrior piped up with a cynical half grin. "Looks like I'll have time to do some shopping in Tehran, get my girlfriend a nice Persian rug …"

The men fell quiet as the helicopter cut across the Caspian Sea that bordered northern Iran.

When the chopper was over Iranian waters, another message

came in from Israeli command. But this one the pilots did not—could not—share with the men they were transporting. "Intelligence sources indicate troop movements within southern Russia, several of the Republics, and also within Turkey and as far away as Sudan and Libya. Major mobilization. Some naval deployment as well. Please observe and report any of the same during your mission."

The helicopter was hovering over the sea, three miles off the coast of Iran. The drop-off point was confirmed by Israeli satellite imaging to have no radar installations and only a few patrol boats. They ran on a predictable schedule. It was 10:15 at night now, and they had a forty-five-minute window before the next Iranian patrol boat would be in the vicinity.

Cannon gave the last-minute reminder to his crew. "Remember, all of us have to swim to the raft. I don't want any bodies floating out there on the waves. We motor till we're a quarter mile from the coast, and then we paddle. Our friends in the Mossad have one of their contacts in-country who is supposed to have a car fueled and waiting for us on an industrial access road about a mile and a half off the beach. Let's hope they left the keys in the car."

Looking out of the open door of the Apache, Jack tossed the large inflatable raft, with its small electric motor, out into the darkness. They saw its blinking light get smaller until it finally hit the water and started bobbing.

As he strapped on his life vest, Jack, the former Navy SEAL, turned to Cannon in the open door. Looking down at the sea below and then back at Cannon the land-loving ex-Ranger, Jack said with a smile, "Welcome to the swim club ..." Then he jumped into the night.

□□□

No one knew how it started. That was usually the case with protest marches like this one. At first, five hundred prodemocracy Iranians flooded the streets of Tehran. Then it grew to fifteen hundred. Many of the shops were still open. Their neon lights were glowing in the night, but their shelves were only half stocked with merchandise.

The protestors were chanting, "Food, not war; food, not war."

The march was five blocks from the warehouse-turned-prison where Joshua Jordan and Dr. Abdu were being held.

Inside, Dr. Abdu had just asked Joshua how he was feeling.

Joshua did not stand up and put his head out the window of the cell as he had done before. He was too weak. Instead he leaned against the open bars as he talked.

"Head hurts. Dizzy. Like someone used my brain for an electric outlet."

"Anything else?"

"Helpless ..."

"Hmm ..."

"I came to help Israel, and I end up here. No escape. My wife and son are back at home ... with this horrible crisis ... I dumped in their lap ..."

Sitting on the dirty concrete floor, Joshua was stunned by how quickly things were ceasing to make sense. He'd always had a forceful personality, able to make things happen, work out problems, find the right avionics to keep things in the air and avoid a crash. But not now. Was it just the pain? He didn't think so. Part of it maybe. But it was also something else.

"My daughter is stranded in Israel. And Iran is planning an attack ... nuclear ... I worry that I may have signed her death sentence by bringing her with me to Israel. Helpless ... helpless ... desperate ... that's how I feel ..."

"Things don't happen by accident ..."

"So you tell me ..." Then Joshua remembered something. "Hey, I thought you said you were going to share some secret about my getting out of here."

"Did I?"

"Don't play games, Hermoz ..."

"No, I'm not. I said I had a secret for getting you out of *your* prison —"

"Exactly ..."

"But this place isn't your prison."

Even in his pain and disorientation, Joshua was starting to get the picture.

"You are imprisoned in yourself, Joshua. Till you get out of that, you'll never be free. That's why you need the key."

"And I suppose you have it hanging on your belt?"

"No ... in my heart." Then Dr. Abdu added, "But if I give it to you, I warn you, Joshua ... while it will cost you nothing ... it will ask everything of you ..."

Then, somewhere outside in the night, they could hear something ... chanting ... crowds. Joshua had heard that before. "Another protest? In the streets?" he asked.

Dr. Abdu said yes and translated the chants for Joshua.

After some silence, Joshua asked, "How can it cost me nothing but ask me for everything?"

"Oh, well," Dr. Abdu answered, "a desperate man may have nothing in his pocket ... or in his soul. Both are empty. Hollow. So he is willing to accept what is freely offered to him. But even a desperate man like you, Joshua, beaten, bloody, imprisoned — even a desperate man has something he has yet to give."

FIFTY-THREE

Word filtered from Iran to its contacts within Hamas in Gaza, at the southern end of Israel, where it bordered the Egyptian Sinai. It was the Persian word *Qiam*, the signal for Arabs everywhere, including the Palestinians in the Gaza, to become part of the Qiam, the "uprising." The Iranian subversives in Gaza didn't know about the impending missile strike. Their order was only to begin the insurgency.

And so they did.

Hamas terror cells rounded up hundreds of supporters and rushed the IDF checkpoints just north of the Gaza, overpowering the IDF officers there.

They received a second message as well: "Take Jerusalem." The implication would have been clear if they had the whole picture. The missiles that Iran had sent into the heart of Israel would spare Jerusalem. That city would now belong to Allah, and an army of Palestinian terrorists would be part of the effort to secure that city for Islam.

ㅁㅁㅁ

In Jerusalem, warning sirens were blaring. The residents of the King David Hotel were rushing down the emergency stairs to the basement, which served as their bomb shelter for the hotel. People were shouting out questions to each other, trying to find out what had triggered the air-raid drill, but no one seemed to know.

Deborah Jordan and Esther Kinney were caught in the stairwell amidst a shoving mass of humanity. They were shoulder to shoulder on the cement stairs, on the level below the lobby when, somewhere farther down the stairs there was a gunshot. Then another. Screams. Someone down there shouted, "Go back up! Go back!"

Now the crowd was turning around, with people toppling off their feet and being pulled under by the crush of the mob. Below, Hamas gunmen had entered the hotel and were randomly shooting hotel guests trapped on the stairway.

Deborah was only ten feet from an exit door leading to the hotel lobby, but the crush of people in the stairwell was crowding the trapped hotel guests against the door, keeping it from being opened.

"Do this!" Deborah shouted to those around her. Then she turned to face the crowd behind her with her arms up in front of her and fists tucked under her chin like an offensive lineman in a football game. Several others followed suit, forming a human defensive chain to hold back the mob that was pushing up the stairs in a frenzy. With the space that Deborah's maneuver had created, a man in the stairwell next to her was finally able to swing the door open.

The crowd, including Deborah and Esther, poured through the exit door and into the familiar lobby, with its blue ceiling and tall square columns. People were scattering in all directions, running for their lives. There were more shots. Now they were ringing out in the lobby from somewhere.

A gunman appeared with a revolver, and he was shooting randomly at the hotel guests.

Deborah called to Esther, "To the pool!"

They dodged across the lobby and down one hallway until they found the door leading to the outdoor pool. It was surrounded by trees and shrubs. Deborah jumped down behind some bushes and Esther joined her. They were out of breath. Deborah surveyed the area to see if it was safe to escape the hotel grounds.

Just then she saw a bearded gunman jogging around the perimeter of the pool, looking for victims. "Stay down," she whispered to Esther.

Deborah peaked through the bushes. Suddenly, a broad-shouldered, clean-shaven man, who looked like a tourist, ran up to the gunman from behind. He locked his forearm around the gunman's throat.

The two struggled. The tourist took him to the ground and slammed the gunman's head on the pavement. Then again. The gunman was still. The tourist took the gun.

Only when he stood did Deborah get a good look at him.

"Ethan!" she screamed out.

Ethan March, gun in hand, whipped around as he recognized her voice. They locked glances. He sprinted around the pool and into her arms.

"Ethan, thank God you're all right!" Deborah was crying as they hugged.

He said, "I thought I saw you running through the lobby. I followed you. Deb, the downtown is chaos — a killing zone. I've got to get you out of here. A tour guide dropped me off on the way to his condo outside the city, just as the sirens went off. No one seems to know what the threat is or what's going on … but there's clearly small-arms fire coming from small groups of terrorists. Nony, the tour guy, was on his cell with his wife, and she said the Israeli army has set up a checkpoint over where she is and it's much safer. He said if I found you, I could bring you to his place. We can camp out with them. But Nony took off after dropping me here. He had get to his wife. We'll have to go on foot over to his condo. It'll be quite a hike I'm afraid. There's not a cab to be found."

"Ethan, this is Esther," Deborah said pointing to her. "My friend who — "

Before Deborah could finish her sentence, Ethan said, "Esther, come with us. You'll be safer."

ⵔⵔⵔ

Joshua was still sitting with his back against the bars. Dr. Abdu was on the floor of his cell, his face at the bars, where his cell met Joshua's. Joshua's head still felt like it had imploded, but his thinking was clearer now.

Abdu said, "So you know it intellectually …"

"Sure."

"About God?"

"Yeah. He's out there ..."

"But in the Bible, Jesus said that even the demons acknowledge that."

"So?"

"Here's the real question. What do *you* think about Jesus Christ?"

"Pretty much the same."

"Explain."

"Thought about it. Haven't told Abby ... that's my wife ... very much about it. Should have though. I worked a lot out in my own head."

"What does your head say?"

Joshua wondered about that. Was his brain really working after all he'd been through? He tried to recall something, just to test his memory, his thinking process. At least that's what he told himself. *Okay, see if you can lay it out logically. Make sure the gears are working ...*

So he started to talk. "Abby's got this pastor. Peter Campbell. He's explained it. You look at the accuracy of the stuff in the Gospel stories ... about Jesus. Historical verification. Credible accounts ... good historical data. And the stories come from eyewitnesses ... the versions of the New Testament passed down ... they're reliable. So you've got that. And the fact that Jesus fulfilled all those prophecies ... a hundred of them in the Old Testament, Pastor Campbell said, delivered centuries before the birth of Christ ... about the miracles the Messiah would perform and even His manner of death. Jesus was the perfect fit. The only fit ... and then there's the people ... who have faith in Jesus ... it's like they've walked into something miraculous. Life changing ... That's what my head's telling me."

On the last point, he had to think about Dr. Abdu, his brutalized, disfigured face, but the man also exuded an inner calm, a peace beyond earthly explanation.

"So," Abdu said. "That is what your head says ..."

"Yeah."

"What does your heart say?"

Joshua paused for a second or two. "My heart? Well ... that's a holdout."

"Too bad, because even though it's all free — gaining salvation, eternal life, forgiveness of your sins, restoration of a relationship with the living God — all of that is totally free and available right now for you, what God wants from you now is *all* that you have to offer Him. God wants *all* of you. Your brain? Certainly. Yes, of course. But your heart as well. Trust in God's Son Jesus Christ by faith, using your brain as well as your heart. My question now is a very simple one for you, Joshua ... are you ready for that?"

There was no response ...

Until several minutes later. Joshua had thought it out. Was all of this just an accident of fate? His being there, in a jail cell in Tehran, next to an Iranian pastor who was talking to him about the Christian Gospel? It seemed as though, in some strange way, for him it had to be in a place like this, on a concrete floor spotted with filth, blood, and cockroaches — though he didn't know why exactly. Somehow it just fit.

For Joshua the time for avoidance had ceased.

A voice came out of Joshua's cell. "Okay. Let's go."

"Right now?"

"Yeah, now."

"I have questions for you," Dr. Abdu said.

"I'm ready."

"Do you believe that you're a sinner, Joshua, that you have broken God's laws, are guilty of sin, and separated from God as a result?"

"That I've offended God? That's a no-brainer ... odd ... never admitted that out loud before ..."

"Do you repent of your sins ... and do you want to receive forgiveness for them? Do you want to come into a relationship with the living God?"

"Hermoz, truth be told ... I've tried to keep this a secret ... tried to keep it screwed on tight ..."

"Secret?"

"Tried hard to succeed at the externals in my life: military career, professional life. But the inside of me ... a pretty dark, lonely, restless place ... is a mess. Morally ... spiritually ... and every other way. I think God's the only one who can fix it."

"Then do you accept the work of Jesus Christ on the cross, the Son of God, who was the only, once-and-for-all, perfect sacrifice for your sins, and who then walked out of the grave three days later?"

"I accept that. I believe that ... as God is my witness I do ..."

"Do you invite Jesus the Christ to come and live inside you through the Spirit of God and to be your Savior and your Lord?"

But Joshua's voice stopped at that point.

There was weeping somewhere, until Joshua realized that the tears were his own. His face was against the cold steel bars. Bowed and broken. Cornered and isolated. Faced with the most important decision he would ever make. In a forsaken place of torture. A jail cell that smelled of urine. A place of heartless cruelty. But one thought surfaced ... this place ... it reminded him of something else. The place of the cross? Where Jesus paid the price for him ... crucifixion. He had known it abstractly, but now it was much more than that. As if he was standing before the crude, bloody cross of Christ. Now it finally seemed to make sense to him. That a place of horror and cruelty could also become the source of all that is good and true. So too this jail cell could be the right place, at the right time, for something miraculously good to happen.

Joshua's words were hardly perceptible: "Jesus come into me ... my Savior ... oh God ..."

Joshua tried to hold back the tears but couldn't.

Then there were no more words.

Until another voice came out of the darkness, from another cell, from another prisoner.

"Dr. Abdu?"

"Yes ..."

"Please, may I pray that prayer to Jesus too?"

FIFTY-FOUR

At the Bushehr nuclear-launch facility in Iran the prelaunch was completed. The tops of the three missile silos, all in a row, opened like the eyes of a triple-eyed dragon. The warning siren was wailing, and the warning lights on each silo were flashing.

The three Qiam missiles had been tested. Their accuracy was absolute. Thanks to Russian engineering assistance, the formerly outdated short-range missiles were now long-range, and at speeds of more than Mach 3, they would outfly the Israeli jet fighters that would try to intercept them. More importantly, each had a new radar system that would send deflecting countermeasures to ward off defensive Israeli ground-to-air missiles.

The three weapons officers, each at the launch panel, listened to the countdown.

Then, with a deadly choreography of hands, they simultaneously reached forward and pushed the green buttons on the panels in front of them. Smoke and fire blew out of the silos as the three nuclear missiles hurtled into the air and on to their trajectories — streaking toward Tel Aviv, Haifa, and Galilee.

ㅁㅁㅁ

Inside IDF headquarters, where they had verified the launch of the Iranian missiles, Israel's military chief bowed his head with his staff. This was the moment of truth.

They prayed the prayers of Nelah. Even though the calendar told

248

them this was not yet the Day of Atonement, the impending threat of annihilation told them that it was.

The order was given at IDF headquarters to launch three separate defensive Return-to-Sender equipped missiles. They would come from sites as far south as the Judean Desert to a base in the far north at Katzrin along the Golan.

IDF radar had picked up the first Iranian nuke heading on a course that looked as if it was in the direction of Tiberias in Galilee. At Katzrin, the first defensive missile blew out of its silo. It was armed with a refashioned Israeli version of the Return-to-Sender laser system.

ooo

The trio of Iranian nuclear warheads flashed over Jordan and neared Israeli airspace.

The IDF had already scrambled several F-15s into the air when the intel alerted them of a potential attack. But that didn't seem to matter. They tried to hit the Qiam missiles with defensive warheads of their own over Jordan airspace, but the effort was fruitless. The missiles flashed by with blinding speed. Israeli ground-to-air defenses were launched along the Jordan River sending up a raft of patriot missiles. But the newly engineered Qiam guidance system had automatic countermeasures built in, along with a frighteningly accurate missile-avoidance system.

The nukes were untouched. Still on course, they were heading for Tel Aviv, Haifa, and Tiberias on the Sea of Galilee.

Tiberias was the closest. It would get hit first.

Amidst the sound of ear-piercing sirens, thousands of screaming tourists piled into buses, attempting to flee the city along the famous sea. But for them there would be no time for escape if the nuclear warhead hit its mark. The rows of hotels and houses would be incinerated all the way around the coast up to Tabha. The blast would level everything in the area, including the ancient city of Capernaum where Jesus had taught in the synagogue and had settled during His initial ministry. It would all be gone. Along with the Sea of Galilee itself. The nuclear fireball would instantly evaporate the water.

The Iranian nuclear warhead was streaking toward the outer border of the Sea of Galilee. At IDF command they stared at their radar screen. A gut-wrenching thought was right there in front of them. Their RTS-armed missile might not be able to intercept the incoming nuke in time. They had done the logistics with Joshua Jordan. There was a minimum angle of encounter required between the laser beam shot from their RTS missile and the nose cone of the incoming nuclear warhead. Their RTS had been fired down from the north, thirty miles away from the projected intersection point with the Iranian nuke. But at the calculated speed of the Iranian missile, the required intercept might not happen. The staff at IDF headquarters could see that now. The Iranian nuke might blow right past their RTS missile.

And hit Tiberias.

Meanwhile, an RTS missile from a site in central Israel was in the air, closing in on the Iranian Qiam rocket heading toward Tel Aviv.

To protect Haifa an RTS missile had been launched from the Jezreel Valley to intercept that nuclear warhead.

The IDF staff watched the screen. The blinking cursor of the Iranian nuke heading toward Galilee. The other blinking dot, their RTS missile heading toward the nuclear missile at an oblique angle.

No one was breathing. It would take only seconds to learn their fate. But the clock seemed to stand still.

Two miles up, the incoming RTS was a thousand feet from the Iranian nuke. But it was heading at an extreme angle. The RTS intercept was not designed to work at that kind of approach.

The laser blasted out from the RTS missile and struck the side of the nose cone of the Qiam missile where the guidance system was housed. But the nose cone of the nuke had also been protected by a Russian antilaser shield.

That was something that the Israelis had prepared for. Their Mossad agents had wiretapped the conversations of Iranian nuclear engineers. So they had upped the capacity of Joshua Jordan's laser. They hoped it could penetrate the Russian-made shield.

The RTS laser beam entered the guidance program of the Qiam

nuke from the side. The data stream from the laser did a light-speed mirror reversal of the trajectory.

The Iranian nuke did a slow U-turn and started back toward its place of origin.

But the Iranian missile had experienced a slow fuel leakage. It would never find its way home. Instead, it would land along the border of Jordan and Syria — without detonating.

The missiles heading for Tel Aviv and Haifa were encountered dead-on by the outgoing RTS defensive missiles. Perfect laser contact was made with the onboard guidance systems in the nuclear warheads. The nukes swung around in an arc and headed back to their launch site.

At IDF headquarters, they saw it all on radar. There was a burst of screaming and cheers and backslapping and weeping. A few of the younger officers hopped onto the tables and bellowed at the top of their lungs.

□□□

Iranian command in Bushehr was tracking the missiles. The officers saw what was happening. They sprinted from their posts and madly scrambled to escape the port city before the devastation hit. They were too hysterical to appreciate the irony: they would have no problem with traffic because the Iranian government, not trusting the local population, had already evacuated the city's two hundred thousand residents two months before the launch, suspicious of sabotage. The city was now a ghost town of empty homes and stores.

All except for the members of the Iranian nuclear project. Now they were careening around corners at seventy miles an hour in their Mercedes Benzes — trying to escape.

But in vain.

The second nuke that had been intended for Haifa would hit Bushehr first.

There was a blinding light. The iridescent cloud expanded over the city, followed by a wave of sonic force and a solar inferno that swept out in a circumference of obliteration that melted down to black glass and ash the entire Iranian nuclear facility as well as the nuclear enrichment building and the launch silos. The second nuclear detonation came from the second missile only a minute later.

The twin mushroom clouds rose ten miles into the sky. When it cleared, the only thing left of the nuclear facility and the surrounding city was a few gnarled pipes sticking out of the ground, a single cement wall, and the reinforced girders of a dozen former office buildings that now jutted out like mangled, steel skeletons.

ㅁㅁㅁ

When the news reached President Mahmoud Ahmadinejad, he was in his palace, surrounded by his advisors. His aides were silent, eying each other. Then the president exploded into an uncontrollable rant. Even at his age he had the energy to do that well. Ahmadinejad, his face contorted with rage, balled up his fists and swung them into the air like a boxer who could not find his opponent.

"How can my nuclear dream be destroyed? Gone ... gone!"

While he was cursing the destruction of Bushehr, somewhere two hundred thousand Iranians were quietly celebrating the fact that they had been forced to move out of their homes and shops in Bushehr because of Ahmadinejad's paranoia. He had, inadvertently, saved them all from destruction.

As the sun began setting over Iran, Ahmadinejad, in his mad fury, cursed the day.

ㅁㅁㅁ

John Gallagher and his makeshift assault crew had dug in at their positions in the woods in the Shenandoah Valley. They had a good view of the metal barn. Now they were swatting bugs and waiting.

Then there was some movement. A man, unarmed, left the barn and walked over to a car. He started it up and walked back to the barn.

A few minutes later the big barn doors swung open. A cart with a crate on top, slightly larger than a refrigerator, was rolled out by four men. They gingerly slid the crate off the cart and into the back of the truck. Then one of the men stayed in the back of the truck. Gallagher thought that he was hooking something up, maybe a remote detonating device.

Then the man in the truck jumped out and locked the back doors. Two men with clip-loaded automatics exited the barn, and they handed an extra one to him.

A fourth man appeared. He was also armed. One of the men turned back as if to reenter the barn, perhaps to close the doors.

Deputy Colwin's voice came over the bullhorn: "This is the sheriff's department ... drop your weapons immediately. Drop them ..."

Then the two-second count, *one thousand one, one thousand two ...*

The men by the barn froze. They lifted their weapons, trying to figure out where the warning had come from.

Gallagher gave Dumpster the signal.

There was a chest-punching boom from Dumpster's 50-caliber that echoed through the valley. The gunman closest to him dropped as if pulled by an invisible cord.

The two gunmen closest to Dumpster saw the flash. Dumpster quickly squeezed off another shot, winging one of the men in the leg and causing him to drop his weapon momentarily. The other gunman yelled out wildly and scattered automatic fire through the woods, back and forth in the direction of Dumpster and Gallagher.

Gallagher unloaded his 357 toward the gunman, but he was moving as he was returning fire, and then skirted around the truck.

Don't shoot at the back of the truck! Gallagher told himself.

Blackie's shotgun was blasting from the other side of the clearing along with the sound of shots being fired by Frank Treumeth and Deputy Colwin.

In the melee, the gunman injured in the leg by Dumpster had crawled under the truck and was clawing his way to the cab. Gallagher tried to get a clear shot at him but couldn't. He yelled to Dumpster, "You okay? Dumpster!" Gallagher thought he heard groaning coming from Dumpster's position.

More shots on the other side of the truck, on his blind side. Then a final furious volley of shots. Gallagher was trying to figure it out quickly. One bad guy down, probably dead. Another injured and under the truck. A third, apparently not hit, was on the other side of the truck somewhere.

Where's the fourth guy?

The answer came. The fourth gunman popped up from his position, crouching under the truck engine, and he frantically opened the cab door and swung himself inside the truck. Then he geared it forward. Gallagher reloaded and blasted several rounds from his .357 into the door as it roared past. He couldn't tell if his shots had found their mark.

Gallagher could see three dead terrorists on the ground. The fourth was driving a truck armed with a nuclear device down the gravel road. Gallagher took off running after the truck, thinking that it might have to slow down at the security gate. He was panting and out of shape, but he kept running. He could see the truck up ahead racing down the dirt road spitting gravel and dirt.

Then something popped out of the woods in front of the truck.

It was Ruby with her Remington shotgun. She fired once into the windshield from her shoulder. The truck kept coming. She pumped it with jackhammer speed and fired again, this time from the hip, again into the windshield.

The truck slowed, swerved slightly, and then rolled to a stop with the front end in the underbrush.

Gallagher ran up, yelling to Ruby to stay clear of the truck. "Great shooting, Ruby. Wow, you're incredible. I married the wrong woman. Listen, I think Dumpster was hit. Go find him back there and help him ..."

Gallagher, holding his handgun, swung the truck door open. The mess inside of the cab told him immediately that the threat was over. By the time Ruby reached Dumpster, Blackie was there. Their Allfones were working again, and they called for an EMT and the sheriff's department to come. Dumpster had been hit in the clavicle, and he was squirming in pain. But in between groans, while they tried to stop the bleeding, he kept saying, "We got 'em ... we got 'em ... we got 'em ..."

Frank Treumeth and Gallagher slowly opened the back of the truck and turned on the overhead dome light. Several thick cables ran from the crate into the cab of the truck. They lifted the top off and looked in.

"Ever seen one of these?" Frank asked, as they surveyed the compact nuclear bomb.

"Only in pictures," Gallagher said. Then he added, "How about we put the top back on, okay?"

□□□

In Union Beach, the truck with the Mexican food markings on its side was still parked in front of the machine shop, fully loaded. Several of the men were milling around.

The assault team had picked up their conversation through their listening device, so they knew they had automatic weapons underneath their jackets. The three-man assault team in the black SUV now had to intercept the truck. The driver slammed the vehicle into gear and sped toward the machine shop, two blocks away. They had to round the large sewage treatment facility to get there.

Inexplicably, a parade of seven septic trucks from the local community had chosen the night hours to pull into the access lane leading to the sewage plant, lining up to unload at the site, two abreast. They were blocking the access road in both lanes.

The driver of the special-ops team blasted his horn. He shouted for them to get out of the way.

The septic-truck driver stuck his head out the window and shouted back a few profanities.

The team could see, off in the distance, that the truck with the nuke was leaving the parking lot of the machine shop. It stopped momentarily and then turned onto the street. It was on a road parallel to the access road by the sewage plant, about a hundred yards away. The driver of the SUV immediately saw that they had only one option.

The three men grabbed their weapons, jumped from the car, and sprinted through a gate in the chain-link fence that cordoned their SUV from the other street. Their legs were windmills as they ran furiously across the grassy grounds of the sewage plant and toward the truck. They knew that they were now in plain sight, but they also knew that if they did not stop this truck, it would get into Manhattan and destroy New York City and a whole lot of its inhabitants.

The truck, which had been rolling about fifteen miles per hour, now sped up quickly. Two men were in the front cab and two were out of sight in the back. The driver glanced over at the three men sprinting toward the truck, who were now about thirty yards away. The lead man for the assault team gave the command, "Drop and fire!"

The three men hit the ground and began firing, two at the tires and one at the driver. The driver fell forward and then was pulled down by his passenger who took over the wheel. The tires were flattened. The truck was slowing and rumbling loudly as it rolled forward, shuddering on shredded rubber.

The three men jumped to their feet and raced furiously toward the truck, shooting as they ran.

But the man behind the wheel had his eyes opened so wildly they could see the whites from their running position. The man in the truck mouthed something. Then he reached under the dashboard. One of the special-ops men saw it as he ran. It was his last utterance.

"Oh my God, no ..."

Then the blinding flash — and the nuclear fireball from the small nuclear device. Heat as if from an exploding star incinerated everything in its blast radius, vaporizing much of Union Beach and those residents who had not commuted out of the small town to work. The blast spread outward in a horrific wave of decimation. It started fires in the adjoining towns. Several miles away, the cars that were traveling on the Garden State Parkway were rolled over by the force of the blast. The sonic explosion whipped the harbor into ten foot waves, which plowed across the lower New York Bay and battered the opposite coast of New York. To the north, the blast was heard through New York City and shook the pavement and rocked office buildings. Electric grids were overloaded, shutting down traffic lights and darkening the marquees and jumbo screens that were usually blazing along Times Square. Pedestrians on the sidewalks of New York screamed when they saw it: the nightmare vision of a nuclear mushroom cloud rising into the sky across the bay, over in New Jersey.

A few miles from Union Beach, Jim Yaniky had been waiting in his Hummer for a report from his three fellow special-ops contractors. It would never come. Instead, the blast blew out his windows and rolled his big car over on its side. He was temporarily knocked unconscious. When he came to, he climbed straight up out of his tipped-over Hummer through the passenger door. He staggered to his feet. Buildings were on fire around him, and cars were scattered as if a tornado had just swept through the area. He felt a powerful easterly wind blowing. But amidst the nuclear horror he didn't calculate the small blessing in that. How could he?

The wind was blowing the radioactive cloud out to sea rather than north into the heart of Manhattan.

FIFTY-FIVE

In Tehran, the crowds spilled onto the streets. The news had spread that Bushehr had been decimated in some kind of nuclear explosion, but the government had promptly cut all of the Internet service for its citizens to try to contain the news of its embarrassing defeat. Rumors spread wildly. Iranians were hearing some theories that Bushehr had been incinerated during a nuclear mishap caused by the Iranian scientists. Was it another Chernobyl? They didn't know. Most of the rioters in the streets didn't care. They were now even doubting the reports of a supposed Israeli attack against Natanz. They had missed their opportunity to topple their own tyrant during the Middle East upheavals of 2011 when the citizens of other nations in the region were overthrowing dictators. This was finally their chance. They had grown weary listening to the eccentric lies of President Mahmoud Ahmadinejad for more than two decades while the people starved or were arrested by the secret police or worse.

They had had enough.

The crowds in the streets numbered nearly thirty thousand. The Iranian army was ordered to quell the protest, but half of the enlisted men refused to respond to the order. They quietly decided that they would no longer serve in a military headed up by a lunatic.

In the middle of the protest were ninety members of the CDCI, the Committee for Democratic Change in Iran. Yoseff Abbas was striding next to his friend whose apartment had been serving as his safe house.

"Over there," Yoseff announced and pointed to a forlorn-looking two-story warehouse. "That is where they are keeping the political prisoners."

His friend touched something under his belt, covered by his shirt, making sure his revolver was still there. He turned to Yoseff. "You are sure this is the special prison?"

Yoseff nodded. His contact in the Israeli Mossad had told him they had irrefutable intelligence about the prison. Yoseff had been promised safe passage to Israel. He didn't want that. All he cared about was the release of his brother and sister, and to get that done, he would have to do this one last thing: encourage the CDCI to stage a raid on the prison that housed political dissidents. It also happened to house the real target of the rescue: Joshua Jordan. None of the Iranians realized that this was the same strategy used by Colonel "Bull" Simmons back in 1979 when he rescued Ross Perot's EDS employees from a Tehran jail. It was Rocky Bridger who had borrowed that page from Simmons's playbook when he laid out the rescue plan for the Israelis.

In the street, Yoseff's friend signaled to his group leaders. Then he said to Yoseff, "You realize the Iranian MOIS will now put you on the list ... because you are part of the CDCI ... no turning back."

There was a funny look on Yoseff's face as he nodded. His friend could not possibly have known that Yoseff was already an enemy of the state, beyond anything the CDCI could imagine.

Over sixty of the CDCI were armed as they stormed the warehouse prison. They broke down the front door and fired shots in the air. There was no resistance — at least, at first. Some of the dozen jailers for the ten prisoners had already left their posts and escaped. Most of those who had remained walked down the hallways with their hands held over their heads. They quickly filed out of the facility and slipped into the night, leaving the keys to the cells behind in their offices.

Three of the jailers, however, were bent on toughing it out. One of them, the head of the torture crew, knew that there would be no escape for him. The citizens of Tehran would track him down when the news spread, and what they would do to him would be worse than death.

As the CDCI rebels climbed up the stairway, they were met by a hail of automatic gunfire. Fourteen protestors dropped to the ground in a bloody heap.

That is when the four bearded American special-ops veterans shouted out their presence in the middle of CDCI mob. Cannon announced, "We're Americans — we've come here to help your cause. Pull back. Go back down the stairs, and we'll get you back upstairs again to save all of your friends in the jail ..."

Jack and Cannon pushed their way through the retreating crowd until they were on the street level. Cannon pulled out two projectile guns with two anchor hooks attached to zip lines. He fired two up to the second-story windows. The hooks held. Cannon, the ex-Ranger, tied the end of the zip lines around a street pole. Then he turned to Jack, his SEAL buddy. "I know you Navy guys like flopping around in the water, but you think you can handle a rope climb on land?"

Jack grabbed one rope while Cannon wrapped his hands around the other. Jack gave a challenge. "On three, big guy. First one up to the window gets a free steak dinner — courtesy of the loser."

Cannon nodded and smiled. One of their team members gave the count. One. Two. Three. The two warriors scampered up the ropes like monkeys. But Cannon got there first. They swung through the busted windows on the floor that housed the jail cells. They had landed in an empty file room. They quietly slipped to the doorway with their weapons ready. They could see the three armed jailers peeking over the railing at the top of the stairs, ready to shoot the next intruder.

Jack gave the signal. Cannon would take the guy to the right. Jack would fire on the two on the left. Jack held up a finger on his left hand. Then two fingers. Then a third.

They both fired a furious volley through the doorway and into the three jailers. One fell over the railing and down the stairwell. The other two crumpled where they stood.

"All clear!" Cannon shouted out. "Come on up." Then he searched the desks until he found the keys for all of the cells.

On the first floor, as they ascended, the rebels saw the torture rooms splattered in blood. They climbed the stairs to the second floor and found Cannon and Jack waiting with the keys in their hands.

Cannon handed them over to the CDIC rebels with a grin. They began to open the cells one by one. When they got to the second-to-last cell, they released Dr. Hermoz Abdu, who cried out, then hugged them and pronounced a blessing over them. Then they yanked open Joshua Jordan's cell. Joshua struggled to his feet.

Just then someone spoke in a voice that Joshua recognized as American. "Sir, I'm a former Navy SEAL, and I've got a message for you," Jack said, helping Joshua out of his cell. "General Rocky Bridger says hello and to tell you that it turns out your wife is an even better leader of the group than you ever were."

Joshua belly laughed and kept on laughing, despite the pain walking.

Then another American stepped forward and said, "Colonel Jordan, I'm Tom Cannonberry, but they call me Cannon. Former Army Ranger. We're going to get you out of here."

Joshua turned and gestured toward Dr. Hermoz Abdu. "Men, this is Dr. Abdu, my friend. He's a marked man here in Iran. We need to take him with us."

But Dr. Abdu waved his hands and said, "No, Joshua, you are very kind, but I am staying here. The people of Iran need to hear about the love of Christ ... how can I leave such a great mission as that?"

Then Dr. Abdu turned and put his arm around another prisoner standing next to him, who was grinning through missing teeth. The man said in halting English, "I follow Jesus now."

Joshua recognized the voice. He was the man who had said the same prayer as Joshua. Joshua smiled and gave him a nod. Then Joshua grabbed Dr. Abdu by the shoulders. There was so much he wanted to say but couldn't. Not now. No time. He could only blurt out, "God bless you, my friend ..."

Dr. Hermoz Abdu returned the benediction, "And may God bless you mightily, my brother ..."

Then the four American special-forces veterans surrounded Joshua like a group of linemen protecting a running back, and they started down the stairs. As they did, Cannon turned to Jack, with a sly grin on his face. "I take my steak medium rare ..."

New York City

Curtis Belltether, the shadowy web journalist and founder of Leak-o-paedia, had been trying to track down Rev. Peter Campbell for weeks. He was aware that before the New Jersey blast, Campbell's widely publicized pronouncements of God's coming apocalypse had caused the media to sarcastically label him "the Deacon of Doom." But now that a mini-apocalypse had actually occurred right across the bay from the media center of the universe in New York, Belltether noticed that the high potentates of the mainstream press weren't giving him the time of day — except for AmeriNews, which had quoted Campbell a few times. Belltether loved this kind of intrigue. He had the notion that Campbell might have something interesting to say about a whole lot of things.

But there was something else. The web reporter had been working a story about the United Nations climate convention and the newly formed global coalition of religions that had become its public relations arm, trying to force new international environmental standards on every nation. Many of his fellow reporters had been tracking the climate revolution, but all from a sympathetic angle, about the need for global preparedness. But when the horrendous New Jersey nuke blast happened, that eclipsed everything in the news business. At least at first. The news coverage that had focused on the crumbling U.S. economy, the gas riots at the pump, the depression-like failure of the American agricultural heartland, the mall bombing, and then the shocking news of President Corland's coma, now gave way to something even more stunning.

The media launched into nonstop coverage of the nuclear devastation to the small town of Union Beach and the damage to its neighboring boroughs. Questions were asked about how it could have happened. Within hours after the tragedy, the innuendos started about a group of private vigilantes — had they tried to interfere with the terrorists and recklessly caused the bomb to be detonated? Perhaps the federal authorities might have stopped the bomb before it arrived in New York, had it not been for this lawless band of private mercenaries?

But now, a week and a half later, some of the global-warming spokespersons were speaking out about the effects of the nuclear detonations on the earth's climate. They predicted that the radiation from the blasts in New Jersey and those in Iran would create a superheating of the atmosphere, beyond even that caused by the recent, unexplained acceleration of average temperatures.

But the more that Curtis Belltether dug, the more he sensed that the real story lay down at the murky, muddy bottom. During his interview with Dr. Robert Hamilton at the University of Hawaii, Hamilton had shown him his hard data on the climate effects of volcanic eruptions. The uptick in the number and the severity of global volcanic events, which had spewed millions of tons of dust particles into the atmosphere, actually explained why suddenly global temperatures seemed to have spiked exponentially. Belltether was particularly interested in Hamilton's complaint that the federal climate agencies had blacklisted him and refused to consider his findings. If Hamilton's theory was right, the increase in temperatures was not a global-warming crisis, but a short-lived trend caused by Mother Nature that would soon even out.

As Belltether kept digging, he saw a fascinating phenomena unfolding before his eyes: an international movement was capitalizing on the climate "crisis" in ways that might change life on earth in radical ways. Belltether was now a dog on a bone, and he would not be sidetracked.

When the Union Beach nuclear disaster occurred, Belltether figured that it would take a miracle to get Pastor Campbell to sit down for an interview. The pastor was working around the clock in the neighborhoods near his Manhattan-based Eternity Church to help those who had been impacted by the blast. Setting up soup kitchens. Locating missing persons. Establishing a homeless shelter in his church. The radiation findings so far for New York City were fairly good news. The strong easterly wind blew most of the radiation out to sea. But Wall Street and the stock market had been shut down and was still frozen in trading status since the blast. The real fear that nobody wanted to talk about because of the grotesque loss of life in the New Jersey attack — eight thousand dead not counting those injured, perhaps critically — was the impending collapse of the American economy.

The United States government had cordoned off most of the New Jersey shoreline surrounding the pitiful, ashen ruins of what had formally been Union Beach. The FBI was performing an "all-out" investigation to trace the groups behind the attack. Secretly, however, they had discovered Jim Yaniky's connection to the disaster and took him into custody. The U.S. attorney general's office was personally conducting the interrogation. The government was quickly starting to mount a criminal case against the Roundtable, and Abigail Jordan in particular, for acts of "vigilantism"; acts, according to the Department of Justice, that had actually provoked the nuclear detonation during their botched citizens' attempt to stop it.

Jessica Tulrude, meanwhile, had finally been sworn in as president of the United States as Virgil Corland continued to languish in a coma. Her strategy had been to keep delaying the formal swearing in until the optimal political timing; her instincts proved to be spot-on once again. It just so happened that now she could officially assume executive power *after* the New Jersey attack. That way Corland would be blamed, and she could avoid political responsibility for that horrible assault on American shores. She immediately ordered the attorney general to forcefully prosecute any "renegade citizens" who might have taken the law into their own hands. By that, of course, she meant the Roundtable, Abigail Jordan, and especially, Joshua.

On a hunch, Belltether painstakingly worked his way through the crush of traffic, police checkpoints, and emergency radiation huts around New York City. Finally he showed up at Eternity Church. He figured that would be a good place to start. Hundreds of people — church staff, the homeless, and volunteers — were milling around. No one seemed to know where Pastor Campbell was.

One elderly black woman heard Belltether inquiring about Campbell and piped up, "You leave him alone," she said. "He's taking a nap down in the church kitchen. Let the man catch some sleep ..."

And with that Belltether immediately charged down the stairs to the busy church basement, where meals were being handed out to several hundred people. He nosed around until he came to a storage room. He cracked open the door. There, curled up on the floor and snoring, was Pastor Campbell.

"Sorry to bother you," the reporter announced, even though he really wasn't sorry and kept nudging the minister until his eyes opened. "Pastor Campbell, I'm Curtis Belltether, the web commentator. I'm doing an exposé on the Global Coalition of Religions and the international climate movement ..."

"Belltether?" he replied bleary-eyed. "Oh, yes. I remember ..." Campbell slowly rose to his feet and dusted off his wrinkled pants and open shirt. "You're going to have to follow me while we talk ... I can't sit around for an interview ... too much to do ..."

"Okay with me. So, first question ... the New Jersey bombing. Eight thousand massacred. The missile strike on Israel and the nuclear detonations in Iran ... isn't this starting to look a lot like Armageddon to you?"

"Armageddon?" Campbell said, as he patted a few volunteers on the back as he walked past. "Hardly. What you're seeing right now are simply shadows of things to come."

"How can you tell?"

"Israel will be attacked ..."

"Already happened. Come on, I'm sure you've read the news ..."

"No, you don't understand, Mr. Belltether. The Bible has already told us precisely what is about to occur. Iran's missile attack against Israel was not it ... no ... the Bible tells us explicitly about a coming war against Israel. The real thing hasn't started yet. But I do read the news, Mr. Belltether, and I believe we will be seeing the beginning of the end unfolding very soon."

Campbell was a fast walker, so much so that Belltether was having a hard time keeping up as they made their way across the church basement, up the stairs, and through the sanctuary. A young Asian man interrupted them to give Campbell a quick report on the church's project to help the New Jersey families impacted by the blast. When he left, Campbell smiled as he pointed to him. "See the young guy there? He stopped by one day to listen to a press conference I was holding here at the church. He never left."

Then Campbell turned to Belltether and put his hands on both of his shoulders.

"Listen to me carefully ... the Bible tells us that the war against Israel will be a defining moment that marks the end of the age — the beginning of the last chapter of life on earth as we have known it. Then it also tells us *who* it is who will be waging war against Israel ... and even something beyond that ..." Campbell's index finger was pointing straight up in the air. His face was illuminated by some interior flame. "Mr. Belltether, the Bible tells us exactly *how* God is going to miraculously intervene. It explains very plainly *how* He is going to do it. And when God intervenes, when that happens, I guarantee you, my friend, it is going to be a wonder to behold ..."

Belltether wasn't going to let it rest there. Sure, he considered Campbell and his fundamentalist prophecy cronies to be crackpots. But he did believe that the real-life formation of a United Nations – backed world religious coalition, one that in lightning speed had gained the support of the most powerful nations on earth, well, that was something surprising, even to him. And in the background, as Belltether was beginning to realize, a few interesting personalities were pulling the strings. He knew that to get Campbell's take on all that, he would have to endure the pastor's ramblings about the end of the world.

So he asked the question that even a cub reporter would ask ... the billion-dollar question: "Tell me, Rev. Campbell, who's going to invade Israel? And exactly what is God planning to do about it? I'd like to hear."

Campbell swung open the front doors of the church, the daylight poured in, and he stepped outside. The pastor turned and said to Belltether, "Anyone who really wants to know had better have ears to hear ..."

"Hear what?"

Pastor Campbell answered with only two words. Belltether had no idea what they meant. At least not then.

The two words were:

Ezekiel's thunder.

PART 3

The Coming Thunder

With Moscow's coffers replenished by the global oil boom, Adm. Vladimir Masorin, Russia's naval commander, has announced ambitious plans to expand the country's primary Black Sea base and establish a "permanent presence" in the eastern Mediterranean for the first time since the Cold War.

Washington Times, August 7, 2007

Russian Federation Navy group's frigate "Ladny" and deep-sea tug "Shakhter" will make stops at the naval base of Taranto from 5 to 8 and Augusta from 13 to 15 September.... The presence of the naval group in the Mediterranean, belonging to the Black Sea fleet, is part of the development of international cooperation between the Italian Navy and the Russian Federation.

World Aeronautical Press Agency, September 2, 2010

A Russian flag in the center of Jerusalem, in such close proximity to the Holy Sepulcher, is priceless.

Sergei Stepashin, former Russian prime minister
and security police general

FIFTY-SIX

In the Situation Room of the White House, Secretary of Defense Roland Allenworth was using a red-dot laser pointer. He was aiming it at a digital wall map of the world, sending the iridescent dot to several points throughout Russia, over to its neighboring republics, across the Mediterranean, to points in the Middle East, and then to northern Africa.

President Tulrude had planned on devoting the majority of the national security meeting to the nuclear attacks on U.S. soil, both the New Jersey massacre and the foiled attempt in Virginia. She had a plan and a political "solution" she wanted to float once again as a cure for these terror attacks. If she could get her national security staff behind it, she could roll it out for America, and she would be viewed as its champion-in-chief. Now Allenworth's report about this Russian thing was a distraction. Her tone was clipped. "So what's the conclusion, Secretary Allenworth?"

"Madam President, we're not sure yet. We are trying to locate a pattern to these large troop movements of Russia and its federation, as well as some of the Islamic nations. It's a complicated picture. There are intense naval movements as well. We're looking for some logical symmetry to them. Our agents are picking up Russian communiqués that indicate this is just a coordinated set of 'war games,' but the question is whether they're giving us a false lead."

"So, you have nothing definitive? Fine. Then keep us apprised ..."

Admiral William Patch, the national security advisor to former president Corland, raised a finger to speak. Tulrude didn't care for him, and she knew that the buzzer was about to sound on Patch's tenure now that Corland was out of the picture. And Patch knew it as well. "I think," Patch said, "that the secretary's warnings are not just theoretical. This could be a major military engagement, possibly to expand the Russian Federation, maybe as a counterpunch against Israel now that it has fended off Iran's attack ..."

But the secretary of state threw a disgusted look at Patch. "What would Russia possibly have to gain by that? Russia would have to be concerned about our reaction to a military offensive like that. Besides, thanks to Madam President's deft diplomacy, our relations with Russia are superb. They've increased oil allotments to the U.S. It's all good ..."

President Tulrude broke in. "Admiral Patch, our ambassador told me just yesterday that he believes Russia was probably going to flex its muscles in that region just to keep Israel and Iran from escalating an already nightmarish nuclear exchange that has occurred between those nations. Frankly, having Russia play policeman in that region is fine with me. The United States has enough problems of our own. We don't need to do that job. In fact, right after the Natanz and Bushehr attacks, didn't the EU Parliament even call for Russia to play — what was the wording — I think it was something like 'the firmest possible security role to ensure peace in the Mediterranean.' Along those lines. Am I right, people? This isn't unusual. Russia's been playing an increasing naval role in the Mediterranean over the last decade. Furthermore, two days ago, as a gesture of goodwill, the Russian prime minister pledged one half billion dollars in Russian aid to help rebuild the New Jersey area and outlying areas. Does that sound like a country that wants to offend us?"

"No," Secretary of Defense Allenworth replied with a smooth-as-glass calm in his voice. "That sounds like a country who wants to bribe us."

Tulrude exploded with a loud caterwaul. "Don't be ridiculous!"

Admiral Patch started to speak, but Tulrude cut him off. "You people would be the first to criticize me if I ignored American interests in favor of some tiny nation in the Middle East. But here I am, saying that America has suffered a nuclear attack, so let's look to our own interests and not waste our time on some tiny nation in the Middle East."

"By that," Admiral Patch said, "you're referring to Israel? America's long-standing ally in a hostile area of the world?"

"Wake up, Admiral!" Tulrude snapped. "We have other allies. Arab allies. Russian allies. Global allies. United Nations as an ally. Check your calendar. This isn't the 1950s."

The room fell quiet. Tulrude said, "Now for a very timely matter. I'm happy to report that Congress is getting close to being able to pass my key proposal, the National Security through Identification Act. And I want you all on board with this."

Helen Brokested, the director of Homeland Security, jumped in. "This legislation is brilliant. It mandates a biological identification tag imprint on the body of every American citizen. The BIDTag. Madam President, you have extolled its virtues before — in this very room, as a matter of fact, when you were vice president. The BIDTag would have stopped those nuclear murderers who set off the bomb in Union Beach and the terror cell in the Shenandoah ... and the Mall of America bombing, as well as the Chicago air disaster. We could have identified each of them when they passed through the airports and train stations and public buildings, because they wouldn't have had their BIDTag imprints. Or if they did, then their backgrounds, criminal records, associations — all of it would have instantly shown up on our screens. This is an idea, Madam President, whose time has truly come."

Tulrude basked in the accolade. "I really do believe this is going to revolutionize national security. By imprinting every lawful American citizen with a tiny laser tattoo, invisible to the eye, painless, that contains all of their biological and personal identification data, criminal record, international travel data, we can screen them, and then we can instantly weed out the bad eggs from the good. After all, people do that when they go grocery shopping don't they?"

A few of her advisors laughed and nodded. Admiral Patch wasn't one of them.

Tulrude put a finer, much more somber point on it. "Eight thousand

Americans dead, ladies and gentlemen, in New Jersey. And the number is growing. Our citizens want some assurance of safety. And I am the President who is about to give it to them."

□□□

At Hawk's Nest, Abigail was finishing up a phone call with Harry Smythe, her attorney. "Any more news about Josh?" Harry asked.

"No, not since the last call from Rocky Bridger, when he confirmed that Josh had been rescued and was out of Iran, thank the Lord."

"Abby, I'm so sorry all of this is falling down on your head."

"I'm trying to focus on the positive ... Josh is safe. Deborah is okay. I talked to her. She's tucked away in a friendly condo outside of Jerusalem. We're working on getting her out of Israel ... but, well, Deb is just like her dad — strong-willed. She's refusing to leave without her father. I guess I can't blame her ..."

"Well, I'll let you know," Harry said wrapping up the reason for the call, "the minute I find out anything about a criminal indictment against you on your involvement in the nuclear incident in New Jersey. Right now it's hard to know where this thing is going."

Abigail's voice cracked. "All those thousands of people. Innocent people in that little town. Killed. And I can't shake the feeling that I'm the one responsible. Harry the nightmares I have, every night, night after night ..."

Harry got tough. "Look Abby. Two things are true. First, terrorists drove that bomb into New Jersey, not you. Get that straight in your head. If Josh were here he'd say the same thing. Brave men tried to stop it. You gave the order, but they volunteered. And brave men died trying. And it looks like the nuke would have gotten into the heart of New York City had it not been for you. And second, where was our government? Why does it take a semiretired lawyer in her log cabin in the Rockies to try to stop a nuclear attack?"

Harry's tone softened just a little. "Abby, you're putting up a brave front, but I can hear the anguish underneath." But then the quintessential Harry Smythe came out. The 'I told you so,' coming from an attorney who never liked the idea of the Roundtable in the first place.

"I just want you to recall, Abby, that you told me yourself that you knew the legal risks. You knew the Roundtable could be prosecuted by a hostile, motivated Department of Justice. Now it's come home to roost. "

She didn't like to hear that, but Harry was right.

After she hung up, she noticed that Cal had slipped out onto the porch and was standing next to her.

"Any news?"

"No," Abby said. "Harry's waiting to see if the grand jury's going to issue an indictment against me and the Roundtable."

"You're a hero, Mom. So is Dad. But I guess that doesn't mean anything."

But Abigail didn't feel like a hero. She had blood on her hands. And the weight of that thought was almost too much to bear. "We do everything we can do. Even when it ends ... in terrible disaster. Then all we can do is stand and wait on the Lord. No matter how difficult ... " She had to choke back tears.

Cal put his hand on his mother's shoulder and squeezed it. "Any news about Dad?"

She regained her composure. "Nothing new. Cal, where in the world is Josh right now? Where?"

The Southern Tip of Azerbaijan

Joshua and the four-man rescue team were exhausted. Cannon looked through his binoculars and nodded. "That looks like a city up ahead. Must be Lerik — the secondary pickup point."

After driving out of Tehran and back north to the Iranian coast, the rescue team and Joshua waited for the Israeli chopper to appear at the rendezvous point near Neka. But the Israelis didn't show. Somehow, the team wasn't surprised. Israel had other problems on its hands. As a result, the five men had to scramble. They had to swipe a powerboat and cross the Caspian Sea toward Azerbaijan. They fully expected the worst, namely, to meet up with Iranian patrol boats en route and then have to fight their way through. But for some reason the Iranian coast guard never appeared. All they could figure was that something big must have happened, some change in Iranian military strategy regarding its coastline.

Just short of the border, they dumped the boat and walked inland, relieved that at least they were close to leaving Iran. They waited until nightfall to cross into Azerbaijan, then walked past the town of Astara and thirty miles north to Lerik.

Jack pulled out his GPS and secured the coordinates. They were now only a few miles from the pickup point, but they weren't expecting an Israeli helicopter this time. The Israelis had summoned help from the Republic of Georgia, which lay to the north of Azerbaijan. Georgia had resisted an alliance with Russia and had secretly coordinated defenses with Israel. But as a former part of the Soviet Union, it retained mutual contacts with the Russian republics. So it was decided by Rocky Bridger and the IDF headquarters that a civilian commercial helicopter from Georgia was likely to raise few eyebrows if it was seen over Azerbaijan airspace. Georgia agreed to the plan and sent a two-pilot helicopter to the new pickup point.

The team looked at their watches. Cannon said, "We have six hours until pickup. Let's find a safe place to crash for a couple of hours."

They found a spot just off the main road. They settled at the edge of a thick forest of trees. Cannon pointed out that the trees were called *demir-agach*, the famous "iron tree," with its orange leaves and fruit. A few of the guys picked some of the fruit off the branches. That was enough, together with the cooler full of food on the boat they had stolen, to help ease their nagging hunger for a while.

From their position they could see the road below. Cars passed. A convertible filled with several dark-haired, attractive girls passed, and the two younger special-ops guys, both of whom were single, cracked jokes. But Joshua couldn't help thinking about Abigail, wondering if she'd been told about his rescue. Surely she had. He had left her behind with so many burdens. And he thought about Cal and was glad he was there with Abby. Joshua was certain that Cal would step up to the plate and be the man of the house in his absence.

And Joshua wondered about his country.

As he lay on the mossy forest floor, he was feeling his age, as well as the effects of the beatings he had received in captivity. But one thought overshadowed even his bone-sickening fatigue and pain. He wished he could simply will the message across to the other side of the planet: *Abby, please know how much I love you, baby ... I'm coming home ...*

Then he was struck with a thought, and he put it into silent words: *God, please let Abby know I'm all right. Keep her safe. Deb and Cal too. Thanks for listening. Amen.*

Down on the road, a few people on horses clip-clopped past. Then it was quiet for more than an hour. Joshua, in his exhaustion, drifted off into a deep, otherworldly sleep.

The quiet was broken, however, with the rumbling of a military convoy that echoed up to the forest — armored Humvees, tanks, troop transports, missile launchers — all rolling down the road.

The team members sat up fast and rigid, like pointer dogs.

Jack was the only one to speak. "Something's about to break loose."

FIFTY-SEVEN

On the Mediterranean Sea

The Russian general had just given the order: "The invasion of Israel and the destruction of the Jewish occupiers shall commence in twelve hours."

Vice Admiral Sergei Trishnipov was enjoying the excellent vantage point from the bridge on the destroyer *Kiev*. He had a nearly three-hundred-degree view of the massive flotilla he was commanding. It had taken years for Russia to rebuild its sagging navy. Now, at last, he would show the world that Russia ruled the seas.

Most of the American press had readily accepted the explanation that this was nothing more than a "joint naval exercise," so when NATO member states protested, Russia and its allies didn't care. Without backing from the U.S., Europe was likely to do nothing, particularly because there was little love for the tiny nation that the Russian-Islamic coalition would be soon invading. Whatever sympathy existed for Israel had now disappeared after its preemptive strike against Iran, which was followed by the RTS-guided nuking of Bushehr.

The Russian-Islamic coalition was ready to make its defense to the world. After all, hadn't an American-led coalition attacked Iraq over its invasion of Kuwait decades before? So why shouldn't a Russian-led coalition of Middle Eastern nations invade Israel over its military aggression against Iran? Russia's long-standing partnership with Syria and its use of the Syrian port of Tartus gave it an ideal launching platform for the naval phase of the invasion.

Trishnipov, who had helped shape the naval operation of the war, liked the plan. Four Russian aircraft carriers from his fleet would launch four hundred MiG fighter jets and bombers over Israeli airspace and pound Israeli defenses. Seven transport ships, carrying three hundred thousand soldiers from the Russian-Islamic alliance, would land simultaneously at Haifa and Tel Aviv. That was twice the size of Israel's entire standing army. Then a dozen submarines and ten heavily armed patrol boats would seal off Israel's coast.

At the same time, the coalition army would begin the land invasion from the north, advancing through Syria and pouring down into Israel. That force consisted of five hundred thousand troops from Russia, Turkey, Kazakhstan, Azerbaijan, as well as other Russian republics. From the south, another fifty thousand troops would blast their way into Israel, from the armies of Libya and the Sudan. Syria, Egypt, and Jordan would tell the world they had no choice but to permit the invading armies to cross their lands en route to Israel or else suffer annihilation themselves, but they would privately celebrate the anticipated decimation of the nation of Israel, that thorn in the side of Islam.

Trishnipov gazed through the window. It was a clear, mild day. He wished he was on the deck, catching the fresh air, instead of locked inside the glass-enclosed bridge. But this is where he needed to be. In full control of the naval invasion. As the vice admiral thought about the slaughter to come, he had to remind himself that he had no particular hatred for the Jews, although he remembered with a chuckle something his father, who had been a Soviet general, once said: "Now that we have run the Jews out of Russia, let them keep running ..."

Within hours, though, there would be no more running. The Jews in Israel would have nowhere to escape. Invasion by sea, invasion from the north and south, overwhelming military power raining death down on the tiny nation.

Once, back at the Russian naval base at Murmansk, Trishnipov had been asked what the soldiers and sailors should expect once the war to obliterate Israel had begun. He had smiled and replied, "It will be like shooting fish in a barrel ... a very small barrel."

Tuscany, Italy

The clandestine meeting was held at Caesar Demas's country house in Tuscany. That site was chosen rather than his main villa in Rome out of concerns for security. His remote estate was nestled into the surrounding hills. His private guards were posted strategically throughout the two-thousand-acre compound. Helicopters circled the property. The driveway, which ambled for a mile through his vineyards, had two separate security gates with armed guards.

Privacy was essential. After all, they were plotting a global revolution.

Demas looked around his sunroom, the one with the large working table and the breathtaking view of the rolling hills brimming with his ripening vineyards. Around the table were Lexes Demitrov, deputy prime minister of Russia, the lovely Andrea Portleva, Russia's ambassador to the U.S., and Gallen Abdulla, president of Turkey.

The meeting was about to end. Demitrov summed up. "So, the timing is right."

"Perfect, it would seem," Abdulla added.

They all agreed. But Portleva, whose specialty, after all, was the U.S., stated the obvious. "America is on its knees, unraveling economically. Politically they are in chaos. And so sad about Virgil Corland's health problems ..." There were smiles all around. She continued. "And then there is the unfortunate nuclear attack in New Jersey. United States is a giant — but with feet of clay. The downfall is coming. So there will be the inevitable superpower vacuum."

Caesar Demas had a question for Abdulla. "And you feel that you can continue to keep the Islamic nations in our coalition, that Turkey can serve as the bridge to our Muslim partners, to Iran, and the entire Arab League, and to OPEC?"

"Yes," Abdulla answered. "Of course, now that Turkey has finally been admitted into the European Union, we can also serve as a liaison between our new alliance of nations and the EU." He could have said more but didn't. The two Russians and the Turk exchanged millisecond glances.

Demas was the only one in the room who had not been informed about the specifics of the joint military offensive against Israel. All had agreed, Demas included, that he needed to be sequestered from the specifics of the impending war. He only knew how it was supposed to play out. Russia's aid in destroying Israel would earn it the endearing support of the Arab League and would grant Russia a preferred seat at OPEC and the promise of Arab cooperation with Russia's expansionist plans. Next, the coalition would begin a takeover of key parts of the African continent and South America, with Venezuela leading the way. With the United States paralyzed into indecision, and licking its own wounds, the only obstacle left to total world domination would be China. If all went according to plan, even China could not withstand a political network so vast that it covered three continents. Pakistan and the Muslims within India would help the cause on the subcontinent. As far as the EU, they had no taste for war and could be counted on to do little to stop the expansion of the Russian-Islamic empire — all except England, of course. By that time, however, Great Britain would be in no position to launch an attack. The Russian-Islamic coalition would negotiate with the English, throw them a few crumbs to keep them placid. Australia might be a problem, but they were so far removed geographically that they could be dealt with down the road.

Caesar Demas had been promised the position of president of the new global alliance of nations with Russia in the lead. Because of that, it was thought wise to keep him out of the "dirty" business of the Jewish genocide to come. When that was over, the shift of global power would begin. The days of America's domination — its leadership of the Western nations and NATO, and its "bullying tactics" in the U.N.'s Security Council — would soon be history.

"Of course, I'm humbled," Demas added, "at the confidence each of you has shown in me."

Demitrov smiled. He was thinking that, for all of Demas's reputation as a ruthless international businessman, a friend of shadowy black marketers, and a tough global geopolitical negotiator who possessed the uncanny ability to manipulate heads of state, he had figured Caesar Demas for something else. While Demas could never conceive of himself this way, Demitrov truly believed that when push came to shove, the billionaire could be made to play an effective marionette at the end of strings that would stretch all the way back to Moscow.

After the meeting, Demas's guests left with their entourages, surrounded by armored limousine security. All except Andrea Portleva.

When he thought they were alone, Demas gathered Portleva in his arms and began to kiss her and fondle her with abandon. She laughed a little but didn't resist.

Portleva, still in his embrace, said in a husky whisper, "So, Mr. Caesar Demas, it appears that your wish is now going to come true."

"What wish is that?"

"Your desire to run the world, of course."

Now they both laughed.

Out of the corner of his eye, he noticed Tomasso, his bodyguard, standing at the front door of the country home. Tomasso quickly jammed his hands into his pockets.

Caesar Demas stared him down and then snapped, "Until further notice, keep everyone away ..."

Tomasso gave a quick nod of his head. "Yes, Mr. Demas. Whatever you say."

FIFTY-EIGHT

In the condo outside Jerusalem, Esther Kinney was on the phone with her husband, Clint, who was still in the hospital.

Deborah Jordan could see that Esther's face had suddenly paled, as if she had received the kind of news that takes your breath away. While she held her Allfone to her ear, Esther made a quick movement with the other hand, as if she was about to bring it swiftly to her mouth, but stopped. Then she lowered it. She managed a struggling smile, told her husband she loved him, and ended the call.

She turned to Deborah, Ethan March, and to the tour guide, Nony, and his wife, Sari, who had put them up in their home. She spoke slowly and with a clear, deliberate cadence. "Well ... I had thought that with the victory ... the great victory with Iran's nuclear missiles turned around ... and Deborah your father's ingenious Return-to-Sender weapon that seemed to have saved Israel — with all of that ... and the reports that the Hamas uprising in Jerusalem had been quelled by police and military ... I had thought we were in the clear ..." Then she fell silent.

"Aren't we?" Deborah asked.

Esther shook her head no. She sat down with her hands in her lap, took a deep breath, and said, "Clint said we should try to find some way out of Israel if we can. If not, to find the safest place, a bunker, a basement. Lock the doors. Arm ourselves. Prepare to fight ..."

Ethan joined in. "Is this an invasion, Mrs. Kinney, a ground war? Is that what he's talking about?"

She nodded. "He couldn't tell me any details except that the intelligence reports indicate a massive assault on Israel ... from every direction ... overwhelming forces against us ..." Then her voice broke.

Nony shrugged and paced, his arms outstretched. "There is no way to leave Israel. No planes. No boats. I have friends with private aircraft, but everything has been shut down since the Iranian attack. I can make some calls ..." There was a long pause. Then Nony said, "But that would mean leaving Israel. Leave Israel?" His voice rose higher. "*Leave Israel?* The land given us by God Himself. No ... no ... this I will *not* do. We will stay. We will fight." Then he turned to Deborah and Ethan. "This isn't your war. I can call some friends. Perhaps there is a chance for you two to escape ..."

Deborah said it before Ethan had a chance, but she spoke for both of them: "This has become our war now."

Ethan added, "Deb, if you say we stay and fight with our friends here, then I'm in."

Deborah's face was pensive, freighted with the weight of what she was about to say. "My father came here for a reason, not just a defense-contracting job. So here it is ... I believe God brought my dad — and all of us — here, to this place, at this time. I'm not sure why, but I know this was no accident. So now we make our stand, right here. We just have to remember somehow that the battle belongs to the Lord ..."

Esther smiled. She exhaled, then fell to her knees and reached her hands out to the others. "Let's ask the God of Abraham, Isaac, and Jacob, the King of the universe ... let's ask Him for victory, for safety, for His divine protection, to see His mighty hand ... and let us pray, friends, that the nations of the earth will see that God is truly God ..."

At IDF Northern War Command in Israel, Ramat David Air Force Base

General Shapiro showed no emotion as his deputy, Lieutenant General Gavi Havrel, was giving his report, but it was a tough act. A half dozen other members of the general's staff were sitting in, so Shapiro had to keep his game face on.

"General," Havrel continued, "the size of the invading army ... the naval flotilla ... all those numbers have been verified."

"And our air defenses?"

"We have F-16s here in the north, ready at your command. With bombing raids, we will try to contain the front amassing at the Syrian border. All the other bases are on high alert. The southern bases are protecting the Ovda Airport at Eilat. If necessary, they will destroy the landing strips so the invaders can't use them. The fighters at Hatzerim Air Force Base are ready to fly. Hatzor base too. And Palmachim base, same thing, and of course that air base is ready to convert to your fall-back headquarters if our northern command here has to ..."

The words caught in his throat. Shapiro heard the same silent word in his own head: *Retreat.*

Havrel finished his thought: " — if our northern command has to evacuate."

Shapiro turned to his diplomatic liaison. "Any word from the prime minister about his contact with President Tulrude in Washington?"

The aide shook his head. "President Tulrude has not spoken directly. She's had her secretary of state relay the message to the prime minister that they are 'carefully evaluating' the situation. We've tried the secretary of defense — he's been sympathetic in the past — but no luck. I think the White House is blocking our access to him."

Shapiro asked. "The United Nations Security Council?"

"A tentative emergency meeting is scheduled for late tomorrow afternoon in New York."

Shapiro's face was ignited now. "That's their idea of an emergency meeting, scheduled for the day *after* an invasion?"

His aide had to add, "Only a *tentative* meeting ..."

"So much for *hasbara*," Shapiro growled. His cynical comment about Israel's efforts to build international support through public relations was met with nodding heads around the room. He had one more question — one last avenue about gathering help before Israel was swallowed up in the invading tide. "How about NATO?"

"They've declined. They say it's not within the boundaries of their treaty obligations."

Shapiro took it in. He could see the grim picture. He was a chess player, looking at a board that simply didn't have enough pieces for him to win. He could delay the enemy on its many fronts, but probably only by hours, not days. He could dance and weave, scramble, hit and run, but what he saw was something he had hoped never to see in his lifetime. So many young men and women — and not just soldiers — were going to perish. Civilians would fight to the death for their homes, which is exactly what they would have to do. Die.

The general turned to his staff. "We still have a few minutes. Why don't each of you call your wives, families, close friends. Report back here in fifteen. That's all."

Their faces showed that they understood. The realization had just sunk in, like having to be told twice that a friend had just died. Everyone knew that they were about to have what might be their last conversation with the ones they loved.

Masada, Near the Dead Sea

A dozen tourists were winding their way along the path that led up the rocky cliffs. Halfway to the top, the guide stopped and started his lecture. He had lost his cell and had been out of touch with the news that day.

"Okay, the place we're going to is called Masada. It's the ancient site where Israel made its final defiant stand against the Roman army after the fall of Jerusalem in AD 70. Armed Jewish rebels and their families occupied the fortress at the top of this mountain. The tenth legion of the Roman army chased the rebels, following them to the wilderness here, and laid siege to the fortress. The Roman army eventually built a ramp on the western slope, so they could overtake the stronghold at the top. So Elazar Ben Yair, the Jewish commander in Masada, made a startling suggestion. He gathered the fighters and their families, about nine hundred and sixty men, women, and children, and told them it would be better to die free than to live as Roman slaves. So they made a suicide pact as the Roman soldiers marched toward their stronghold ..."

Then the guide stopped. Something had caught his eye. He shielded his eyes from the sun and peered out over the desert below, to Highway 90 that ran alongside the Dead Sea and led to Masada. The tourists turned to see what he was looking at. There, on the highway, was a slow, snaking caravan of cars, bumper to bumper, making their way to the ancient site of Masada. Some cars had already parked near the tour bus in the parking area. Families were getting out, lugging suitcases, food, supplies — and weapons.

One Jewish man, with his wife, son, and daughter, was hiking double-time up the path and had already caught up to the tour group. Two Uzi machine guns hung from his shoulders. His family followed him with large backpacks and boxes. His young daughter carefully cradled the blue and white flag of Israel.

The man stopped next to the tour group. His face had an immovable resolve to it, hard and flinty, like the face of the cliffs that led to the ruins above them. His eyes met those of the tour guide. They did not need to say aloud what was clear to both of them.

The man with the machine guns spoke to the tourists, "My friends, I suggest that you leave this place as quickly as possible. For your own safety ... unless you are prepared — all of you — to die with us."

FIFTY-NINE

"I've got bad news and worse news ..."

Abigail braced herself. "Keep going, Harry."

"The grand jury has just returned a multiple-count criminal indictment against you, Josh, and each member of the Roundtable."

"So much for freedom of association," she muttered. Abigail was incensed that the government would know the identities of the members, when they had worked so hard to keep that information confidential. "How did they find out?" But Abigail already knew the answer. Fort Rice had once interviewed an attorney for possible inclusion in the group. Fort hadn't realized it, but the attorney was a mole, a confidant of Jessica Tulrude's. So the crumbs weren't hard to trace.

"I'm sorry, Abby."

"What are the substantive charges?"

"As you predicted, only one, in every single count: seditious conspiracy."

"So what's the worse news, Harry?"

"I've talked to Attorney General Hamburg. He says he's willing to dismiss the charges ..."

Abigail waited for the *but*.

"... but there's a hitch."

"There always is."

"He says all the members — each of them — has to cooperate."

Abigail had already figured it out. "This can't be happening ..."

"I'm afraid it is."

"The attorney general wants them to testify against Joshua — to knife him in the back?"

"Not just that."

"It gets worse?"

"Hamburg says the same goes for you."

She couldn't respond, at least not at first.

Harry filled in the blanks. "I know what you're thinking ... the husband-wife privilege not to testify against each other. But Hamburg says he'll be satisfied if you merely nail Josh with things said in the company of others, where the privilege would be waived anyway — "

Abigail cut him off. "Tell the attorney general — and, Harry, I want you to quote my words exactly — that I will rot in jail, in the worst cell in the world, the filthiest hellhole in the prison system, before I lie about my husband ... before I turn on him. Have you got my position on that?"

"I figured you'd say that." Then he added, "Sorry, Abby, but as your attorney I had to disclose what Hamburg said. Frankly, it made me sick to my stomach."

"I can appreciate that, but you can take Tums for that. My problems are more complicated than indigestion."

Before clicking off, Harry said, "One last thing, Abby. We need you to turn yourself over to the authorities. You know the routine: handcuffs, media photographers, the whole nine yards. Then the initial court appearance. It'll be a feeding frenzy for the press."

"Can you buy a little time?"

"A day or two, max."

"Don't worry, I'm not going into hiding. I'll produce myself ... if it comes to that. I just need time to think. And to pray."

After the call, Abby dashed down to the barn where Cal was watering the horses and mucking the stables. He dropped his bucket and leaned back against the wooden slats of the stable, as Abby told him what Smythe had said. She could see the fear in Cal's eyes, but he didn't waver. He asked her to clarify something. "Mom, you told me once about that lawyer who was a mole ... who spilled the information about the Roundtable ..."

"Allen Fulsin, a D.C. attorney. He had connections to the vice president's office."

"Something sounds unethical about that. Or am I wrong?"

"No, your instincts are right, Cal. Fulsin was interviewed regarding his serving on the legal committee for the Roundtable. That's attorney-client privilege. Then Fulsin gave the information to the White House to use against us. Probably to Jessica Tulrude who is the one who had the ties to Fulsin."

"Can't we use that to get the case dismissed?"

"Maybe. If we can show that the White House deliberately used Fulsin as a spy in his capacity as an attorney initiate for the Roundtable. But Fulsin didn't learn much about us. Just some background stuff — who we are, the members, that sort of thing. But I'll take whatever we can get as a defense. I just have this sneaking suspicion ..."

"What?"

"Call it woman's intuition ... that if we dig deep enough into Jessica Tulrude's attitude about us, Josh and I, and the Roundtable, we may hit pay dirt. On the other hand, maybe I'm just grabbing at straws."

Abigail silently chewed on that for a moment ... the fact that Allen Fulsin was known to have ties to Jessica Tulrude when she was vice president. *There might be something there. It keeps coming back to Tulrude.*

She turned to Cal. "When you're finished with our four-legged friends, come on up to the house and clean up. You and I have work to do. You're going to be my paralegal. You're the guy who changed his major to poli-sci, remember? You're about to get an advanced course in the collision between law and politics."

Cal smiled and nodded.

As Abigail trudged back to the lodge, she began to let herself go a little emotionally. She had wanted to be confident in front of her son. But when she privately allowed herself to see the trouble she was in, she suddenly felt as if she were slipping down, farther and farther, being slowly sucked into quicksand.

God, give me wisdom. Help me keep my mind straight. And please, protect Josh ...

She was shaken out of her prayer by the ringtone of her Allfone. It was Rocky Bridger.

"Abby, there's news about Josh. Plan A — being picked up in northern Iran by an Israeli helicopter — didn't happen, but don't worry, there's a plan B — an alternate pickup site farther north. I'm told that Josh and the team are okay. They're waiting right now at the secondary rendezvous point."

She whispered, "Thank You, Lord."

"Now, something else. This is classified, but you need to hear it. I don't want you seeing this on the evening news first ..."

"Evening news?"

"There's a monster invasion underway — right now. May be breaking in the next few hours or so. Ships are gathering in the Mediterranean. Armies massing in the north in Syria and in the South in Egypt. A Russian-led coalition, Abby. They're going to attack Israel."

Abigail reeled. She stopped at the front steps and dropped down on the first step. Deborah, the one that she thought was safe, was now in the crosshairs of a war. "Deb ... my Deb ..."

"I've tried to make contact with her, Abby, but the Israelis have locked down satellite communications. I'm trying to get to her through IDF command, but as you can imagine, they're preparing for an all-out invasion."

Rocky's voice stumbled. "Abby, I'll stay on this until I get answers — about Debbie and Josh. Hang in there, dear. No one's giving up."

After the call, Abigail sat listless for a moment and stared at the immovable mountains that pierced the blue sky. She could only voice a trembling whisper from the Psalms:

> *But the lovingkindness of the Lord*
> *   is from everlasting to everlasting*
> *   on those who fear Him,*
> *And His righteousness to children's children ...*

□□□

The Airspace Near the Turkish-Syrian Border

Grigori, the Georgian pilot of the MI-26 Halo helicopter, was on his radio. Neither the special-ops guys nor Joshua, as they sat in the jump seats, could understand what he was saying, but they could read his face and body language. It looked like there was a complication. Grigori and his copilot talked back and forth during the radio conversation.

The pickup in Azerbaijan had been flawless. The saving grace was that the helicopter was branded with a Black Sea Petro-Chem sign on the side, and the Georgian Ministry of Commerce had alerted the Russians, Turks, Syrians, each of them that one of their commercial aircraft was off course. The coalition said they would allow it to travel through their airspace but couldn't guarantee its safety. Not ideal, but a plan. The idea was to transport the Americans directly back to Israel with a drop-off point in Israel, near the Syrian border. They'd been assured that everything had been cleared with the Israelis.

But then, midflight, the pilot, in broken English, announced something disturbing and cryptic in his deep Slavic accent. "Sorry so much … but headquarters say that there is big trouble in Israel … you now all have to go to my homeland, Georgia. Maybe then fly to Berlin. Maybe then from there to United of States."

Joshua asked, "What kind of big trouble?"

"War breaking out … some kind big trouble war. Dunno anymore."

That was all that Joshua needed to hear. "My daughter's back there. I need to go to Israel. We've got to stick to the plan, the drop-off point … the original plan … up on the Golan Heights, just like we planned. Do you understand? There's an Israeli helicopter that's supposed to be waiting for me there. You said so yourself, Grigori."

"Yes, but, oh, I dunno … can't do that maybe."

Cannon joined in with Joshua. "Oh, yes, you definitely can 'do that maybe.' You're going to stick to the plan, Grigori, like our friend says. We all go with the original plan. Savvy?"

So Grigori called his superiors. When he was done with his long radio call he half turned to his passengers. "Okay, here it is going to be ... I got the okay to take Mr. Jordan to drop-off point but has to be real quick."

Joshua gave a satisfied nod.

"But rest of you, no ... can't do. You commandos have to go to Georgia with me. Then fly to Berlin like I say before."

"Unacceptable," Jack shouted out. "Totally unacceptable. We stick with Josh the whole way."

"Look," Grigori shouted back, "I have orders. You don't want it this way, then you get it no way. When I stop in Turkey to refuel, I kick you all out. You want that? I don't think Turks will be happy with you."

Cannon turned to his team. He whispered, "Any of you guys know how to fly a helicopter?"

They all shook their heads no.

The ex-Ranger chuckled and muttered, "Gee, what kind of special-ops team are you guys anyway? Well, I was hoping." He lowered his voice and added, "We could sort of disable our friend and his copilot and fly to Israel according to plan. I'm getting a bad feeling about this."

Joshua said in a low voice, "I was trained on a Blackhawk, but man, that was a long time ago. Look, let's stand down for a second on that idea. Let me talk to the pilot."

Then Joshua shouted up to the pilot. "Hey, Grigori, what's the problem with *all* of us being dropped at the Golan Heights, just like we planned?"

"Headquarters says ... you four guys there ... you are commandos, right?"

Joshua still didn't get it. "Yeah, these guys are commandos. So what?"

"Headquarters says that if I drop commandos while war is about to start big time, that's bad idea ... not going to happen. Then someone says that Georgia is part of war ..."

The dawn was breaking. "Okay," Joshua said to the team. "I see what he's saying. Look, when we get to the checkpoint, there should be an Israeli helicopter waiting. If there is, I jump out. Job done. Mission accomplished."

Cannon smiled. "Or we get to the rendezvous point and we all jump out together. What's Grigori going to do. Shoot us?"

"Yes!" Grigori said over the two-way intercom that had been left on. "I will shoot you."

Jack rolled his eyes. "We've been had."

The copilot had unbuckled his seat belt and was in the aisle, pointing his handgun at the Americans.

Grigori ordered them to hand all of their weapons to the copilot. "You be good boys. Don't want blood all over my nice helicopter."

The team reluctantly disarmed themselves.

Cannon was unhappy. "Like I've been saying, this is starting to stink."

But Joshua didn't see the problem. "You don't have to hold my hand, guys. You've saved my life. I'll never forget it. But once I'm in the Golan, I can take it from there. Okay?"

Jack said, "But what about this 'big trouble war' that Grigori's talking about?"

Joshua tried to dismiss it. "What's new about that? Israel's always got some shooting match going on with one of its Arab neighbors. Look, like we already heard from the CDCI rebels, Israel has already kicked Iran back over the goalposts with the nukes they turned around. Game over. So how bad can things be?"

SIXTY

On board the *Kiev*, Russian Vice Admiral Sergei Trishnipov had just conferred with his invasion chiefs. In thirty minutes he would give the flight order for his jet fighters, in squadrons of fifty each, to head toward the Israeli air bases. Early intelligence indicated that the ships' electronic radar-masking systems had worked, that they had become invisible to Israeli radar. The IDF had been successfully tricked about where the first wave of the naval invasion would take place and believed it would be much farther south.

At the same time, a dozen bombers, with fifty MiGs protecting them, would soon begin battering Haifa, with a similar formation bombing Tel Aviv.

In the north, near the Syrian border, General Viktor Oragoff, who would lead the Russian troops, and General Izmet, commander of the Turkish army, were meeting in a makeshift command center in a farmhouse. The map of Israel was laid out on the table.

General Oragoff was making sure the Turks were on the same page. He leaned over the table and pointed to the northern tip of Israel. "We enter here, between Nimrod's Castle and Tel Dan. We secure entrance onto Highway 99, and then our fastest mechanized units must race south to Highway 90 and then take 90 south. Our tanks will be right behind to clean up the resistance. We blast down 90, and in the first five hours I want to take the Hula Valley and enter Galilee. Along the way we should be able to pick up support from the local Hamas groups embedded in Nazareth and farther south at Nablus. They will start liquidating the Jewish resistance for us. Understood?"

Izmet nodded.

Oragoff straightened up. "Then we push south to Jerusalem, followed by the dirty business of mopping up pockets of resistance, burning down houses, shooting any Jews that are left ... that sort of thing. I would like to be able to begin a slow pullout in a few weeks. I'd like to see my home in St. Petersburg in two or three months. We'll leave an occupying force, of course ... two hundred thousand from Russia, another hundred thousand from the rest of the coalition. That should do it."

Over the Mediterranean Sea, Approaching Port Said, Egypt

The Israeli Air Force was now about to break radio silence.

"This is blue leader one. Blue leader one. Maintain elevation and flight pattern."

The sixty other pilots of the Israeli F-16s and the F-15s guarding them acknowledged. They were flying low to avoid radar detection. It was still dark, but a sliver of red was starting to appear on the horizon.

The captain in the lead fighter was expecting to see landing ships at any moment or some sign of a massive naval flotilla arriving at Port Said. Presumably the enemy would then construct a launching platform for an invasion from the south. It didn't make sense to the captain; it seemed too far south, but HQ had ordered it as a first strike. He figured their intel was on target.

This first sortie was to deal a devastating blow to the invading navy.

Something showed up on the captain's radar. Two ships, three miles ahead. Maybe it was just the tip of the spear. The captain wondered out loud, "There have to be more than this. Where's the invasion?"

Then suddenly he saw more blips on his screen. Ten ships. No, twenty-five ... thirty ships. This was it.

He gave the order, and the jets closed in for bombing formation. Two miles. One mile. One thousand feet.

The first wave thumbed the release buttons, as the first two ships came into their guidance screens, and sent their missiles into the vessels.

They could see the two frigates burst into flames.

But there was nothing else they could pick up on visual. Suddenly the other blips on their screen disappeared. The IAF fighters, as well as IDF headquarters, had been fooled. One of the two ships had been a recon vessel equipped with radar imaging that was designed to send phantom signals of multiple ships that didn't exist.

"Save your missiles," the captain shouted.

"Where's the rest of them?" one of the pilots asked.

But he wouldn't get an answer. Seventy MiGs flown by Libyan pilots swooped in on them from their flank, sent from their air base in Qantara, Egypt.

Then the antiaircraft defenses set up around Port Said opened fire, sending flack out to the Mediterranean, side pinning the IAF formation in.

The Libyan fighter pilots, though specially trained by the Russians, were still no match for the Israelis. In the first fifteen minutes of the dogfight, twenty-seven MiGs had been shot down. Only six Israeli jets had been downed. For the next twenty minutes the air battle would continue. Four more IAF fighters would be lost.

But the primary aim of Israel's enemies had been achieved.

Sixty-one out of Israel's three-hundred-fighter-jet fleet had been waylaid to the extreme south, distracting them from the main thrust of the invasion, keeping them far away from the path of the incoming Russian-Islamic forces — where the real killing was about to begin.

SIXTY-ONE

"Where is the United States in all this? Our government refuses to rescue my husband, and now this." Abigail sat in the great room of Hawk's Nest in front of the wide-screen Internet television. The screen was divided into six quadrants, each with a separate broadcast. She paged from one to the other. On the right-hand column, a news ticker scrolled through the headlines. "Who's going to help Israel? My daughter's over there!" Abby said.

Cal, sitting next to her with his laptop on the coffee table, looked up. "They still haven't given us anything new, right?"

"Just that there's some kind of fighter-jet skirmish over Egypt. Nothing else."

"Mom, I keep trying to get Debbie on her Allfone ..."

"Don't bother. They've said Israel has blocked international calls." Then she added, almost to herself, "Deb, honey, where are you? Are you safe?"

Cal waited a few minutes before broaching the next subject. "Mom, we need to talk. You've got a court appearance in two days in federal court in Manhattan."

"Yes," she said. "In the same courtroom where years ago they tried the blind sheik for the first bombing of the World Trade Center, and other terrorists after that." She looked at her son, who was glued to the computer screen. "So, is your mother a terrorist too?"

Cal went snake-eyed. "Absolutely not. There's something very wrong going on in this country. When patriots try to stop catastrophes because their government won't, and then they get treated like the enemy."

"Where is your father at this point? Rocky Bridger doesn't know, Washington won't tell me, and Israel is being invaded."

"Mom ..."

Abigail broke out of her thoughts and looked at her son. Cal was managing a half smile.

"You know what Dad would say if he were here?"

Abigail's eyes softened. "Tell me."

"He'd say, 'Execute the flight plan unless you have a better one.' How many times have we heard that? He went to Israel for his part of the plan. You stayed here for yours. Defending against this unjust criminal case is just part of what we have to do here. And one more thing, something my mother always says ..."

Now she let go with a smile herself. "What's that?"

"God is always in control, even when life isn't."

She studied her son. "Your dad would be proud of the way you've helped me."

Cal's eyes darted away for an instant, then he broke into a grin. "That's our specialty in this family, isn't it? Rescuing each other from disasters?"

They both let out a nervous laugh. It was a welcome relief, if only for a few moments.

"So," Cal went on, "I've been looking at the criminal indictment that Harry emailed us, the one against you, Dad, and the Roundtable. First, they name every member of the Roundtable, even though you said some of them didn't participate in the plan to stop the nuke."

"I think I know why. The prosecutor's trying to split us up, divide and conquer. There's an old saying in criminal defense work: Last to plead, first to bleed. The key is to get members of the group to rush forward and cut favorable plea deals with the government in return for information that can be used against the other defendants. The last holdouts are the ones who get hammered in court. So they'll put pressure on people like Fort Rice and others — agreeing to dismiss in return for their cooperation. But you know who the real target is."

"Dad?"

"Exactly. I've talked to each member of the Roundtable. They're scared, of course. Leander is the worst. But so far, they're hanging tight, willing to fight this thing. No deals."

"Mom, I've looked at this seditious-criminal charge they've filed. Here's the bottom line. The Indictment reads, 'The defendants conspired to oppose by force the authority of the United States by creating a vigilante paramilitary group purportedly to stop a nuclear attack, but instead provoked the detonation of a nuclear device causing widespread death, serious injury, and property destruction.'"

"What's your thought?"

"Doesn't something jump out?"

"Let me guess ... one phrase?"

Cal nodded.

Abigail finished the thought. "The phrase is 'oppose by force the authority of the United States,' that we somehow used our special-ops guys — courageous men who died trying to stop that nuke, who saved hundreds of thousands of lives if that truck had made it to New York City — that we used them to 'oppose the authority' of the government."

"So somehow we need to show," Cal said with his eyes closed and the muscles in his face tensed, "that we did not *oppose* the lawful authority of the federal government."

"Which we do," Abigail said, "by showing that our government refused to honor its sacred duty to protect American citizens, disregarding our many pleas, those of John Gallagher and Pack McHenry, that a nuclear catastrophe was on its way."

"In other words," Cal said summing up, "if the government abandons its authority, we can't be guilty of opposing it."

Abigail leaned back and lifted an open hand toward Cal. "Well done, Mr. Jordan. Let me urge you to think seriously about going to law school!"

After that, they disappeared into their own thoughts. Abigail knew that her defense would mean uncovering the seamy underbelly of Washington politics, and there was no tougher game of hardball anywhere.

Cal said, "So where do we start?"

Abigail's answer caused even her to catch her breath. "By doing the very thing that every attorney who has ever lived counsels his client never, ever to do ..."

The White House

President Tulrude neared the end of her phone call with Secretary of Defense Roland Allenworth. As usual, it was not a pleasant conversation.

"Madam President, all I'm asking is that we release a statement of intent to send our Sixth Fleet to a staging area in the Mediterranean for naval exercises."

"Ro, that's a statement I won't authorize. You might as well issue a public statement saying that the U.S. is itching to join this war. Why else would we send our navy so close to the Russian flotilla?"

"Not true. Our presence could be a deterrent. It could defuse this whole invasion — "

"Or suck us into another war in the Middle East. Are you crazy? This conversation is over."

When Tulrude hit the End button on her console, Hank Strand, her chief of staff, was standing in the center of the Oval Office, trying to keep his chin up. "You wanted to see me?"

"I'm sure you've heard the scuttlebutt."

"I'd prefer to hear it from you."

"You're being reassigned. New title — deputy to the press secretary."

"From chief of staff? That's a huge demotion."

"Don't look at it that way, Hank. I need someone I can count on to keep an eye on our press secretary. He made some comments last week in that press conference I didn't like."

"So now I'm your full-time spy, ratting on your staff? That's a step down. Way down."

"Call it anything you want."

"You know, even back when I was Corland's man, I was always really your man."

"Many thanks. But loyalty only goes so far."

"I just want you to know I'm unhappy about this."

Tulrude snapped back. "If you want to be a chef, get used to the heat."

Hank Strand turned to leave, assuming the conversation was over, but there was a smirk on his face — as if it wasn't the end of the matter as far as he was concerned.

Again Tulrude's console blinked red.

Her executive secretary announced over the intercom, "Madam President, it's Attorney General Hamburg."

"Can't take it now."

"He says it's urgent."

"What about?"

"The Jordan prosecution case."

"Okay." Quickly Tulrude turned to Hank Strand, who was still lingering at the door. "That's all, Hank."

Strand exited, nodded to the secret service agents outside, and closed the door behind him.

President Tulrude clicked on the attorney general.

"Madam President, it's about the criminal case against the Jordans and their Roundtable ... This has been your priority — "

"And it better be yours too. What's the problem?"

"Abigail Jordan. This could be a tough fight."

"You're kidding. She'll be a pushover."

"I've been in Washington legal circles for a long time. Abigail Jordan may purr like a house cat, but she bites like a tiger."

"You have the full power of the United States government behind you and — "

"This isn't about power — "

"It's *always* about power — it starts there and ends there."

"But what about *justice*? We can't forget that these people were trying to save America from a nuclear attack."

"They picked the wrong way to do it. Just because a bank robber plans to feed the poor, does that give him a pass?"

"And I can't think of a single jury in America that would buy into that as a closing argument."

"Then come up with better one. You're the attorney general."

"And it's my responsibility to execute the laws of this nation faithfully. I'm just warning you that if we push this case, some very sensitive information might end up coming out."

"Is that a threat?"

"No, it's a fact. Abigail Jordan and her lawyer are smart. They'll demand release of information about why you ordered us not to pursue Joshua Jordan's warnings to President Corland about a nuclear threat."

"Ever hear of executive privilege?"

"The Supreme Court, even one that favors you, doesn't like executive privilege being used to cover up personal wrongdoing. Look what they did to Nixon in the Watergate case."

"Wrongdoing? *Wrongdoing?* Don't ever use that word in my presence. Besides, Corland's going to take the rap for that."

"But you pulled the strings. We all know Corland gave the order that Jordan's nuclear concerns be investigated — but you did an end run. You made sure the investigations went nowhere. Sure, you had a plausible defense — maybe — that Jordan's credibility on national-security issues might be questionable, but *you* made the call."

"You're way out of bounds, mister!"

After a pause, Attorney General Hamburg delivered this warning: "I just felt I had to put you on notice, Madam President. If this case continues, it may end up to be a political nightmare."

"Sweet dreams, General Hamburg."

SIXTY-TWO

The long guns of the armored divisions of the Russian-Islamic coalition had been stationed in Jordan near the border with Israel. The Jordanian government filed a formal protest with the United Nations, saying that it did not consent to a "military occupation." But everyone versed in Middle Eastern politics knew it was a ruse.

Then the shelling of the suburbs of Tel Aviv from the 200 mm guns in Jordan began. Apartment buildings, homes, and government buildings on the outskirts of the fashionable Mediterranean city started exploding and crumbling into dust.

The IDF staff in the Tel Aviv headquarters was sent into a reinforced bunker. They decided to send fighters from the Ramat David Air Base to pummel the gun positions on the other side of the Jordan River, but before they were airborne, nearly two dozen Israeli jets were damaged or destroyed by the incoming shells, which were also aimed at the air base.

As the enemy coalition expected, the IDF also sent fighter jets to control the airspace over Tel Aviv, expecting an air attack on the city. The first wave of enemy planes was launched from the decks of the Russian aircraft carriers at dawn. Fifty bombers and MiG fighter jets engaged the IDF jets in a ferocious air battle. Most of the MiGs were destroyed or routed. But not until they had dropped enough bombs to devastate downtown Tel Aviv. The streets were crawling with citizens running for their lives, seeking shelter amidst the screaming air-raid sirens. In the art museum, the most priceless pieces had been quickly locked in an underground vault; the rest were run down the stairs by volunteers who then placed them in waiting vans. The hospital was hit and was now running on emergency generators.

But the toll on the air force was crippling. Half of Israel's forty jets had been lost in the battle for Tel Aviv. Parachutes of the ejecting Israeli pilots floated through the sky. At IDF central command, General Shapiro knew that losing so many fighters so early could spell doom for any chance of victory.

Then came the news of the enemy's advance in the north. The Russian-Islamic coalition was moving toward the Israeli border. Soon they would be at Tel Dan.

So the order went out for a hundred of Israel's F-16s and F-15s — a full third of their entire air force — to get airborne and head north. But when they arrived, they were attacked on both flanks by Russian MiGs, one sortie from the sea and one from across the border in Syria. Thirty-seven of the IDF fighter bombers got through and dropped enough bombs to slow down the invasion, but not for long. When it was over, the Russian-Islamic army of a half million troops had lost only eighteen thousand soldiers on the ground. General Viktor Oragoff was elated. In his words, "Those are acceptable losses. More than acceptable."

But the Israeli Air Force had been crippled. General Shapiro watched as his chess pieces rapidly disappeared on the war-ravaged board.

The Israelis blasted deep trenches in Highway 90 along the Hula Valley in an effort to slow down the invader's armored divisions. But the Russians had anticipated that. Their engineering division was equipped with portable titanium steel mini-bridges that could be unfolded and dropped over the trenches so that the troop movements would not be slowed.

From the vantage point of General Viktor Oragoff and General Izmet over the ground invasion in the north, and from the perspective of Vice Admiral Sergei Trishnipov in his sea command on the Mediterranean, nothing was going to stop the coalition from ripping the land of Israel out of the dead hands of the Jews.

The big artillery shells lobbed from the coalition army in Jordan started arriving in the suburbs of Jerusalem. The air-raid sirens blew.

Ethan, Deborah, Esther, Nony, and his wife, Sari, scrambled down the stairway, already jammed with residents, to the reinforced basement below. The apartment tower was shaking. Distant explosions erupted every ten seconds on the streets outside. By the time the five of them had reached the bunker, the shelling was getting closer. The walls vibrated, and cement dust floated down on them from the joists.

Deborah grabbed Ethan's hand and held it tight. They found a spot in the corner and sat by themselves. She said, "I've got to talk to you."

"Shoot."

"I've found myself having some pretty powerful feelings for you. That's a dangerous thing for me ..."

Ethan, trying to play the alpha male, said, "You certainly picked a strange time to tell me that! But don't worry, sweetheart; I'll get us out of this."

"No, you don't understand. You're a wonderful guy — more than wonderful. What you've done for me, well, there's no way I can tell you how much that means. But I'm not sure this is going to work ... between us."

Ethan felt as if he'd been hit in the gut. "I don't understand" was all he could say. Still, this didn't really feel like a complete surprise.

Deborah had a hard time looking at him while she talked. "I tried to talk about this once before, at Hawk's Nest. Maybe I should have pursued it more. I'm sure it's my fault. I let my feelings get in the way, led you on. Now you're right in the middle of this because of me."

"I'm not clear. Tell me straight."

"It's about the differences between us. And something about you."

"My life's an open book. Some of the pages are a little ripped, but it's open."

"Okay, Ethan, I have to know for sure where you're at with God."

Ethan was taken aback. He knew Deb was an ardent Christian. He'd heard her talk about religious stuff, her beliefs. And there was that talk about God she'd tried to get into on their picnic together.

Okay, yes, he'd changed the subject — on purpose. He'd dodged it. So now it was truth or consequences.

He said, "Well, let's just say — "

Just then a shell struck the courtyard outside the condo tower. They could hear glass shattering and walls collapsing above them. Ethan listened for more. It was quiet for a moment.

"Right now," Ethan said, looking up at the ceiling, which was still dropping flakes of plaster, "it'd be nice to have the Big Guy up there as a close friend! Can you pull some strings to get the shelling stopped — "

"Ethan, I'm serious."

"I am too — about not getting blown up."

"I'm talking about you, personally, what's in your heart."

Ethan's face changed. He dropped his cocky smile. Deborah was not going to let it drop. He could see that. And he had to admire her for it. "All right, look," he said. "I haven't exactly spent a lot of time thinking about the mysteries of God. I just haven't. I'm a doer. I'm an action guy. Religion sometimes — and pardon me for saying this — seems like it's all about praying and reading the Bible and keeping real quiet in church. Hush, hush. So what's the point?"

"At least you're honest."

Ethan could see the disappointment in her face. "So after all of this, you're going to ditch me because I'm honest?"

"No, not at all. But I can't get into a serious relationship with you, emotionally, romantically, because of something else."

"And that would be ..."

"The Bible says that when people receive Christ they become new creatures. There's a spirit that's born in you — His spirit. That's what happened to me. You're a great guy. You're a hero, Ethan ... coming over here for me. And I get this feeling that God has great plans for you, something incredible. But you haven't made the decision to follow Christ. Not yet. A couple of miles from here, Jesus Christ walked, preached, died, and then amazed the whole world. He walked out of a tomb to prove He was the Son of God — our Redeemer. As scary as this war is ... and believe me I'm scared ... what happened with Jesus, why He came in the first place — it's more important than any of this. So the question is, are you willing to follow Him, receive Christ, receive His forgiveness of your sins, let Him turn you into a new creature?"

Ethan's head bobbed back slightly. "This is pretty heavy."

"Maybe. But it's something that separates us right now. Even worse, until you make that decision, it's going to separate you from God."

Ethan nodded. He was getting the picture. "I think I'm going to take a pass on this, Deb. Maybe I need to change in some ways, okay, but I'm not seeing the need to take the same path that you did. I'm sorry."

Deborah turned her face to the side. "I told myself I wouldn't cry . . ."

"I'm sorry."

"No, it's not you," she said. She lifted his strong hands to her lips and kissed them. Then she let go. "It's me. I should have known better."

Just then the upper level of the condo tower was hit with a spine-shaking explosion. The lights in the bunker dimmed and then went out. They sat in darkness until a few people with flashlights and lighters lit them.

In the dim, flickering light, Ethan could see the tears streaming down Deborah's face.

SIXTY-THREE

Curtis Belltether had been gathering tidbits from some of his news contacts about the war in Israel. For a split second he wondered what he was doing on Wilshire Boulevard, in Los Angeles, instead of trying to get a scoop on what was really happening in the Middle East. Or maybe covering the breaking news about Hank Strand, the president's chief of staff, who had just abruptly resigned from the White House to "pursue other opportunities in the private sector," whatever that meant.

But as Belltether strode to the front desk of the Hilton Hotel to ask about a guest who was staying in the big penthouse upstairs, he remembered why he was there. He was working on a piece about the unification of world religions and how it was the force behind the global-warming movement, and this was the last hair on the dog's tail for his investigative report.

This climate piece would be the second of two blockbuster exposés he would soon be publishing. The first one, which he'd already finished, uncovered what really happened when the Chicago flight was shot down by terrorists. He had discovered that the Return-to-Sender system on that jet had not failed after all. The fact is it had been disabled by the airlines because they mindlessly thought that FAA regulations required it.

But Belltether was running short on cash. He needed to fund some travel for the rest of his climate report. So he started looking around for a publication that would buy the RTS article. He had contacted Phil

Rankowitz, the retired television exec who ran AmeriNews. To his joy, Rankowitz jumped at the offer to buy the piece. When Belltether further found out that RTS designer Joshua Jordan and his wife, Abigail, were friends of Rankowitz's and that they were all connected with a group that had launched AmeriNews in the first place, Belltether knew the article would be a perfect fit.

Belltether already had a title for his second article: "The Gods of Climate." The guy he was about to interview in the L.A. Hilton was practically the "Zeus" in this new religious-environmental movement.

The web reporter announced himself at the front desk. "I'm here to see Alexander Coliquin." The desk clerk gave Belltether a second glance and left her post to go to another phone to check on something out of earshot. Belltether had tracked Coliquin down in Los Angeles where he knew that the Romanian ambassador was scheduled to address a large convention the next day sponsored by something called the "World Religious Unity Coalition for Climate."

Thirty minutes later, Belltether was sitting in one of the burgundy velvet chairs in Coliquin's massive suite, and the two were engaged in a conversation that hadn't gone anywhere. Yet. The reporter found the guy to be every bit as charming and intelligent as he'd heard. Coliquin did not allow any taping but permitted Belltether to take notes.

Toward the end, the writer honed in on his subject. "I find it ironic that you're leading a global religious movement about climate."

"Oh?"

"I've heard from several sources that you're actually an atheist. Is that true?"

Coliquin's eyes lit up and he laughed. "Not at all. I'm a firm believer in the divine supernatural."

"From what I can determine, this is the closest thing that history has ever seen to worldwide cooperation among all religions. You must be very proud."

"Pride is not what I am about. It is simply the right time now for us to put aside petty differences, the things that separate us — like dogma and doctrine — so we can achieve something remarkable, like saving the planet."

Belltether was about to light up a cigarette, but Coliquin politely asked him not to. "Hotel rules," he said. "Also, I don't care for smoke."

The reporter complied. "Where are you going with this international union of religions?"

"Toward a more perfect world, a safer climate, a future for humankind that won't spell disaster. Don't you want that too, Mr. Belltether?"

"Sure, but I just wanna know when I buy my train ticket where it's going to take me. I'm trying to get a fix on your destination, your ultimate goal. I'm not seeing it yet."

"You should come to one of my orphanages or my leper colony. You'll see what my goal is."

Belltether said only, "Hmmm." He jotted some notes and then added, "You know, a month ago I actually traveled to one of your Romanian orphanages, in the Village of Coplean, the one you founded after the floods there killed a bunch of families, and a lot of kids had been left homeless."

Coliquin maintained a smile, but there was an almost imperceptible flicker of his eyelids.

"There's a bishop in a Christian church in the village," Belltether continued, "who had very strange things to say about you. He says he knows you and that the people in the town who tried to speak out against you had a habit of disappearing."

Coliquin laughed. "People disappear for a lot of reasons." But then his expression changed to a look of paternal gentleness. "A person who really tries to do good, like I'm doing, sometimes steps on the toes of those in the power structure. And then the local power structure strikes back. Hurtful things can be said. But as for those who speak lies against me ... I forgive them."

Belltether said nothing, but his pen never stopped.

Coliquin added, "In fact, the exact same thing once happened to a famous man named Jesus. Wouldn't you agree?"

□□□

Grigori kept muttering to himself and shaking his head as the helicopter cut across Syrian airspace. They could see the troops massing on the ground below. Then they passed over several crashed fighter jets. They couldn't tell at first who they belonged to. There were smoldering piles of smashed aircraft and trails of black smoke spiraling up from the wreckage.

Then they spotted a parachute on the ground. It was dancing and rippling in the wind. Nearby was an injured Israeli pilot, surrounded by enemy troops.

"Hey, I think that's a downed Israeli," Joshua cried out. "We could try to —"

"Forget about it!" Grigori shouted. The Georgian pilot was gesturing wildly. "Lucky we don't get shot ... boom, boom ... right out of sky ..."

Nobody was going to debate the point. Joshua and the team had all been waiting for the first missiles to come flying. After all, they were passing through a war zone.

Grigori and his copilot checked their bearings.

"Okay. Soon be leaving Syria and crossing Israel border. Golan Heights coming up. Pickup point dead ahead. Thanks for flying Georgian Airlines." Grigori laughed.

Now the fear was that the Israelis would blow them out of the sky. As they crossed into Israel, they saw the multiple lines of barbed-wire fence along the DMZ corridor as they followed the brown rolling hills on the Golan plateau. The barren landscape was dotted with yellow and red signs warning of land mines.

They passed over a defensive line of Israeli antiaircraft guns and makeshift bunkers where the IDF was dug in along the border. As the helicopter passed, the soldiers scrambled to their posts. Grigori pointed to the long barrel of the big gun that was being wheeled around to track them. He started swearing loudly in his mother tongue.

They waited.

But no incoming fire. Nothing.

"Thank You, God," Joshua muttered.

"So the Georgians are friendly with Israel after all," Cannon said with a smile.

A few miles past the last Israeli defensive outpost, they came to an open plateau surrounded by a few scruffy trees. On the ground, was an Israeli Blackhawk helicopter. The rotors were slowly idling, cutting the air. They could see a pilot in the cockpit.

Joshua peered down. "Only one pilot?"

Cannon joined in. "Looks like the newer generation, the faster ones. Doesn't need a three-man team like the older models."

Grigori started bringing his big helicopter down about fifty yards from the Blackhawk. When they were on the ground Grigori turned and said, "Joshua Jordan, I want you know something ... that I read about you. I know all about you. You're good man. You have big luck, okay?"

Joshua stepped up to shake his hand and his copilot's too. Then he grabbed the hands of each of the four special-ops guys, one by one.

"I owe my life to every one of you. I'll never forget what you did."

Joshua had a momentary hesitation as he studied the faces of the four Americans. Was it a fear for their safety or for his own?

Jack said, "Be safe."

"God's speed, Colonel Jordan," Cannon said. Then he saluted.

Joshua saluted back and then slid down from the helicopter and started jogging toward the Blackhawk.

The Georgian copter lifted straight up in a whirl of dust. By the time Joshua reached the Blackhawk, Grigori had piloted the commercial helicopter out of sight.

Joshua climbed into the open door and sat in the passenger seat. The pilot had the sun visor of his helmet down. There was a smile on his face. But something didn't seem right. Joshua glanced behind the pilot's seat. A tarp was spread out over something. He looked again. Two fingers of some dead man's hand were sticking out.

When Joshua looked back, the pilot was pointing a handgun directly at Joshua's chest.

The pilot flipped his sun visor up. Suddenly Joshua felt a queasy feeling of weightlessness and the shock of recognition as he stared at the face of the deadly assassin in the pilot's seat.

When Atta Zimler addressed his stunned passenger, there was an oily tone of arrogance to his voice. "Good to see you again, Joshua

Jordan. Sorry to leave you so abruptly last year at the train station in New York, but I had to slip away before your idiot police and FBI got any closer. You had to know I would never give up ..." Zimler was enjoying himself. "... that I would come after you no matter how long it took, that I would never allow you to win. Admit it. You knew deep down it would come to this. Shortly you are going to give me your computer password to the RTS design files — which will then make me obscenely rich."

Then Zimler gave a wave with his .45 caliber Glock 39. "So come on. Let me hear you say the words: 'Mr. Zimler, sir, you win ...' "

SIXTY-FOUR

The first third of the Russian-Islamic coalition ground troops had already poured over the northern border of Israel and were massing south of Tel Dan. Hundreds of Russian tanks, mobile missile launchers, and troop transport trucks were smashing their way toward the main highways that would take them south through the heart of Israel and on to Jerusalem. Mobs of Hezbollah gunmen had joined the invasion along the way. In other suburbs near the northern border, they had surrounded homes and hit them with unending mortar fire to help the invasion. Now the Russian and Turkish tanks were rumbling past them, and the Palestinian terror groups were screaming in delight and cheering them on till they were hoarse. The downfall of Israel was imminent.

The word in Jerusalem was that enemy troops would be at the outskirts of the city by nightfall. Thousands of the Orthodox Hasidim had swarmed to the Western Wall in the Old City section. A sea of black coats moved rhythmically in prayers from the *Nusach Sefard*. Their prayer locks slowly bobbed as their voices cried out to God, weeping, pleading. One Rabbi broke from the prayer-book recitation. The cry of his voice was from the book of Job: "Terrors are turned upon me: they pursue my soul as the wind: and my welfare passes away like a cloud. And now my soul is poured out upon me; the days of affliction have taken hold upon me." Those were the words of his mouth, but his heart was crying out, "When, oh God, when will Your strong arm show itself?"

In the Mediterranean, the huge troop transport ships were only three miles from the beaches of Tel Aviv and the port of Haifa. The Israeli fighter jets had mounted a valiant attempt to destroy the ships, but the Russian MiGs were too many. The Israeli Air Force had been compromised by having to send their fighters simultaneously to defend all four of their borders against overwhelming forces. Now the IDF jets were arriving only sporadically, coming at the massive armada in squadrons of three. They were trying to hit the ships with missiles and were spraying their decks with machine-gun fire. But the MiGs in groups of a dozen at a time would descend on them and chase them off. Hundreds of amphibious launches, all of them crammed with soldiers from Russia, the Slavic republics, and Turkey, were ready to begin motoring from the ships to the Israeli coast. All they needed now was the go signal from the naval command.

But for some reason, that message had been delayed.

At the bottom of Syria, near the Israeli border, General Viktor Oragoff was in an armored staff vehicle at the back of the invading army. He was on his satellite phone with a group of scientists in Moscow.

When he clicked off, he turned to the major sitting next to him. "Send the message to the front immediately. We are holding our positions. No advance. Not yet. We wait ..."

Turkish General Izmet in the backseat couldn't fathom it. He leaned over the seat. "Why? We can't afford to waste time and give the Jews more time to regroup. We have them on the ground with our boots on their necks. Wait? No, this is not good — "

"I'm in command," Oragoff barked. "Just fifteen minutes. Then I'll get the word back from Moscow, and we can proceed."

"Word about what?"

Oragoff couldn't tell him. Not yet. The snafu he had just discussed on the phone was almost laughable, but the high command in the Kremlin insisted they had to sort out some data first, about some absurd concern that the scientists and the eggheads must have cooked up. Oragoff thought it was bunk, but he couldn't tell that to his Turkish counterpart. So he played along with his superiors in Moscow. General Oragoff looked at his watch. If he didn't hear back in fourteen minutes, he was giving the order for the land invasion to resume — with or without Moscow's approval.

So, the eighty-mile-long caravan of military equipment and troops, stretching from Syria and into the north of Israel, came to a halt. The invasion forces on the Syrian side near the Golan Heights and in Jordan also stopped, waiting for General Oragoff's order to continue the merciless attack.

The invading forces from Libya and the Sudan, which had begun rolling through the crowds of cheering Palestinians in Gaza, were about to start assaulting the perimeter of IDF military defenses around the suburbs of Jerusalem. The line of the invading Libyan-Sudanese armies stretched back through Gaza all the way to the Sinai desert on the Egyptian side. But they were also ordered to halt, waiting for General Oragoff.

The war, at least for the next few minutes, had come to a strange, eerie pause.

□□□

In Hawaii, Dr. Robert Hamilton sat in his office. He felt sick. His wife had urged him to go home after his chemo treatment. Just the day before, he had received a belated invitation that should have lifted his spirits. He was being given a small slot at the next global-warming conference in Buenos Aires to address his controversial theories. But that is not where his mind was.

Instead, it was on the most recent computer data in front of him. He pushed the pile of papers away and turned to Finley, his young assistant. Hamilton pointed at the stack of printouts. "Is this accurate?"

Finley nodded, still slack-jawed at the readings that he himself had first detected.

"Where is the center of this thing?"

"It's so big that I can't even isolate it."

Hamilton picked up the phone and quickly dialed a number in Washington, D.C. He demanded to talk to the chief meteorologist at the National Oceanic and Atmospheric Administration. Maybe he would listen.

He was put on hold. When the secretary got back on the phone, she told him the chief was not available; he was addressing a climate convention in Chicago.

Dr. Hamilton screamed into the phone, "This is a catastrophic event! Do you understand? This is Dr. Robert Hamilton from the University of Hawaii, and I'm telling you that a disaster unparalleled in recorded history is about to take place! Do you understand what I am telling you?"

The secretary hung up.

"What about the international agencies?" Hamilton muttered to his assistant.

"Where do we start?" Finley responded.

Hamilton suddenly understood. He had tried to stay analytical, to focus, but he stammered at the prospect of what was about to happen. "With something this big, ... who do we warn?"

000

In the Blackhawk helicopter, Atta Zimler trained his handgun on Joshua. He glanced at his watch. Then Zimler, a man in complete control, smiled at his hostage. "I have two minutes. Then we take off. Everything is precisely timed. The Iranians at the Syrian border have a nice little place prepared for you. You thought you were so clever with your clumsy escape from Tehran, but this time I'm handling things. I'm going to help them get the RTS information from you. The Iranians are amateurs. I'm not." Zimler's eyes lit up. "So, Joshua Jordan, the American hero, are you prepared for my brand of pain? Are you prepared to die?"

Joshua stared him in the eye. "Funny you should ask ..."

"You think I'm joking?"

"No. I know you're not. Only this time — us meeting together — is different. Yes. I am prepared to die."

"Fine. I can accommodate you."

"You couldn't possibly understand."

Zimler grinned. "Try me."

"This time ...," Joshua began in a quiet voice, "this time I have peace with God."

Zimler shook his head. "You're pathetic."

"I don't want to die, and if given the choice, you know I'd take your life to save mine."

"Now that's the old Joshua Jordan I know —"

"No, not the old person. I've trusted my life to Jesus Christ. Things are different now."

"Different? Really?"

Zimler pressed the barrel of the gun against Joshua's cheek.

"See?" Zimler said. "Nothing's different. Nothing's changed, Jordan. Same story. You're the one who's trapped. And I'm the one in control."

Something that Abigail always used to say, a favorite phrase, flashed into his brain like a neon sign in Times Square. He bulleted back, "I'll tell you something about control —"

But he couldn't finish his sentence. Something was happening. The helicopter, which was still idling on the ground, seemed to be swaying slightly. There was a rumbling noise underneath them.

Zimler pulled his handgun away but kept it trained on Joshua with one hand, while he snatched a pair of handcuffs from under the seat and tossed them on Joshua's lap. "Put them on your wrists." But while Zimler barked his order he gave a quick glance out the side window to see what was going on. The shimmying stopped.

"I said, put them —"

But he didn't finish the sentence. The big jolt came. The Blackhawk tipped crazily down on Zimler's side at a thirty degree angle. The cockpit door on his side, which he had not yet closed, swung wide open. Zimler grabbed onto the doorframe to keep from tumbling out.

The ground rumbled and shook. The Blackhawk jolted again so suddenly that Zimler started tumbling out the open door. He was halfway out but still hung on.

Joshua swung around and with his right foot and gave a powerful kick to Zimler's torso, so hard that the assassin's head whiplashed as if he were in a rear-end collision. Zimler flew through the open door and down onto the rippling, shimmying ground.

Zimler tried to stand, but Joshua could see that the ground was vibrating and shaking too violently. Then another major jolt. This time on the other side, and the helicopter swung back almost righting itself.

Between Zimler and the Blackhawk a long, craggy wound ripped open in the earth. There was a deafening thunder beneath the ground, like the groaning of something torn asunder.

The gun had fallen out of Zimler's hand. He jumped backward to avoid the huge crevice, moving farther away from the Blackhawk. Now he was just trying to avoid the abyss that was widening in front of him.

There was a look on Zimler's face. For a millisecond, Joshua saw it. Zimler looked down at his feet as the rumbling came again, and it was an expression of sheer terror.

The earth gave way beneath Zimler like a collapse of fragile snow, as the ground on which he was standing disintegrated. Zimler plunged headlong into the crack in the earth. As he tumbled down, his final screams were enveloped in a toxic cloud, the hot gasses from the reddish-white column of molten lava that was rising up to meet him.

Joshua jumped over to the pilot's seat. He looked at the complex of controls in front of him. *What do I do? Think, man. Remember. The cyclic. Grab the stick and get us out of here.*

With one hand he pushed the throttle down to power the idling rotors up to maximum speed. Then he grabbed the cyclic stick and tried to pull the helicopter skyward. But it was all too clumsy, and while the helicopter lifted it started veering off wildly to the side. The helicopter was airborne and was gaining elevation slightly but at an extreme angle.

Joshua jacked the cyclic stick the opposite way, this time tilting the helicopter the wrong way, toward the Syrian border. But his collective control was good and he was climbing, though he had the nose of the helicopter too far down. He was remembering the finesse he needed on the stick. *Slow it down. Careful, small touches.* And the torque controls as well. The Blackhawk straightened, and he slowly turned it back toward Israel. He torqued the nose back up to a level position, then looked down at the earth opening below him and the rising steam and smoke.

He gunned the turbines to full speed. He might just make it. It was starting to come back to him now. He was moving farther into Israel and away from the earthquake tremors back on the Golan. Something unearthly was about to blow. The newest Blackhawks could do two hundred and forty miles per hour. He glanced back at the Golan. The whole plateau on the Syrian side seemed to be rising up like a grotesque mountain being birthed with black smoke pouring out of the cone that was forming at its zenith. Then he looked back again and saw another one several miles beyond that farther into Syria also belching black smoke. And another smoking cone rising up in the hills beyond that. Like some prehistoric picture of the formation of the earth, the planet seemed to be in the throes of upheaval.

Joshua tried to keep the helicopter on course as he gave one final glance back toward the Golan. He saw red fiery bursts of flame and smoke rising up from the Syrian hills. He was no geologist, but the vision of every famous volcanic disaster he had ever read about, multiplied by ten, was now directly behind him. He checked his airspeed. One hundred eighty miles per hour and climbing. He knew he had to get clear of whatever was coming next.

Faster. Faster.

Two hundred and ten. Two hundred and thirty. He was about to hit maximum speed.

And then it happened. The horizon behind him exploded in a red cloud of fire and flying rock. He could feel a rush of wind punching the helicopter from behind violently forward and out of control. The Blackhawk's nose dipped forward, and everything shuddered and shook as an explosion of smoke and debris caught up to Joshua's helicopter and daylight was turned into night.

SIXTY-FIVE

General Oragoff had no way of knowing that the commanders of Israel's defenses had already resigned themselves to defeat. General Shapiro and those in IDF headquarters had desperately tried to defy the odds. The Israeli forces had thrown themselves at the advancing enemy with reckless, heroic abandon, but it was now clear that there was simply no chance of victory, not in the face of the coalition's monolithic invasion force that threatened to carpet Israel like a toxic cloud.

Oragoff had waited long enough. Time was up. He turned to his aide and was about to announce the resumption of the invasion. The general had scoffed at the Russian geologists who had been talking on the phone with him. They had ranted about the possibility of some strange, tectonic shift that they were beginning to detect deep within the earth's core, beyond anything they had ever observed, and that it was likely to hit the Middle East along fault lines and ancient, long-dead volcanic beds. They were predicting the most intense activity in a strange pattern, virtually creating a circumference around Israel's borders. For Oragoff it was ridiculous. *Scientists should stick to test tubes and microscopes. Leave the battlefield to me.*

He opened his mouth to speak — but General Oragoff would never give the order.

His armored vehicle was suddenly lifted into the air. The major next to him and the driver both screamed.

In the backseat, Turkish general Izmet cried out, "What is going on — ?"

General Oragoff only had time on his open communication line to yell, "We're under attack—" before he realized that the attack was from the earth below.

Their vehicle was on the precipice of a mountain of steaming, smoking rock that was rising up from the ground and into the air. It was undulating like a crazy teeter-totter as it was thrust up higher and higher on the tip of a volcanic mountain that was being birthed in a violent, thundering act of labor. Then the rising stopped. It was quiet for a few seconds.

The general frantically tried to open the door to climb out.

Then the volcanic cone blew wide open. The armored vehicle containing General Oragoff and General Izmet and their staff was blown two miles up into the sky in the middle of an expulsion of fire, smoke, spewing lava, and boiling rock.

More than a hundred MiG jets had been circling the Syrian-Israel border to provide air cover for the advancing troops. There was no radar warning, no escape. The blast from the volcano that was a hundred times more powerful than the nuclear detonation over Hiroshima vaporized them instantly.

The miles of tanks, troop carriers, ammo transports, and missile launchers had been waiting for a go signal that never came. Half a million troops had only time to utter a momentary cry of horror as the sky that seemed to have caught on fire was now falling on them and burying them under hundreds of feet of white-hot ash, lava, and giant pieces of rock. Vehicles tried to bolt off in all directions, but as the tremors shook the earth, the ground opened up under them, and they fell headlong into the deep, shifting crevasses and were crushed like ants in the gears of a grist mill.

The long extinct volcanic regions in Syria, Jordan, and Egypt had suddenly erupted. All of them—simultaneously—in a coordinated series of explosions that defied all scientific explanation.

At the very tip of the advancing front, the colonel in command of the Russian-Islamic invasion was watching. He could only see, behind him now, a series of massive columns of smoke reaching up into the atmosphere, and it covered the horizon like a grey, billowing curtain of death.

The colonel tried to phone central command. Nothing. He tried to call General Oragoff's staff, but the lines of communication were down. A billion tons of burning debris and gases blown into the atmosphere had disrupted electrical transmissions. The only message from the general to the rear, an interrupted one, was that they were under attack.

"This is a trap!" he cried. "The Jews have blocked our view with these clouds of dust. They are attacking us from the rear — "

But the major next to him tried to protest. "Those are our troops behind us, yes?"

"No, they must have repositioned. That must have been why General Oragoff was giving the order to halt. Send the word. Fire our missiles through those clouds so we can kill the Jews before they have us pinned."

Three minutes later, the missile launchers emptied their deadly warheads into the clouds of smoke. What they did not know is that the remaining troops from their own army that had survived the initial volcanic blast were running through the smoke, soot, and ash toward the front in an effort to escape, and right into the barrage of Russian missiles that were now dropping on them with a horrendous series of flashing explosions.

The colonel gave the order to retreat in a lateral direction across Israel. They were to head for the sea. But neither the colonel nor the remainder of his army would ever begin the retreat. Earthquakes shook the ground in aftershocks. The earth ripped open under the troops and swallowed them whole.

The ring of earthquakes and volcanic explosions spread along Jordan's border with Israel and ran down to the Sinai in the south and into Gaza. There the invading Libyan and Sudanese armies were trapped in the same conflagration of fire and rain of automobile-sized boulders that were dropping from the sky. Earthquakes ripped the ground open underneath their troop lines. Some men, in lighter and faster military vehicles, tried to escape back across the Sinai, but lava flows racing at fifty miles an hour were covering the desert, trapping the fleeing troops and melting the tires of the trucks and then trapping the screaming soldiers under a tidal wave of liquid fire.

The skies along all of Israel's borders were filled with miles-high plumes of smoke and gas. It poured from the mouths of dozens of long-extinct volcanoes that had just been awakened in a frightening fury of power, as if an unseen finger had just flicked a switch. Then flashes of lightning started to appear in the columns of smoke. As the black volcanic ash fell from the sky in sheets, the rains began — tumultuous downpours at the Syrian borders, and at the Jordanian and Egyptian borders as well. And then the hail — huge hailstones the size of soccer balls came crashing down on the retreating armies. In the monsoon of rain, the retreating trucks and tanks became mired in the mud. The fiery lava raced toward them at heats so high that the falling rain evaporated just above the lava flows. The soldiers on foot tried to scramble for cover from the monster hailstones that were smashing down on them with the force of bowling balls.

Out in the Mediterranean, Vice Admiral Trishnipov had lost communication with central command, but he was determined not to lose the glory of his grand invasion by sea. So he gave the order. Hundreds of launch boats full of soldiers began motoring for the Israeli coast to commence the coastal invasion. The sea was crammed full of Russian ships in Trishnipov's massive armada: cruisers, aircraft carriers, destroyers, patrol boats, and submarines prowling under the surface.

Trishnipov was in the admiral's bridge when he suddenly saw it approaching.

And when he did, the panic that rose up inside of him nearly froze his heart into ice. It told him instantly, intuitively, that there would be no escape.

And there wasn't. The colossal seismic disruptions had sent simultaneous shock waves into the Mediterranean, and had caused the high chalk cliffs at Rosh Hanikra at the Israeli-Lebanon border to collapse into the sea. Now, hurtling toward the Russian naval flotilla, was a three-hundred-foot-high wall of water, a tidal wave that was traveling at terrifying speeds and mounting in height along the shallows of the Israeli coastline where the naval armada had anchored.

Trishnipov only had seconds to search wildly around the bridge for a life jacket. *Maybe* ... But it would be in vain. The wall of water as high as a skyscraper crashed into the huge naval vessels and tossed them around like toy boats in a bathtub. Trishnipov's ship capsized in a one-hundred-and-eighty-degree rotation, and then, while it was upside-down, it sank with all hands. Mammoth aircraft carriers rolled onto their sides in one huge, groaning motion while the MiG jets parked on them slid down the upright decks and crashed into the sea. The conning towers of the ships were the last visible sign of the naval invasion, until at last they too disappeared under the rolling waves.

□□□

In Washington, D.C., Abigail Jordan strode up to the podium at the National Press Club. Phil Rankowitz had set up this event for her on short notice. Abigail hadn't told Harry Smythe what she was about to do. Not that she wanted to blindside her own lawyer. But she knew Harry. His well-intentioned reaction to her plan might end up inadvertently undermining it. She couldn't take that chance.

Abigail Jordan was about to drop a megaton political bomb.

She looked out over the room. It was standing room only, and several reporters were shouldering each other, trying to get a spot in the doorway.

Abigail began, "I will be appearing in federal court in Manhattan tomorrow, charged with a crime, as is my husband, an American hero, who has become a high-value target of a politically motivated, mean-spirited prosecution. Ironically, we have been charged for trying to save Manhattan from a nuclear attack. As it turns out, Manhattan was spared. But tragically, Union Beach, New Jersey, and several small surrounding towns were not, as well as four brave American volunteers who tried to stop that nuclear bomb and who died saving other Americans. Now the real question is this: why do ordinary Americans citizens, civilians like me, feel compelled to create their own system of national defense? Isn't that the province of our government? It is. Isn't the defense of our nation a first-order priority? It should be. The preamble to the Constitution says that our republic was created to 'provide for the common defense' ..."

Abigail unfolded the piece of paper. She took one more glance at it before she continued. As she looked out at the reporters and television cameras, she saw Phil Rankowitz standing in the back. He nodded in her direction and gave her the thumbs up.

"But did our government fail us?" Abigail asked. "Or was my husband, Joshua Jordan, myself, and others — were we all exactly what the criminal indictment charges us to be ... reckless vigilantes running a 'shadow government' and guilty of sedition, interfering with the lawful authority of the United States of America?"

She laid the piece of paper on the podium.

"I am here because I have been wrongly accused, along with my husband and our close friends — maliciously charged. But ladies and gentlemen, right here ... right now ... I bring charges myself. I hereby charge the White House ..." Then she paused. "No, let me be specific. I hereby charge Jessica Tulrude, sitting president of the United States, with having willfully obstructed an investigation into a real, present, and imminent nuclear threat against our country."

The reporters had been instructed in the normal protocol, to wait until after Abigail finished her remarks before launching into question-and-answer, but this was no normal press conference. Hands flew up like those of brokers on a commodities trading floor. Several of them started shouting out her name.

She picked one in the front, a female reporter.

"You are a trial lawyer yourself, so why have you decided to come out publicly like this? Isn't that abnormal, perhaps even unethical for a lawyer? And where is your attorney? Why isn't he here?"

"By my count, you've asked five questions. I'll give you one answer. No comment, Miss, ever, on my choice of strategy or my relationship with my lawyer."

Another reporter shouted out. "Why isn't your husband here to defend himself?"

"Because he's over in Israel trying to defend them from annihilation, while I was back here with several patriotic Americans trying to save New York and Washington from annihilation."

A female reporter cried out, "The way you talk sounds like you fancy yourself some kind of superwoman. Don't you think that pretending to be a comic book superhero can put citizens at risk, like those poor people in Union Beach?"

Abigail had to take a moment before answering. The hostility of the press corps almost took her breath away. "There's nothing super about us or what we were trying to do. Just imagine for a moment: you're walking past a burning house when to your amazement you find that the fire department has been ordered *not* to show up. Tell me ... wouldn't you try to save the kids hanging out the upstairs windows?"

Another reporter barked out, "A lot of us consider our firemen to be heroes. So, by comparing yourself to them, are you saying that you think you're a hero? Or are you implying that firemen are not doing their job — "

"I would have thought that only an Olympic gymnast could do a midair twist like that. The way you've twisted my words deserves some kind of gold medal."

That evoked a few chuckles from the crowd. But just as quickly another barb was tossed her way. "It's been said that you and your husband have an agenda to destroy this administration at any cost. Wouldn't you say that the accusations you made today are just more proof of that?"

"Only if my accusations are false."

"Are they?" a voice shouted out.

The room suddenly shut down as if a vacuum had just sucked all the noise out. Someone coughed. More silence.

Then Abigail answered. "I have proof, ladies and gentlemen." Then she glanced once more to the paper on the podium. She cleared her throat, took a sip of water, and continued. "Two days ago I was prepared to tell you that Jessica Tulrude's wrongdoing was limited to collaborating with a Washington, D.C., lawyer by the name of Allen

Fulsin. She used him to penetrate a lawful organization of patriotic Americans of which I am one, and she used him to try to maliciously build a case against our group. But then, yesterday, I came into possession of something else. Something remarkable. I am about to read you an email from Jessica Tulrude addressed to Attorney General Hamburg. At the time she wrote it, Ms. Tulrude was our vice president. You judge for yourselves whether my accusations are true.

"Although it was originally encrypted, it was decoded and readable by the highest-level White House staff, including the chief of staff to the president. Here is what it says:

> "Joshua Jordan is a corrupt and untrustworthy source of information regarding an alleged nuclear plot against the United States. His own motives as a private defense contractor, among many other reasons, render his information unreliable and useless. President Corland's informal remarks about investigating this so-called nuclear plot against America ought to be treated as an aberration. And perhaps another indication of his worsening medical situation. Any investigation that gives credence to Mr. Jordan's nuclear fears will cast doubt about your office, General Hamburg, and your fitness as attorney general."

In a sports bar in Georgetown, Hank Strand, recently resigned White House chief of staff, sat with a plate of ribs in front of him. He'd been drinking heavily. Several different ball games were being televised on every one of the web televisions in the place, except one. The TV right in front of Strand. He had demanded that the bartender change the channel on that television set to the news. He said he was expecting some big news from a press conference at the Press Club.

On the screen, Abigail Jordan was reading Jessica Tulrude's email, which Hank Strand had hand delivered to her twelve hours ago.

When Abigail finished reading the email, the news channel flashed a picture of President Tulrude on the screen.

Hank Strand lifted his glass to her image as if proposing a toast.

"Remember, Madam President ... loyalty only goes so far ..."

In the White House, President Tulrude was catching Abigail Jordan's press conference, along with her press secretary and new chief of staff.

Her profanity-laced screams could be heard all the way out to the White House lawn, where a staffer was walking her French poodle.

In the Press Club, one last hand went up. The reporter was holding the special journalist edition of the Allfone, the one with instant international news and video feeds. "Mrs. Jordan," the reporter called out, "You said your husband's in Israel?"

"Yes. He was taken by force by the Iranians, but he was able to escape and should be back in Israel by now. I heard that yesterday. Hopefully he's joined up with my daughter who is over there as well. Why do you ask?"

"Mrs. Jordan, there has been some kind of terrible disaster ... during this invasion of Israel. There's been this massive catastrophe over there ... I don't even know how to describe what I am seeing on my video feed. Do you know if your husband is all right?"

Abigail was momentarily at a loss for words. All she could muster was one word.

"*What?*"

SIXTY-SIX

In downtown Jerusalem thousands flooded the streets. Somber at first but chattering wildly, asking each other, "What exactly has happened?" They were getting the reports now. Accounts of the destruction of the invaders. At the moment of their near-certain destruction, when the IDF seemed on the verge of obliteration, the borderlands of Israel had exploded. Long-extinct volcanic beds had erupted as earthquakes ripped through the enemy troop lines in the Egyptian desert, in Jordan and Syria. And they were even hearing that the naval invasion off the coast of Israel had been swallowed up in a wall of water from the tremors of the earth.

The bewildered crowds now started smiling. Hugging. Cheering.

The minute that Nony and his wife, Sari, received word at their condo of the destruction of the invading hordes, they joined the cheering crowds in downtown Jerusalem. Deborah Jordan, Ethan March, and Esther Kinney were fast-stepping along with them, laughing and cheering with the ecstatic mob. By the time they approached Ben Yehuda Street, the whole downtown district had erupted into joyous pandemonium.

Music blasted into the square from an open shop. Young Israeli soldiers, who still had their machine guns slung over their shoulders, danced in the streets with the bearded Orthodox. Affluent brokers grabbed hands with parents who had children in tow. Shopkeepers linked arms with Knesset legislators as they sang wildly together. The cacophony had spread to the adjoining Mesilat Yesharim and King

George streets and to every other surrounding avenue. Confetti was shimmering down from the balconies where the apartment dwellers were waving flags of Israel and tossing colored streamers. Everywhere there was laughter — and tears.

Deborah was crying and singing and laughing in the street along with Esther Kinney, and Nony and Sari. Ethan too was laughing but standing off to the side, watching it all. A young man, perhaps twenty, a Yeshiva student in a hat with the beginnings of a short scraggly beard, and a girl with him in a long skirt and a babushka on her head, were dancing with their hands in the air. They grabbed Ethan and brought him into their celebration. He humored them with a few awkward steps. Then he raised a hand to say good-bye and stepped away.

Before long, the swirling, dancing celebration started to quiet down. Hands were being raised. The air was filled with shouts to the God of Abraham, Isaac, and Jacob, thanking the Lord for the greatest miracle since the parting of the Red Sea, for the most spectacular show of God's power and sovereignty ever displayed before the eyes of the human race.

In the crowd, a local Messianic pastor in a prayer shawl was looking skyward. His face was radiant, mouth slack, and his eyes looked deeply into an unseen place. He had the look of awe and wonderment, that in his own lifetime he had just witnessed the culmination of a divine promise. Then in a triumphant shout, he began to recite the passage from the second chapter of the first book of Samuel, verse ten. Like the twist of a telescope lens, it suddenly brought into focus the image of all that had just taken place.

> *Those who contend with the LORD shall find themselves*
> *shattered;*
> *Against them He will thunder in the heavens.*

Then he stopped. His voice quivered. There was a catch in his voice as he recognized that the millennia of waiting would soon be over. The pastor finished the rest of the verse, with its heralding of Jesus the Christ, King of Kings and Lord of Lords, and His coming again in power.

The LORD will judge the ends of the earth;
  And He will give strength to His king,
  And will exalt the horn of His anointed.

Esther grabbed Deborah, pulled her aside, and they hugged. "Oh, how I wish your dad was here!"

Deborah nodded with a look that struggled to be optimistic. Surely in the midst of such a great miracle, God would have safely delivered her father. "Esther, your husband said he was sure that the helicopter should have picked Dad up on the Golan, before the volcanoes and earthquakes, right?"

Esther hugged her again. But there was so much that they didn't know.

On a sidewalk nearby, leaning against a signpost, Ethan was still trying to smile. But the fact was that Deborah had shut the door on their future together. Even when the bombs were dropping and the whole world was exploding around him; and even after that, as all of Israel was breaking into this celebration, he couldn't shake that fact. He had gone through other relationships with women. A lot of them. Why was this so different, so difficult?

And another thing baffled him — the stupefying way that this war had ended. He had been a flier in the U.S. Air Force. For him, battles were won or lost by superior air power or by overwhelming forces on the ground or by a winning military strategy. But this ... exactly how could he explain the victory here?

The word *miracle* was on everyone's lips. They were shouting it from the rooftops. Why couldn't he? It was as if Ethan was standing on the outside of everything, looking in, through some great, impenetrable wall of glass. It was as if he were sealed off, a silent witness to the joyous mayhem and the mass worship that surrounded him.

Ethan found himself imprisoned in a strange state of isolation, and it rocked him to his core. If it weren't for Deborah, a few feet away, smiling and praying aloud and singing, Ethan would have slipped away from Ben Yehuda Street and set off in the opposite direction. To where, he didn't know.

□□□

At Ramat David Air Base, General Shapiro had received the reconnaissance reports from every corner of Israel. He double-checked the data. It was true. At the point when the battle seemed lost, while Shapiro himself was searching for a photo of his family so he could have it close to him when the end came, that is exactly when the massive enemy invasion was decimated by simultaneous earthquakes and volcanic eruptions that had cordoned off the tiny nation and protected it. The scavenger birds, he had been told, were already flocking to the places where the carcasses of the hundreds of thousands of dead soldiers lay. Yes, that too would have to be attended to. The months and months of burials for all of the enemy dead. And then there would be the cleanup of a hundred miles of destroyed military equipment and the mountains of volcanic ash that covered the boundary lands. There was already a rumor about a scientist who had suggested a theory on how to handle that. It might all be burned as a source of energy.

Shapiro couldn't bother with that right now. Clearly Israel had been saved. There would be plenty of time for celebration, and to ponder the unimaginable that had just occurred, but now was the time for the solemn business of assessing the damage and locating the dead. The airfield had been devastated. From Ramat David alone, Shapiro had lost thirty-two pilots, along with several of his officers who were killed in the horrendous shelling from the guns on the Jordanian side.

Shapiro walked out to the tarmac to survey the scene. The mangled, smoldering wreckage of jets was strewn across the fields. The runway itself was pocked with deep jagged-edged bomb craters. One of the general's aides trotted up to him. He pointed to the far end of the base where a thin column of black smoke was rising up.

"Sir," the aide said, "we've got an aircraft down out there, just had a bad landing. It's one of ours."

They hopped into a Jeep and sped to the far end of the airstrip. Shapiro was expecting the worst: one more young, dead IAF pilot.

At first, as they approached, Shapiro couldn't figure out what he was looking at. This wasn't an F-16 laying in a heap of smoking metal. The wreckage, he soon realized, was that of a Blackhawk helicopter. Fuel was spilling out where the tanks had been hit by projectiles.

The general's Jeep pulled to a stop a hundred feet away. The dented outside shell of the cabin and fuselage of the helicopter, blackened with oil and soot, looked as if it had been hit with battering rams and then sent through a blast furnace.

His aide warned him, "Be careful, General — that fuel could ignite."

Shapiro nodded. "Call the fire guys, but right now we've got to see if there's a live pilot in there somewhere."

Then they noticed something. Had the door on the pilot's side of the twisted wreckage just moved? It moved again. Then with a grinding metallic groan, it opened.

A hand reached out.

Joshua Jordan tumbled out of the wrecked helicopter and onto the ground. He was blackened with oil and smoke. He slowly raised himself to a half-standing position and tried to limp away from the wreckage. His leg was soaked with blood.

Shapiro jumped from the Jeep before his aide could restrain him. He rushed up to Joshua and grabbed him, holding him up and preventing him from collapsing.

The general shouted out to his aide, "Get a medic here, and I mean now!"

After the aide sprinted to the Jeep and phoned for a medivac, the general, still propping up Joshua, looked back at the smoking wreckage of the Blackhawk. From the burnt scorch marks on the helo it was clear to the general that Jordan had just come from the area of the volcanic decimation. Then the general muttered something that Joshua was too dazed and in too much pain to hear: "There is no earthly reason you should have survived that."

□□□

In his hotel room, Curtis Belltether was sitting on the couch. On the coffee table was a package with a mailing label and postage on it. Next to it, Belltether had laid out his notes from his interview with Pastor Peter Campbell, along with his notes from his other interviews, including the one with Alexander Coliquin. He also had a copy of his completed article entitled "The Gods of Climate."

The flat-screen Internet TV showed images of the ring of volcanic destruction that ran along Israel's borders. Overhead video images showed the miles of incinerated military trucks and tanks that had been destroyed in the wake of the volcanic eruptions. Smoke and steam still rose from the volcanic cones. Belltether studied the screen. The sky-cams showed craters and caverns the size of football stadiums, which had cracked open during the earthquakes and swallowed battalion after battalion of the armies sent from Russia and its republics, and from Turkey, Sudan, and Libya.

Belltether drummed his fingers on the coffee table as he studied the screen and then glanced down at his notes. He nervously cranked his neck back and forth. Part of him wanted to just step away and get some air, maybe forget what Pastor Peter Campbell had told him as they talked together in New York. But something much more powerful kept him reading those portions of that interview.

He knew he didn't really have to reread it; he had that particular interview with Campbell locked in by heart. Now, in light of everything that had happened, and the shocking images on TV, how could he ever forget? But he had to read what the pastor had said just once more, just to make sure he wasn't dreaming.

During the interview, Campbell had been like a perpetual motion machine. He never stopped. He walked through the outer perimeter of the nuclear blast, ducking in and out of the emergency help centers that his church had provided for the homeless. Belltether was out of breath just trying to keep up. Campbell would occasionally poke his head into the portable radiation scanning tents that the government had set up. He'd thank the workers, who all seemed to know him, and he would spread some encouraging words.

But even at that fast clip, Pastor Campbell was deep in thought as he explained it all to Belltether: "There are two great events, preludes to the final stage of the end of days. First, the rapture. Jesus Christ will take His church, and by that I mean every person who trusts in Christ as Savior. Good reason, my friend, for you to make your decision about Christ today. I truly believe it's close. Then after the rapture, the world will experience the worst period in human history — the seven-year tribulation. At the center of it will be the Antichrist, the demonic temporary ruler of the planet who will appear to control it all."

Belltether was tracking. "Okay, and the second event after the rapture?"

"Bible scholars have argued over whether this second event will happen after the rapture, or just before. It's my judgment that it will probably happen *before* the rapture."

"So, what's this event?"

"I call it Ezekiel's thunder."

"You'll have to explain that one ..."

"Book of Ezekiel in the Old Testament. One of God's prophets. Chapters thirty-eight and thirty-nine. Someone called Gog is described as the leader of a nation called 'Magog,' which is said in the Bible to be a great land in the north. In chapter thirty-eight God tells His prophet that this nation of Magog, which seems to be a clear reference to Russia and its neighboring republics, is going to be the leader of a deadly coalition of Islamic nations. That prophecy tells us they will come against the nation of Israel in a ferocious war."

"Coalition of nations? Like ..."

"They're actually named in that part of Ezekiel. You can look it up yourself. Those nations can be identified by matching them historically to their present-day counterparts. Libya today was called 'Put' back then. Then there's 'Persia' — that's modern-day Iran. 'Cush' is described in Ezekiel too. That would be Sudan today. 'Gomer and Togarmah,' also called 'Beth-togarmah,' those are the areas now in modern-day Turkey, and so is 'Meshech.' "

"What happens in the war?"

"Something amazing. The enemy armies are poised to cover Israel, we are told, literally like 'a cloud,' they are so numerous. There's seemingly no hope for Israel. Then God intervenes in a stunning, incredible, miraculous way. God causes so much confusion that we are told in verse twenty-one of chapter thirty-eight, that 'every man's sword shall be against his brother.' In other words, in the melee created by God to protect Israel, the enemy actually helps to destroy itself, to fire on its own troops."

"So, where's the big miracle?"

"Verse twenty-two."

Belltether smirked. "Sorry, Reverend, I must have misplaced my Bible."

But as he said that, the reporter thought it odd that a memory bubbled up to the surface: that black-covered Bible that his mother gave him for this twelfth birthday. He wondered where it was. Probably in an attic somewhere or thrown away with his other middle school books.

But Campbell wasn't fazed by Belltether's wisecrack. He knew verse twenty-two by heart. "Ezekiel says that God will destroy the enemies of Israel in that day by 'great hailstones, fire, and brimstone.' And just before that, in verse nineteen, we're told there will be 'great shaking in the land of Israel.' So, Mr. Belltether, you tell me ... what does that sound like to you?"

"You're the Bible scholar."

"Fire and brimstone, volcanic eruptions; shaking of the land, earthquakes. That sounds logical doesn't it?"

"No, actually it doesn't. The whole thing sounds like science fiction on steroids." That's what the reporter said out loud, at least, but he didn't say what he was really thinking. In a world where the Jersey coast had just been nuked and where New York barely escaped destruction itself, Belltether was ready for anything.

Campbell smiled. "When God says He will do a thing, it doesn't matter that He has said it through His prophet twenty-five hundred years ago. If the Lord says it will happen, then it will happen." Then he added, "And why will God do it? The Lord makes it clear through His prophet Ezekiel. He does it all to let people like you and folks around the world know that He is God. Right there in Ezekiel chapter thirty-eight, verse twenty-three. When all the dust has settled from this miraculous rescue of Israel, the Lord speaks and says, as He does repeatedly in that part of Ezekiel: 'Thus will I magnify myself, and sanctify myself, and I will be known in the eyes of many nations, and they shall know that I am the Lord.'"

In his hotel room, Belltether finished looking at his notes from that interview and dropped them on the table. He stared out into space. A shiver ran down his back, as if a gentle breeze had unexpectedly brushed against him.

Then he shot up from the couch and started rummaging wildly through the dresser drawers. He ran to the bedroom, and from the nightstand he retrieved a Gideon's Bible. He thumbed around in the Old Testament until he finally stumbled on the book of Ezekiel. His hand was shaking. He found this all too incredible and was trying to calm himself. *What's the matter with you, Belltether? You act like you're about to meet a ghost. Just read the Bible verses for yourself. Just do it.*

He sat back down with chapters thirty-eight and thirty-nine of Ezekiel opened on his lap. He read the exact verses that Campbell had cited, the prophecies of Ezekiel given two thousand five hundred years before.

There it was, in black and white. The description of the exact nations that would come against Israel. The massive size of the invading army. The whole thing would look hopeless from Israel's standpoint — and it would be. Belltether had received the media reports from the war front. Israel hadn't had a chance. Their own generals were getting ready to die with their boots on because they saw absolutely no hope. But it wasn't hopeless. The unimaginable miracle *would* happen. Just as the invading forces were entering across the borders, a freakish series of volcanic eruptions and earthquakes had burst through the earth's crust, encircling the tiny country — as if someone had drawn a circle of fire around Israel, as if someone were saying, "You shall not pass." All the details were spelled out in the prophecies of Ezekiel: "brimstone, fire, a great shaking in the land" — which is exactly what had happened in the fiery conflagration of volcanic explosions and earth-shattering quakes.

Belltether's hands were trembling.

Another memory came to his mind. His mother used to walk him as a boy to Sunday school every week. She would quiz him when it was over: "Okay, Curty boy, what did you learn about the Lord Jesus today?"

He was clever enough to spout back what she wanted to hear. But what had he really learned? Then the years of ruthless, hard-boiled cynicism followed, and a life that had taken some rough turns. But he had never forgotten them, those Bible lessons as a child. Maybe he needed to be a boy again to figure this all out.

He dropped down to the ground, onto his knees. Curtis Belltether had some unfinished business from thirty years before. He started praying.

"God, it's me, Belltether. We haven't talked since I was a schoolboy and my mom made me go to church camp and Sunday school. That was a long time ago. I remember looking at that picture in the Bible, of Jesus on the Sea of Galilee stopping the storm and stilling the waves. I somehow knew back then it was all true, but I walked away anyway — don't know why — and I've been walking ever since. Going nowhere fast. But I'm back. You're too big for me to ignore anymore. I want Your Son Jesus Christ to take over now. I should have done it long ago, but I'm doing it now. I believe in Him, and I need You to save me.

When Belltether was done, he stood up. He had to smile. He thought of something. *Too bad Mom's dead. She'd be so happy.*

Then he snatched the package off the coffee table, blew out of his hotel room, and took the elevator to the lobby. He asked the desk attendant to mail the big envelope for him. Then he added, "This has to go out immediately."

Belltether took the elevator back up to his floor. As he did he couldn't avoid the eerie, unmistakable feeling of completion. Finality.

He walked back to his hotel room. He was going to take his room key out to unlock the door, but it was already slightly ajar. Wow, he thought, *I guess I really was in a hurry to get that package mailed.*

When he walked into the room something wasn't right. His notes, his tape recorder, and the copy of his completed article — all of them had been on the coffee table. They were missing.

Belltether whirled around just in time to see the barrel end of the handgun fitted with a silencer pointed at his forehead. There was a surprised look on Belltether's face, but there wasn't the usual look of hopeless panic or fear that the gunman's victims usually had. The man holding the gun, Tomasso, the bodyguard of Caesar Demas, thought that was strange.

Belltether didn't have the chance to say a word, but he had already done his praying. Any attempt to talk Tomasso out of killing him would have been useless.

Tomasso didn't hesitate. He pulled the trigger, and Belltether dropped backward. The gunman had to take one last look at his dead victim on the floor as he puzzled over Belltether's final reaction.

The killer had already coldly collected all of Belltether's notes, tapes, and finished article and stuffed them into his small briefcase. He tucked the gun away, and with briefcase in hand he quickly slipped out of the room, down the elevator, and out of the hotel.

SIXTY-SEVEN

In a Television Studio in Los Angeles

The cameras were rolling, but the conversation had just stopped. The production director in the control booth was squirming and muttering to himself, "Come on, say something ..."

The host of the television program, Bernie Bellows, was seated in the middle of his famous round table on the studio set. On his left, Dr. Nigel Huntington, the Oxford philosopher and usually bellicose atheist, was looking more passive than usual and taking a long, languid drink of water. Across the table from him, Christian theologian Dr. Maxwell Thompson was waiting for an answer to his question.

Bellows smiled and was about to interject something, just to fill the dead air. But Dr. Thompson hopped in first. "Dr. Huntington, what I'm asking is whether you are familiar with the mathematical odds worked out by a Nobel Prize – winning mathematician at your own university, at Oxford? The odds that those long-extinct volcanoes and attending earthquakes in the Middle East would explode precisely and exactly, as if on cue, just as the coalition armies and navy were about to invade Israel. Bernie, I think you have the graphic; can you put it on the screen?"

With that, Bellows clicked a button, and his set backdrop became an illuminated screen. There was an outline of the nation of Israel, with little red flame symbols designating each volcanic eruption and a lightning bolt representing major earthquake activity. An arrow represented each attempted enemy army or navy advance. On the graphic, at each exact attempted invasion point, there were symbols for volcanic eruptions and earthquakes.

Thompson couldn't help but laugh. "Dr. Huntington, look at this. Down in the Sinai, the armies of Libya and Sudan advancing toward Israel from the south, see the arrow? Notice how the arrow is cut off by the lightning bolt of a major earthquake and two volcanic eruptions. Then over at the Jordanian border with Israel, the armies of the coalition are stopped right at the border of Israel by the same thing. Total destruction. The armies trying to cross over through the Golan Heights from Syria, stopped in their tracks by eruptions, earthquakes—incinerated. Same story ..."

Huntington had both his hands in the air, waving them. "Don't bother. We all know the story. We've seen the news so you don't have to bore us."

"Then," Thompson continued, "up in the north of Israel, the big army push from the Russian coalition—earthquakes, volcanic ash and lava, hurtling boulders blown out of the volcanoes. Wiping them out, just at the perfect time, as if directed in perfect military precision. And what the earthquakes and volcanic fireballs didn't accomplish along Israel's borders, the giant hailstones falling from the sky did. Now, your Oxford mathematician, working jointly with a geologist, computed the odds of all of this happening the way it did to be eight hundred trillion to one. Conservatively speaking. But that's just the start—"

"Let me talk about odds—"

"Please, Dr. Huntington, let me finish. Those odds don't even take into account the fact that these events were predicted twenty-five hundred years ago in Ezekiel chapters thirty-eight and thirty-nine of the Bible. That additional factor was loaded into the world's fastest computer several days ago at Cray, Inc. up in Seattle. That computer can do ten quadrillion operations per second. It is still working the question, trying to come up with a number large enough to indicate how infinitesimally small the chances are that such a prediction could have come true purely as a matter of random chance."

Huntington was trying to look unimpressed. "Statistics, odds—

they're valid in themselves from a mathematical standpoint, certainly, but you're missing the point ... the earth was started with just those kinds of odds — "

"Exactly! Which means that it takes more of a leap of faith to believe that life started on this planet randomly than it does to believe it was set in motion by a Creator God. More relevant to our discussion, it takes more wild speculation to swallow the idea that the rescue of Israel that we have witnessed was just by chance, than to believe the truth — that God Himself orchestrated this victory for Israel so that the world would see that He is God. It is God's most spectacular evidence of Himself to date. You have to ask yourself, if this proof of God doesn't do it, if it doesn't satisfy you, then exactly what manner of proof would? That's a question you refuse to answer, Dr. Huntington. So, my prayer for you is that you take this opportunity to get right with God, pull down your wall of philosophical obstructionism and admit the truth. God is there. That when it comes to dramatic miracles of biblical proportions, God has broken His silence, and He is calling you to believe that He sent His Son, Jesus Christ, to earth, according to the Scriptures — and that He is coming again."

Bernie Bellows broke in. "Our time is up. But we clearly have to admit that something extraordinary has happened as a result of these events in Israel. Churches in America have tripled in attendance. Reports of spontaneous Gospel revivals breaking out — right here in Los Angles, Seattle, Las Vegas of all places, Denver, Omaha — stories of divorced couples coming back together ..."

The credits started rolling across the screen, but Bellows wasn't done. He kept reading from his notes while he shook his head in disbelief. "Despite the devastation here at home in New Jersey from a nuclear attack — thousands of lives lost — and the fear from these massive geopolitical events and the major outbreak of war across the ocean, people seem to be responding to some kind of movement of the spirit. Revivals in St. Louis, drug rehab centers emptying, criminals turning themselves in after confessing, more revivals in New Orleans, Boston, New York City, Albuquerque, reports of gangs in the projects of Chicago coming to Christian faith, more revivals in Pittsburgh and Philadelphia, Milwaukee, Columbus, Akron, Indianapolis ..."

In a Villa Outside of Rome

Caesar Demas had locked himself inside his sprawling estate off the Villa Salaria. He had spent the day on the phone, frantically trying to connect with the Russian prime minister, but he couldn't get through. He was allowed only a minute on the phone with the deputy prime minister, Lexes Demitrov, who said simply, "Our losses have been exaggerated by the Western media. We are regrouping our coalition. No need to worry, Caesar. Our plans for global dominance are still on track."

Despite several attempts, Demas never got through to Gallen Abdulla, the president of Turkey. Demas was beginning to wonder whether the press reports about Abdulla's committing suicide might be true, or the other reports that hinted that he may have been assassinated.

For Demas, it was never a matter of hitting bottom. He believed in his own almost supernatural ability to keep himself aloft, to manipulate, to conquer. He was already contemplating a new global coalition that he could head up. It was already in discussion. All he had to do was to make sure that some of the international upstarts, like Alexander Coliquin and a few others, didn't get there first. Demas hadn't come this far to settle merely for being one of the world's richest men. He was convinced that his destiny lay far beyond that.

He decided he needed a drink. He walked out of his library and headed toward his paneled bar.

His wife was seated in her wheelchair just outside of the library. Demas was about to brush right past her when she said something. "Caesar ..."

He stopped. Momentarily he wondered why she had a blanket on her lap on such a warm day. She pulled her Allfone from beneath it. It had a photo on it. She shoved it in his direction.

Demas snatched it and looked at the photo on the little screen.

It showed Demas in a passionate embrace with Andrea Portleva, the pretty Russian ambassador.

"You take me for a fool," his wife said.

"No," he responded unruffled, "I take you for a crippled fool." Then, offhandedly he added, "Why would you believe this anyway? Anyone can Photoshop this kind of trash. Who gave this to you?"

He didn't notice that she had slipped her hand back under the blanket and had pulled out a handgun. But as soon as he saw it, she had his full attention. He knew he had to start sweet-talking her, as he had done so often before, so he could get within range, grab the gun, and slap her silly.

But there was no chance for that.

With both hands on the gun, his wife aimed for the upper-left quadrant of his chest and squeezed the trigger. The blast startled her. Caesar Demas was knocked a half step backward as he grabbed aimlessly for his heart, where the blood was now pumping out through his shirt. A half second later he was on the floor. He didn't move.

In her wheelchair, his wife laid the gun in her lap. With a sneer, she answered the last question Caesar Demas had on his lips before he died.

"I got the photo from your own bodyguard, Caesar. I got it from Tomasso."

◻◻◻

On a private island near Bora Bora, Alexander Coliquin too had been working the phones. The events in the Middle East had spurned wild speculation. The whole balance of geopolitical power seemed to have been knocked off-kilter.

But Coliquin had calmly kept his course straight. He was unflustered. This most recent war and the defeat of the Russian-Islamic coalition only *looked* like a historic game changer. But Coliquin knew better. While the attention of the world was obsessing on this supposed "miracle" for Israel, he was going for a much longer-term change for the world.

His Allfone rang. It was Henry, the deputy climatologist for his global religious coalition for climate change.

"Mr. Coliquin. This business over in Israel. Still trying to figure this out."

"What exactly are you trying to figure out?"

"Well, sir, the effect on public perception. The media is all over this business about volcanic activity along Israel's borders. The earthquakes. A massive anomaly. Sure I admit that ... but it distracts from the fact that we are on the tipping point of a global catastrophe because of climate change. People are going to forget ..."

"I don't think so."

"You don't?"

"Of course not."

"Well, then there's rumors about Dr. Robert Hamilton's findings."

"Don't worry about him. He's got cancer. Won't last long. And he's been discredited, hasn't he?"

"Sure. Yes. He's a crackpot. But the problem is that his theory about climate change being due more to volcanic particles than to carbon emissions — that's technically correct. I mean it is true that when volcanic aerosols get shot straight up miles and miles they can affect the ozone by altering chlorine and nitrogen chemicals in the stratosphere."

"So?"

Henry paused. "Well, it seems obvious doesn't it? If global temperatures are increasing because of natural factors like volcanic eruptions, then it takes the emphasis off of what we are saying about controlling global industry and everything else so we can shut down all carbon emissions."

"Look, Henry," Coliquin replied slowly, "roll with this. So volcanic eruptions can cause global temperatures to rise. That's actually good for us. Talk that up. The point is that we continue telling the world it's heading for a cosmic environmental crisis. That's the point we have to sell. Then after a while, the public will get tired of talking about this volcanic episode in Israel, as the public always does. And when that happens, then we return to the original argument that global warming is caused by carbon emissions, and we go back to beating that drum. Don't fret so much."

"Well, then there's this Belltether story ..."

"Oh?"

"You know, Belltether, the Internet snooper, the guy who leaks all this stuff on his own website. Word has it he's interviewed Hamilton, and even worse, he's about to do some exposé about the federal climate agencies trying to censor him from letting his findings get out to the public, and then trying to cover that up."

"You forget your history ..."

"Like what?"

"Back in 2009. The whole *climategate* scandal. The leaked emails of climate experts, which exposed some of their scientific biases about the cause of global temperature increase and their total disdain for any alternate theories. But then a couple of well-publicized investigations were mounted in the years after that to exonerate them. And after a while, the thing went away."

"So, you're saying don't worry about it?"

"What I'm saying is that when it comes to Mr. Belltether's supposed Internet article, I would definitely not worry about it. Leave that to the conspiracy theorists. Let's keep the ball rolling forward. So how are we coming with my meeting at the Vatican next week, and with the Greek Orthodox leaders after that?"

"I should have the dates locked in by tomorrow."

"Excellent. And the new Dalai Lama?"

"He's all over it. Very excited. No problem."

When Coliquin was done with his phone call he was buzzed that he had a visitor. When his secretary identified who it was, Coliquin said he wanted to see him right away.

In a few minutes, the visitor was standing in front of Coliquin's bamboo desk. Behind Coliquin was an open lanai leading out to swaying palm trees and the blue ocean beyond that.

"Nice place to work," the man said with a smile.

"For the time being," Coliquin remarked. "While the world is expounding on the Israel thing, I'm staying out of the public eye, getting some real work done." Then Coliquin got to the point of their meeting. "So, what about Caesar Demas?"

"Seems his wife shot him to death, after seeing pictures of his cavorting with another woman."

"You don't say," Coliquin replied with mock surprise. "Well, so much for his plans to run for king of the world. It's actually better for him this way. Divorce would have been simpler for poor Caesar, but probably more painful."

They laughed.

"And Belltether?"

"Done."

Then Tomasso handed the little briefcase to Coliquin and added, "Everything that Belltether was working on should be in there, including his tapes and notes of your interview with him and his stuff on the problems with your orphanages in Romania."

"Well done."

Tomasso smiled and said he'd like to hit the beach for a few days before leaving.

After he left, Coliquin made an international call to Baghdad, to his manager for international development. After chatting for a few moments, Coliquin asked how the project in Iraq was going, and the manager replied, "About that one hundred acres owned by the U.S. government ... the State Department says it should be able to transfer the parcel to your global foundation. Then we can begin construction on your international headquarters."

"That's what I've been waiting to hear."

"Only, we need a name for the project."

"That's simple. I've always been a student of history," Coliquin explained.

"So ... the name?"

"Why, New Babylon, of course."

SIXTY-EIGHT

One Week Later

In the courtroom of the U.S. District Court in Manhattan, federal judge Wendell Tierney was giving the government lawyers an astonished look. "If I understand you then, you're asking this court to permit you to dismiss all the charges against all of the defendants, including Abigail Jordan? All of the defendants dismissed except one ... all dismissed but her husband, Joshua Jordan?"

Assistant Attorney General Gowers had flown in from Washington to make the pitch to the judge. "Yes, your honor, exactly."

"And these are not negotiated pleas but are outright dismissals?"

"That's correct."

The judge took a second to flip through the court file. Then he turned to Harry Smythe and Abigail Jordan, who were seated at counsel table. "Mr. Smythe, I assume your client, Mrs. Jordan, has no objection to having the charges dismissed against her and the other members of this political group of hers?"

Harry Smythe turned to Abigail. She clearly had something to say. "Your honor," she began, "I believe that these charges were false and meritless from the beginning. I think these dismissals are happening because the White House is fearful of what we would be able to show at trial about the conduct of President Jessica Tulrude. I was reluctant to be dismissed from this case unless my husband got the same benefit. My husband, Joshua, however, has urged me to accept this dismissal, so I am agreeing, even though the government, for some inexplicable reason, is still hanging on to the criminal charges against my husband. This looks like a vendetta to me."

Harry Smythe, sensing an oration from Abigail on the subject of her husband's prosecution was imminent, cut in at the microphone: "In other words, your honor, we have no objections to the dismissals."

Judge Tierney closed the file on the bench in front of him. "Fine. Dismissals granted. What is the position of the Department of Justice on Mr. Jordan's case?"

Gowers stepped back to the microphone. "Mr. Jordan is currently in Israel. We will be asking Israel to cooperate with us so he can be extradited to the United States for trial."

Judge Tierney knew the tough reputation of Israel in opposing controversial extradition cases. "Good luck with that," he noted with a tinge of cynicism.

After the hearing, Harry and Abigail walked out a side entrance with the help of a friendly court clerk, so they could avoid the cameras and reporters.

Harry said, "You know they can now subpoena you because you're not a defendant and force you to testify against Josh?"

"Sure ... assuming it ever comes to trial."

But Harry Smythe was thinking about another legal wrinkle. "... And realizing that Josh will not have to face a trial unless he's returned to the United States. You and I know full well that Israel will protect him and block his extradition to the U.S." Then he paused, realizing what he was saying. "This is going to be rough on you, Abby. His best chance is to stay where he is. If he comes back here, he could spend the rest of his life in prison. At the same time, the United States has a material witness order against you, preventing you from leaving the country while your husband's case is pending. So it seems that the government has successfully kept the two of you separated at the opposite ends of the world. Wow, talk about cruel and unusual punishment ..."

As Abigail walked out into the sunlight, she looked between the buildings to the sky, which was blue and cloudless, but her vision was obscured by tears. In an impassioned voice she whispered, "Josh, dear, when? When are we going to be together?"

Stepping to the curb, Harry began looking for a cab. After a few minutes a taxi pulled up. Harry opened the car door and waited for Abigail to climb in. By that time Abigail had a sly, confident smile on her face as she wiped the tears with a manicured finger. She stepped confidently to the cab.

Harry Smythe, exasperated, said, "Okay, Abby. I know that look. You've got something else up your sleeve that you're not going to share with your lawyer ..."

○○○

Deborah and Ethan were hanging on the railing of the military ship, looking out over the water. Ethan was listening intently. Then Deborah stopped talking and pointed to something far off. It was the skyline of New York City looking faint and miniature in the misty distance.

"America," she sighed. "Home."

She turned to look at two other people standing at the railing, out of listening range. Deborah wondered aloud, "What's going to happen to them?" And she nodded toward the man and the woman with their heads leaning against each other.

Ethan looked at the couple, then turned back to the sea. "Oh, I wouldn't worry about them. If there was ever a couple that could get themselves out of this mess, it would be your parents."

At the other end of the railing, Joshua leaned on a crutch, a reminder of his helicopter crash in Israel. Abigail had his arm tightly tucked in hers.

"Gotta hand it to you," Joshua beamed. "I've got a pretty smart wife." He looked up to the blue and white flag of Israel that was snapping in the breeze over the deck of the Israeli military ship. "So we're here at the border of international waters, just within United States jurisdiction, so you haven't violated your material witness order. And I'm on an Israeli ship with one of their ambassadors on board, so I'm outside of the reach of the United States and technically still within the sovereign state of Israel. Yeah, you're smart ..."

"No, not smart enough," she said. "When our rendezvous ends in an hour or so, I get on a boat with Deborah, Cal, and Ethan and head into New York harbor. But you sail back to Israel. Josh, how do I stop that from happening?"

"Easy. I enter the United States with you, turn myself in, and take on the White House and the Department of Justice."

"Easy? Courageous but foolish. They'll detain you without bail. You'll be stuck in jail for at least a year waiting for trial. Meanwhile the Tulrude administration will kick into overtime with the full force of the federal government trying to destroy you. The truth won't matter to Tulrude. And if you're convicted, you'll die in prison."

Joshua smiled, "So let's forget about all the legal stuff. Let's talk about something pleasant. And carefree ... like that envelope you said that Phil Rankowitz received in the mail."

Abigail had to smile at her husband's smart-aleck sense of humor. She pulled the package out of her purse. "Here it is. Your copy of Mr. Belltether's article, and all his background research on Alexander Coliquin and his global initiative to unite the world's religions around a global-warming agenda. He must have mailed it just before he was murdered. The way that Belltether put it, Alexander Coliquin could be poised to execute a plan for global control. Phil's going to post the whole thing on AmeriNews."

"And you think he's the one? Coliquin, I mean?"

"I shudder just thinking about it, but if he is ..."

"I know what you're thinking ... evil personified."

But Abigail studied her husband. "That's putting it mildly. The Bible describes that 'lawless one' as a genius in multiple areas: a demonic polymath, good communications skills, political savvy, a master of economics, military strategy, and administration. He's got it all. And even the ability to appeal to the religious yearnings of the human race. Josh, we have to let God handle this," she added with a somber kind of resolve. "This is way above our pay grade. I mean it, Josh. We leave this one alone. Okay?"

"I agree. God's going to handle it. Since I prayed in that Iranian jail I've been reading my Bible every chance I have. I get what you're saying about the sovereignty of God, but shouldn't we at least make ourselves available ... to join Him in the effort if He calls us?"

"I'm not sure exactly what God would call us to do, Josh."

Joshua ventured a thought about that. "It just goes against every fiber of my training ..."

"What does?"

"To sit by and watch the enemy gain a foothold, to give the devil the high ground."

She shook her head and giggled. "My husband has been a follower of Jesus for just a few weeks, and already he's talking like a country preacher!" Then Abigail moved in closer to her husband. "Kiss me."

He smiled and pulled her to him with one arm. It was a long kiss and said more than they could have explained. Then Joshua pulled his head back and asked, "Where's Cal? I need to talk to him."

"He's up on the bridge with the captain. They're giving him a personal tour of the ship — VIP treatment. You forget, your son has a father who's a national hero over in Israel."

Abigail said she'd spare him the clumsy trip up the stairway with his crutch and would fetch Cal herself. A few minutes later, Cal was next to Joshua at the ship's railing. Abigail gave them time together and sauntered over to Deborah and Ethan.

Joshua turned to face his son, with the rolling waves at his back. "I'll be in Israel for a while, trying to figure out which way to go with my situation."

"How about I go to Israel with you? I'll just stay on board the ship. I've brought my passport."

"I wish you could. Cal, I've missed you something fierce. But things being as they are, you need to finish up at Liberty University first. And I need you by your mother's side. She's going to need your support and advice. Frankly, you're the only person I can trust to do that while I'm away."

Cal was going to question that. After all, Deborah was practically a military clone of her father, or at least Cal had always thought so. But now he was starting to understand something about his father.

"Besides," Joshua added with a grin, "now that you're talking about going to law school, I can't think of a better mentor for you than Abigail Jordan — America's smartest lawyer."

Cal smiled and nodded. "Okay. I'll do it."

Joshua turned back to the sea and put his arm around his son's shoulder. He could hear his wife laughing with Deborah and Ethan farther down the deck.

He felt good that at least right now his family was all together — and safe. With Joshua's feeling that history was rushing to a conclusion and his sensation that time was vanishing between his fingers like loose sand, he would never take that for granted. Not ever.

□□□

The private room at Walter Reed Hospital had Secret Service agents posted outside. Inside, there was a nurse on each side of the bed. The patient, Virgil Corland, the former president of the United States, whose executive powers had since been transferred to Jessica Tulrude, had been in a coma for months. His attending physicians were now calling it a "persistent vegetative state."

Suddenly the two nurses snapped to attention, flagpole straight. The distraught former first lady, Winnie Corland, entered the room, escorted by the attending physician. She had just come from a private meeting at the White House with President Tulrude.

"I know how hard this will be for you," Tulrude had remarked as they strolled in the Rose Garden, "but soon your suffering — and Virgil's — will be over."

Winnie gave Tulrude a quick, restrained hug when she was about to leave. But in the back of her mind she thought how bizarre the illogic of Tulrude's last statement was. *If Virgil is suffering, then that must mean that he's not in a persistent vegetative state. Which means we shouldn't pull the plug.* Yet one fact was undeniable. Three years before, Corland had signed an irrevocable medical directive, ordering that all life-support systems be removed if he ever fell into that kind of state.

Winnie also thought back to Virgil's complaints about Tulrude. How many times, around two or three in the morning, would he slip into bed in the private quarters of the White House and whisper to her about his mistrust of Jessica Tulrude? His favorite tag for her was "that scheming wife of Macbeth."

The attending physician reached out and squeezed Winnie's arm. "I believe we are ready, Mrs. Corland. Would you prefer to leave the room?"

She shook her head no. Then she had to fight back the tears that were threatening to overwhelm her. Winnie Corland wasn't thinking about the implications for America or the impact on the world for that matter, though there would clearly be ramifications. Now she was facing only her own private pain.

The two nurses reached to the switches controlling the ventilator and the oxygen. That would be turned off first. They would keep the lines for the sedative open until the end, to control "involuntary movements" that might appear distressing to Winnie. But Winnie wasn't watching the nurses. She had her eyes riveted on something else. On her husband. She would watch him until the end.

The nurse reached for the control panel.

"Wait a minute!"

The nurses jumped a little at Winnie's shout. She scurried up to her husband's side. "His eyes," she called out pointing to his face. Virgil Corland's eyes, which had seemed so fixed and unmoving for months, were now roving from one point to another and seemed to be taking in the room. Then Corland blinked and muttered something unintelligible. Winnie kneeled next to him, her face awash with tears that were rolling down her cheeks. "What did you say, darling? Talk to me ..."

The doctor tried to urge her away from her husband, explaining that this was not at all unusual and talking obtusely about something called "locked-in syndrome." But all of that was about to become irrelevant. Because the immobile patient in the bed suddenly had a voice.

Virgil Corland spoke three garbled words. "Had a dream ..."

Winnie was dumbfounded. She burst into tears and cradled his head. "Tell me, dear, what dream, sweetheart?"

Virgil Corland tried to enunciate. His lips were dry. He tried again. Finally some words came out. Four of them. They were faint, raspy, and parched, as if they had just arrived from some dry and desolate place. Yet at the same time they seemed to possess the power of a prophet's cry in the wilderness.

"The King is coming ..."

Discussion Questions for

THUNDER OF HEAVEN

1. When Joshua finally makes his life-changing decision about God, his physical surroundings help him realize something important about the sacrificial death of Jesus Christ. What was it that Joshua came to understand? How did his miserable surroundings help him to realize that?

2. Deborah had to make a tough decision about her relationship with Ethan March. Did Deborah make the right decision, and why or why not?

3. Abigail had to struggle with the fact that, despite her best intentions to save New York, the New Jersey tragedy occurred anyway. Do you think she was morally responsible for that tragedy? Was the legal outcome in Abigail's criminal case a just result?

4. Remember the scenes that show protests in the streets of Tehran, Iran, near Joshua's jail cell? That part of this novel was written back in 2010, many months before the surprising outbreak of so many popular uprisings in numerous Middle Eastern nations in 2011. Do you see similarities? Differences?

5. President Virgil Corland, according to his Chief of Staff, Hank Strand, seemed to have been changing his attitude, his outlook, and some of his policies. What do you think was behind those changes?

6. Vice President (and later President) Jessica Tulrude was a strong advocate for the mandatory use of the BIDTag — a "biological identification tag," to be inserted on human skin through a non-painful laser "tattoo" — the tag would contain personal data such as social security number, date and place of birth, criminal record or terrorist ties, etc. and could be detected from a distance by government scanners, supposedly as an antidote to terrorism. In making that argument she pointed to several terror attacks on American soil as fictionalized in our novel. What kind of attacks would it take before the majority of Americans would be willing to accept a national security device such as BIDTags? Do you see any prophetic, Biblical significance in such a personal, mandatory identification system?

7. Massive disasters occur in this novel near the borders of Israel, and as a result, that nation is miraculously rescued. How do those events relate to the Old Testament prophetic book of Ezekiel, chapters 38 and 39?

8. What is the attitude of the White House in our novel regarding the nation of Israel? Is that approach similar to or different from the attitude of the American government today? How does that attitude compare to the position of the American people?

9. Russia plays an important role in the events of this novel. If you had to chose, would you view present-day Russia as mostly a friend and ally of the United States or as a potential enemy?

10. The America depicted in this futuristic novel is suffering catastrophic financial problems, and partly because of that, it has entered a new stage of global unification politically and economically with the other nations of the world. If we use a scale of 1 – 10, with 10 being a complete and total unification of the United States with the other governments of the world, what number would you assign to America on that scale today?

Edge of Apocalypse

#1 New York Times Bestselling Author Tim LaHaye and Craig Parshall

The End Series by *New York Times* bestselling author Tim LaHaye and Craig Parshall is an epic thrill ride ripped from today's headlines and filtered through Scriptural prophecy.

In this adrenaline-fueled political thriller laced with end times prophecy, Joshua Jordan, former U.S. spy-plane-hero-turned-weapons-designer, creates the world's most sophisticated missile defense system. But global forces conspire to steal the defense weapon, and U.S. government leaders will do anything to stop the nation's impending economic catastrophe—including selling out Jordan and his weapon.

As world events set the stage for the "end of days" foretold in Revelation, Jordan must consider not only the biblical prophecies preached by his wife's pastor, but the personal price he must pay if he is to save the nation he loves.

Available in stores and online!

Revelation Unveiled

Tim LaHaye,
coauthor of the bestselling
Left Behind Series

The biblical foundation for the bestselling Left Behind Series ... In *Revelation Unveiled*, Dr. Tim LaHaye, coauthor with Jerry Jenkins of the bestselling novels *Left Behind* and *Tribulation Force*, reveals the scriptural foundation of this series. *Revelation Unveiled* explains such critical topics as: the Rapture of the Church, the Return of Christ, the Great Tribulation, the Final Battle against Satan and His Hosts, the Seven Seals, the Millennial Reign, the Seven Trumpets, the Seven Bowls of Wrath, the Great White Throne, the Destruction of Babylon, the New Heaven, and the New Earth. Previously titled *Revelation Illustrated and Made Plain*, this revised and updated commentary includes numerous charts. With simple and accessible language, *Revelation Unveiled* will help you better understand this mysterious, final book of the Bible and its implications.

The End Series

EdgeofApocalypseToday.com

#1 New York Times *Bestselling Author*
Tim LaHaye and Craig Parshall

EdgeOfApocalypseToday.com is the blog of Tim LaHaye and Craig Parshall, authors of the *New York Times* bestselling The End series of novels. Their blog not only regularly reports on current events that intersect the futuristic themes of their novels, but also analyzes those events that have a special relevance to prophecies in the Bible. Their blog site will give you a perspective on the headlines of the day that you will be unlikely to find anywhere else.

Subscribe to the blog today to keep informed!

ZONDERVAN®
.com

Prophecy Books by Tim LaHaye

Are We Living in the End Times?

Charting the End Times

Charting the End Times Study Guide

Revelation Unveiled

The Popular Bible Prophecy Commentary

*The Popular Encyclopedia of Bible Prophecy The Rapture:
Who Will Face the Tribulation?*

Tim LaHaye Prophecy Study Bible

Understanding Bible Prophecy for Yourself

*These and other LaHaye resources are available at:
www.timlahaye.com*

Share Your Thoughts

With the Author: Your comments will be forwarded to the author when you send them to *zauthor@zondervan.com*.

With Zondervan: Submit your review of this book by writing to *zreview@zondervan.com*.

Free Online Resources at
www.zondervan.com

Zondervan AuthorTracker: Be notified whenever your favorite authors publish new books, go on tour, or post an update about what's happening in their lives at www.zondervan.com/authortracker.

Daily Bible Verses and Devotions: Enrich your life with daily Bible verses or devotions that help you start every morning focused on God. Visit www.zondervan.com/newsletters.

Free Email Publications: Sign up for newsletters on Christian living, academic resources, church ministry, fiction, children's resources, and more. Visit www.zondervan.com/newsletters.

Zondervan Bible Search: Find and compare Bible passages in a variety of translations at www.zondervanbiblesearch.com.

Other Benefits: Register to receive online benefits like coupons and special offers, or to participate in research.

ZONDERVAN.com/
AUTHORTRACKER
follow your favorite authors